HOW *to* USE

Microsoft®
FrontPage® 2002

Paul Heltzel

SAMS

201 W. 103rd Street
Indianapolis, Indiana 46290

Visually
in Full Color

How to Use Microsoft® FrontPage® 2002

International Standard Book Number: 0-672-32140-8

Library of Congress Catalog Card Number: 00-111514

Printed in the United States of America

First Printing: May 2001

04   03   02   01   4   3   2

Trademarks

All terms mentioned in this book that are known to be trademarks or service marks have been appropriately capitalized. Sams Publishing cannot attest to the accuracy of this information. Use of a term in this book should not be regarded as affecting the validity of any trademark or service mark.

FrontPage and Microsoft are registered trademarks of Microsoft Corporation.

Warning and Disclaimer

Every effort has been made to make this book as complete and as accurate as possible, but no warranty or fitness is implied. The information provided is on an "as is" basis. The author and the publisher shall have neither liability nor responsibility to any person or entity with respect to any loss or damages arising from the information contained in this book or from the use of programs accompanying it.

Acquisitions Editor
Betsy Brown

Development Editor
Alice Martina Smith

Managing Editor
Charlotte Clapp

Project Editor
Elizabeth Finney

Copy Editor
Mary Ellen Stephenson

Indexers
Erika Millen
Sheila Schroeder

Proofreader
D. West Ponder

Technical Editor
Dallas G. Releford

Team Coordinator
Amy Patton

Interior Designer
Nathan Clement

Cover Designer
Nathan Clement
Aren Howell

Page Layout
Heather Hiatt Miller
Ayanna Lacey
Stacey Richwine-DeRome

Contents at a Glance

	Introduction	1
1	Getting Started with FrontPage 2002	2
2	Creating Pages	18
3	Working with Text	40
	Project 1: Creating a Personal Page	60
4	Connecting Files with Hyperlinks	66
5	Working with Graphics	82
6	Creating the Page Layout	112
7	Working with Webs	144
	Project 2: Creating a Company Home Page	174
8	Adding Multimedia	180
	Project 3: Creating Dynamic Animations	192
9	Enhancing Pages with Components	198
	Project 4: Creating a Simple Intranet	214
10	Creating Forms	220
11	Preparing to Publish	240
	Glossary	262
	Index	268

Table of Contents

Introduction *1*

1 Getting Started with FrontPage 2002 *3*

How to Open and Exit FrontPage 2002 4

How to Navigate the FrontPage 2002 Interface 6

How to Change Views 8

How to Use Toolbars 10

How to Use FrontPage Help 12

How to Get Help from the Answer Wizard 14

How to Use the Task Pane 16

2 Creating Pages *19*

How to Create a New Web Page 20

How to Create a New Web Site 22

How to Use Page View Tabs 24

How to Choose and Apply a Theme 26

How to Modify a Theme 28

How to Choose a Browser for Preview 32

How to Preview a Page 34

How to Save and Name a Page 36

How to Close and Retrieve Pages 38

3 Working with Text *41*

How to Enter Text 42

How to Pull Text from an Existing File 44

How to Format Text 46

How to Change the Style of a Paragraph 48

How to Align and Indent Text 50

How to Create Lists 52

How to Make a Collapsible Outline 54

How to Spell Check a Page 56

How to Use and Edit WordArt 58

Project 1 Creating a Personal Page *60*

4 Connecting Files with Hyperlinks *67*

How to Use Hyperlinks View 68

How to Set and Edit Hyperlinks 70

How to Create Internal and External Hyperlinks 72

How to Create Bookmarks 74

How to Link to a Movie or Audio File 76

How to Change the Look of Links 78

How to Follow a Hyperlink 80

5 Working with Graphics *83*

How to Import an Image 84

How to Find and Insert Clip Art 86

How to Import a Scanned Image 88

How to Set Picture Properties 90

How to Crop Images 92

How to Rotate Images 94

How to Resize and Resample Images 96

How to Link Graphics 98

How to Adjust Brightness and Contrast 100

How to Add Text to an Image 102

How to Create a Transparent Image 104

How to Wrap Text Around an Image 106

How to Create an Imagemap 108

How to Use the Drawing Toolbar 110

6 Creating the Page Layout *113*

How to Choose and Modify Backgrounds 114

How to Sample a Custom Color 116

How to Align Elements with Tables 118

How to Merge and Split Table Cells 122

How to Add and Remove Rows and Columns 124

How to Change Table Borders 126

How to Change a Table Background 128

How to Insert and Customize Horizontal Lines 130

How to Build Pages with Frames 132

How to Modify or Delete Frame Borders 136

How to Set Links in Frames 138

How to Insert an Inline Frame 140

How to Position Elements Precisely 142

 7 Working with Webs *145*

How to Work with a Predesigned Site 146

How to Save and Retrieve Web Sites 148

How to Import an Existing Web Site 150

How to Use Folders View 152

How to Add and Remove Pages 154

How to Create a New Page from an Existing Page 156

How to Move or Copy Pages 158

How to Find and Replace Text in a Site 160

How to Use Navigation View 162

How to Create Shared Borders 164

How to Automate Navigation 166

How to Insert a Page Banner 170

How to Use Tasks View 172

Project 2 **Creating a Company Home Page** *174*

 8 Adding Multimedia *181*

How to Insert a Video 182

How to Set a Background Sound 184

How to Use Java Applets 186

How to Use a Plug-In 188

How to Create a Page Transition 190

Project 3 **Creating Dynamic Animations** *192*

 9 Enhancing Pages with Components *199*

How to Add a Custom Link Bar 200

How to Create a Hover Button 202

How to Rotate Banner Ads 204

How to Set Pages to Load Automatically 206

How to Include a Scheduled Picture 208

How to Add a Top 10 List 210

How to Add a Photo Gallery Component 212

Project 4 **Creating a Simple Intranet** *214*

 10 Creating Forms *221*

How to Use the Form Page Wizard 222

How to Use a Predesigned Feedback Form 224

How to Insert a Search Form 226

How to Create a Guest Book 228

How to Design Your Own Form 230

How to Create a Drop-Down Menu 232

How to Modify Form Fields and Menus 234

How to Save or Mail Form Results 236

How to Connect a Database to Your Web 238

11 Preparing to Publish *241*

How to Find a Web Service Provider That Supports FrontPage 242

How to Use a Web Service Provider That Doesn't Support FrontPage 244

How to Check Your Site's Health with Reports View 246

How to Repair and Update Links 250

How to Spell Check the Entire Site 252

How to Back Up a Web Site 254

How to Publish Your Site 256

How to Track Visitors to Your Site 260

Glossary *263*

Index *268*

About the Author

Paul Heltzel has created Web sites for the Discovery Channel, MCI, and the Discover Card. During the heady dot-com days of the late '90s, he served as a reporter and editor for PC World Online in San Francisco. He has contributed articles on technology to the *Washington Post*, *Windows* magazine, CNN Interactive, and the *New York Times* on the Web. He lives and works from his home in Chapel Hill, North Carolina.

Dedication

For Deborah

Acknowledgements

Thanks to Betsy Brown, Nathan Clement, Elizabeth Finney, Aren Howell, Amy Patton, Dallas G. Releford, and Mary Ellen Stephenson. Thanks in particular to Alice Martina Smith, who deserves a high five for her thoughtful comments and thorough editing.

Tell Us What You Think!

As the reader of this book, *you* are our most important critic and commentator. We value your opinion and want to know what we're doing right, what we could do better, what areas you'd like to see us publish in, and any other words of wisdom you're willing to pass our way.

I welcome your comments. You can e-mail or write me directly to let me know what you did or didn't like about this book—as well as what we can do to make our books stronger.

Please note that I cannot help you with technical problems related to the topic of this book, and that because of the high volume of mail I receive, I might not be able to reply to every message.

When you write, please be sure to include this book's title and author as well as your name and phone or fax number. I will carefully review your comments and share them with the author and editors who worked on the book.

E-mail:	**webdev@samspublishing.com**
Mail:	Mark Taber
	Associate Publisher
	Sams Publishing
	201 West 103rd Street
	Indianapolis, IN 46290 USA

The Complete Visual Reference

Each chapter of this book is made up of a series of short, instructional tasks,
designed to help you understand all the information that you need to get the
most out of your computer hardware and software.

 Click: Click the left mouse button once.

 Double-click: Click the left mouse button twice in rapid succession.

 Right-click: Click the right mouse button once.

 Drag: Click and hold the left mouse button, position the mouse pointer, and release.

 Pointer Arrow: Highlights an item on the screen you need to point to or focus on in the step or task.

 Selection: Highlights the area onscreen discussed in the step or task.

 Type: Click once where indicated and begin typing to enter your text or data.

Drag and Drop: Point to the starting place or object. Hold down the mouse button (right or left per instructions), move the mouse to the new location, and then release the button.

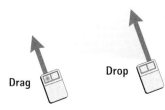

Drag   Drop

Each task includes a series of easy-to-understand steps designed to guide you through the procedure.

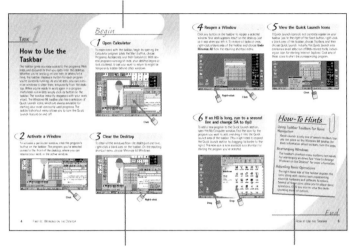

Each step is fully illustrated to show you how it looks onscreen.

Extra hints that tell you how to accomplish a goal are provided in most tasks.

 Key icons: Clearly indicate which key combinations to use.

Menus and items you click are shown in **bold**. Words in *italic* are defined in more detail in the glossary. Information you type is in a **special font**.

If you see this symbol, it means the task you're in continues on the next page:

Introduction

*E*verybody has a story to tell. Whether you want to get people excited about your business or show off your vacation snapshots, FrontPage 2002 can help you get your message across on the World Wide Web. If you already own FrontPage, you're halfway there. Now, perhaps, you want a little guidance.

If your storytelling requires a tight budget, you're in luck. FrontPage is an ideal program for anyone who wants a professional-looking Web site without the hassle and expense associated with hiring professionals. Soon you will see how painless it is to enter text and graphics on the page and publish your Web site on a server. No Web server? We can help you with that, too (see Part 11, "Preparing to Publish").

Because managing the elements of your story requires a lot of thought, FrontPage acts like a faithful production assistant. From checking your spelling to gauging the size of your audience, FrontPage keeps a watch on all your site's files. Rename a page, and the program takes note, updating all your *hyperlinks* (the text and images you designate to connect one file to another). When you need a new look and feel for your site, make a few selections from the list of *themes*, and FrontPage takes care of the rest. At any time, you can change the colors, fonts, and graphics in your site. You get to handle the big picture. FrontPage takes care of the details.

This book was created to get you up and running quickly. There's no extraneous background information, just tasks and projects that help you build useful and eye-catching documents. Figures accompany each step so that you can see exactly where to click, type, or smack the side of the computer to get things moving in the right direction.

Whether you read this book from beginning to end or start somewhere in the middle, you will find out how to build the following:

- A personal home page
- A corporate home page
- A simple company *intranet* (a fancy word for a Web site used only by your co-workers)

Learning FrontPage is a great way to start publishing on the Web because no other Web editor makes you look so good with so little effort. Soon you'll be recognized as the Web-publishing mogul that you always knew you could be. Just remember the little people when you make a big splash at your premiere.

Task

1 How to Open and Exit FrontPage 2002   4

2 How to Navigate the FrontPage 2002 Interface   6

3 How to Change Views   8

4 How to Use Toolbars   10

5 How to Use FrontPage Help   12

6 How to Get Help from the Answer Wizard   14

7 How to Use the Task Pane   16

Getting Started with FrontPage 2002

*S*o you're ready to stake your claim on the Web. Good for you. By purchasing FrontPage 2002, you've chosen a powerful and easy-to-use tool to get the job done.

Because FrontPage closely resembles a word processor, you'll have no trouble creating attractive sites without learning *Hypertext Markup Language* (HTML)—the "coding" that actually makes a Web page work. Intuitive buttons and windows guide you through page building, with a little help from this book, of course. We'll start with a quick look at the interface and show you the basics for creating and publishing pages. Along the way, we'll check out the toolbars and explain the different ways to view pages when creating and managing your Web site.

New in this edition of FrontPage is the Task Pane, which offers quick access to often-used features. If you use the pane, you can more effectively copy and paste text, find files, and quickly start a new page or Web site (see Task 7 for more on the Task Pane).

When FrontPage opens, it displays a blank page by default; you can type on that page, but note that you have not yet created a Web site. The details of that job are given in Part 2 of this book, "Creating Pages."

As you get your feet wet in working with the program, you'll inevitably run into problems: A page won't load, or a feature that worked yesterday seems to have a mind of its own today. Some of the tasks in this part show you how to get assistance when your deadline is fast approaching. ●

How to Open and Exit FrontPage 2002

FrontPage smartly lets you lay out pages and then move, copy, or delete them. You'll find all these features in one interface, saving you from launching separate programs to view your creations and manage files. This task shows you how to fire up FrontPage and get started.

Begin

1 Launch FrontPage

From the **Start** menu, choose **Programs, Microsoft FrontPage 2002**. (For some installations, you may find the **FrontPage** option under the **Office 2002** option.) FrontPage opens and displays a fresh, blank page. You might see a dialog box asking whether you want to make FrontPage your default HTML editor. Click **Yes**, if you want to associate your HTML files for editing with FrontPage.

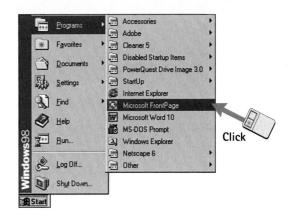

Click

2 Explore the Interface

Take a look at the program's toolbars and menus. Like most Windows programs, the FrontPage interface is standardized so that you can acclimate quickly to the FrontPage environment.

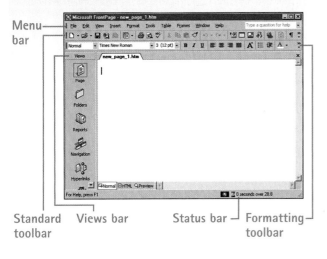

Menu bar
Standard toolbar
Views bar
Status bar
Formatting toolbar

3 Try Typing Something

A blank page launches the first time you start the program. Type in some text, if you like, to get a feel for the program. (Notice that if you type a word the FrontPage dictionary doesn't recognize, the word is underlined with a wavy red line, just as it would be in Word or similar word processing programs.) If you have worked with FrontPage before, it will open the last Web site you worked with. If this is the case, click the **Page** icon in the Views bar and then press **Ctrl+N** to open a brand-new page.

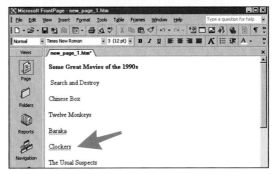

4 Save Changes

Save the changes you have made to the page: Choose **File**, **Save** from the menu bar. The **Save As** dialog box appears.

Click

5 Choose a Filename

In the **File name** field, type a descriptive name for the file you are saving (such as **test-page**). Note that FrontPage supplies the **.htm** file extension for you. Click the **Save** button. For consistency, it's a good idea to type all your filenames in lowercase letters. Also, avoid using spaces in your filenames. Some Web servers can't recognize page names with spaces.

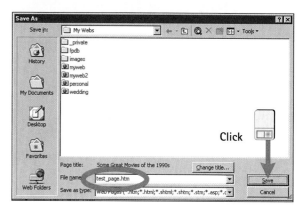

Click

6 Close FrontPage

To exit FrontPage, choose **File**, **Exit** or click the **Close** box (the **x** in the top-right corner of the title bar). The program closes with your work safely stored on the hard drive.

Click

How-To Hints

Create a Desktop Shortcut

You can start FrontPage from your desktop (instead of from the **Start** menu) by creating a shortcut. If you use Windows 98, open the **Start** menu and select **Programs**. Right-click **Microsoft FrontPage** and drag the selection to the desktop. Release the mouse and select **Create Shortcut(s) Here** from the pop-up menu. If you prefer, drag the shortcut to the Quick Launch toolbar until you see a thick, vertical line, then let go of the mouse. (Your Quick Launch toolbar displays a line of small icons, in between the **Start** button and the system tray—where you see the date and time.) If you use Windows 95, try this: Find the FrontPage program file, named **FrontPg.exe**, on your system. (On my system, the file is in **C:\Program Files\ Microsoft Office\Office10**.) Right-click the **FrontPg.exe** filename and drag it to your desktop. When you release the mouse, choose **Create Shortcut(s) Here** from the pop-up menu that appears.

End

How to Navigate the FrontPage 2002 Interface

This task looks at the most frequently used features of FrontPage 2002 by touring the toolbars and menus you use to design your pages. In this overview, we'll create a simple Web site that will let you design and publish your pages. Microsoft refers to Web sites created with FrontPage as *Webs*. Managing Webs is important, and we'll dive into the details later in this book; for now, let's focus on working with a single page within a new Web we'll create. For more details on Webs, look at Part 7, "Working with Webs," and Part 11, "Preparing to Publish."

Begin

1 Start a New Web

Start by creating a new Web, which lets FrontPage handle the publishing process. Click the **down arrow** to the right of the **New Page** button in the Standard toolbar and choose **Web**.

2 Select a Template

In the **Web Site Templates** dialog box that opens, select the template you want to use to create the Web. For this example, select **One Page Web** to create a Web site that will have only a single Web page. Then click **OK** to continue.

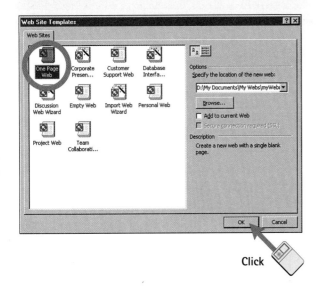

3 Make Sure That You're in Page View

Most of your time in FrontPage is spent in **Page** view, where you enter text and insert images. Make sure that you are in **Page** view by clicking the **Page** button in the **Views bar** on the left edge of the screen. You can use toolbar buttons and menu selections to edit the pages (such as resizing a graphic or adding a cool highlight effect to text).

4 Start a New Page

Whenever you want to add a new page to the Web site you are building, click the **New Page** button in the Standard toolbar to open a blank page. Even if you choose the **One Page Web** template, you can add more pages to your site later.

Click

5 Set a Theme

Type some text onto your new page. Now let's make it look sharp. To give all the pages in your Web site a similar look and feel, you can use a *theme*. To select a theme, select **Format, Theme**. In the **Themes** dialog box, select an option from the left pane and view a preview of that theme in the right pane. For this task, I picked the **Network Blitz** theme. Click the **OK** button to apply the change to the current Web site.

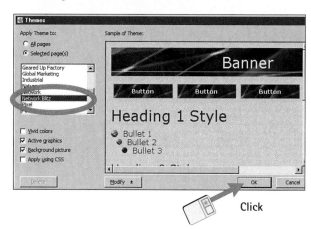

Click

6 Understand the Page Tabs

With the **Normal** tab selected at the bottom of the page, you can edit your pages. Click the **Preview** tab to see how the pages will appear in a browser. Click the **HTML** tab to go behind the scenes to view the code that actually generates the page. (You don't have to deal with the **HTML** tab unless you want to.)

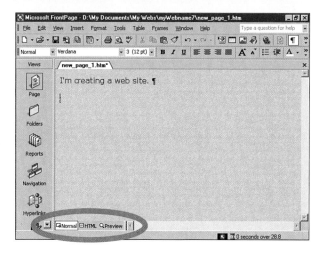

7 Put Your Site on the Web

Although there are a few more steps you must take before you can see your site on the Web, now you understand the basics of using FrontPage. When you finish developing your Web pages, you can publish them to a Web *server*. The **File, Publish Web** menu option transfers pages from your local hard drive to the hard drive on the server you specify. When FrontPage finishes publishing, your pages are available for others to access over the Internet.

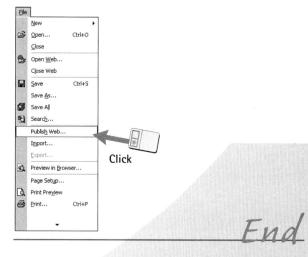

Click

End

How to Change Views

To help keep your site organized, FrontPage offers six views for creating and managing pages. Most of the heavy stuff happens in only two of these views: **Page** view (where you begin adding and working with Web pages) and **Folders** view (where you manage all the pages, images, and folders in your entire site). Depending on the view, the **menu bar** can change, offering choices that relate only to the current view. In this task, you learn what each view is used for and how to jump between them. In later tasks, you'll work with the views in more detail.

Begin

1 Introducing the Views Bar

The **Views bar** lets you jump from one view to another. Right-click anywhere in the **Views bar** to display a shortcut menu with which you can change the size of the icons or hide the bar. Bring the **Views bar** back by choosing the **View, Views Bar** menu option.

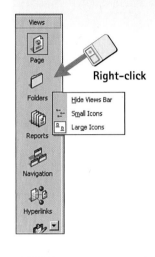

Right-click

2 Choose Page View

Click the **Page** button in the **Views bar** to open **Page** view. In this view, you create pages and preview your work.

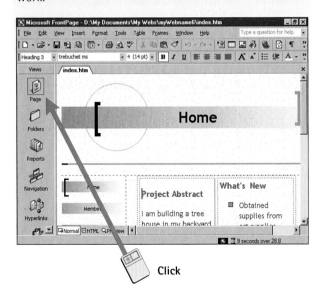

Click

3 Choose Folders View

Click the **Folders** button in the **Views bar** to see a Windows Explorer–style tree of the files and folders in your site. In this view, you can move, copy, and delete pages.

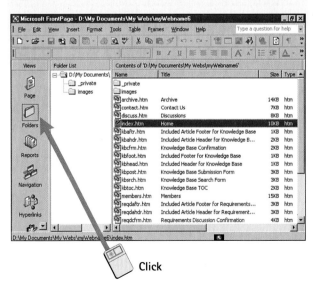

Click

4 Get a Site Report

Click the **Reports** button in the **Views bar** to see a summary of your site. **Reports** view shows which of the pages in your site have problems (such as poor download speeds or unused themes that are taking up space unnecessarily).

Click

5 Choose Navigation View

Click the **Navigation** button in the **Views bar** to view your pages in a flowchart-like display. In **Navigation** view, you can rearrange pages and automatically link them together.

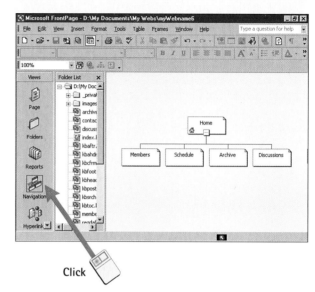

Click

6 Choose Hyperlinks View

Hyperlinks view graphically shows how other pages in your site relate to the current page. Click the **Hyperlinks** button in the **Views bar** to see how your pages are connected. This view also identifies links to other sites on the Web.

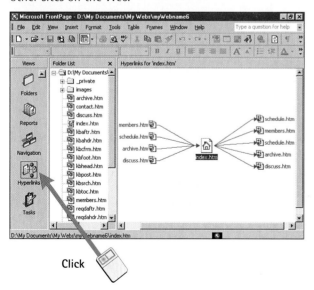

Click

7 Choose Tasks View

Click the **Tasks** button in the **Views bar** to create a to-do list for your site. If you work with others, you can assign tasks to members of your team. Everyone working on your project can view the tasks and check them off as they are completed.

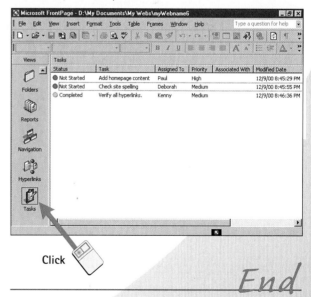

Click

End

How to Use Toolbars

It's easy to get frustrated when you can't find the menu command you need. Fortunately, FrontPage lets you accomplish most common tasks with the click of a tool-bar button. The **Standard** and **Formatting** toolbars appear by default; this task explains how to view—and hide—these and other toolbars you use at various points in your site building.

Begin

1 Find Out What a Tool Does

The "tools" are really the buttons on the toolbar. To see the name of a tool, point to its button with your mouse, but don't click anything. The name on the tool appears in a *ScreenTip*, which looks like a hovering, yellow sticky note.

Standard toolbar

Formatting   ScreenTip
toolbar

2 Display or Hide a Toolbar

To display a toolbar, choose **View, Toolbars** from the menu bar and then select the name of the toolbar you want to show from the list that appears. Toolbars on display have a check mark next to their names. To hide an open toolbar, choose **View, Toolbars** and select the toolbar you want to hide.

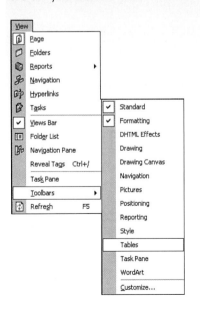

3 Position a Floating Toolbar

When you open some toolbars, they may appear to "float" over the main FrontPage window. You can repo-sition a floating toolbar by clicking and dragging its title bar. The toolbar stays in its new position until you move or hide it.

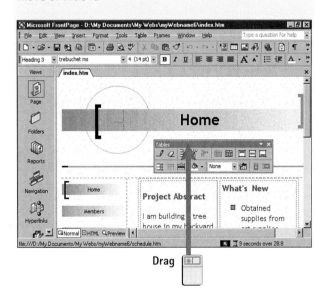

Drag

4 Dock a Floating Toolbar

To "dock" a floating toolbar to a fixed position, drag the toolbar until it "snaps in place." The toolbar is "in place," for example, when it becomes a piece of the large menu/button area at the top of your screen, where features such as the **File** menu and the **Print** icon appear. You can also dock toolbars at the left, right, or bottom edge of the screen.

The Tables toolbar has been docked here.

5 Move a Fixed Toolbar

You can move any docked toolbar to a floating position, where you might find it easier to access. Move the mouse over the left edge of the toolbar until the pointer changes to a four-headed arrow. Now drag the toolbar wherever you want it to go.

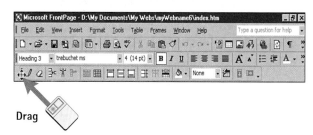

Drag

6 Add or Remove Buttons

You can customize a toolbar by adding and removing buttons. Click the **Toolbar Options** tool (the down arrow at the right edge of the toolbar), select **Add or Remove Buttons,** and then select the name of the toolbar. A list of toolbar buttons appropriate for that toolbar appears. Buttons that appear on the toolbar have a check mark next to their names. To remove a button from the toolbar, click its name in the list. Click the name of a button without a check mark to make that button appear on the toolbar.

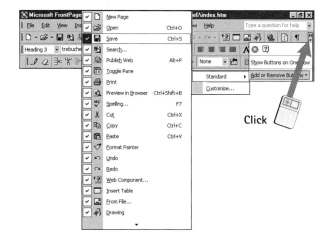

Click

How-To Hints

Turn Off ScreenTips

If you find ScreenTips more annoying than enlightening, you can turn them off. Select **Tools, Customize** from the menu bar. In the **Customize** dialog box, click the **Options** tab and deselect the **Show ScreenTips on toolbars** option.

End

How to Use FrontPage Help

No amount of clear direction on my part can change one invariable truth: FrontPage will eventually do something that confuses you beyond belief. Where do you turn when FrontPage confounds you? Try searching the built-in Help system, which offers several easy ways to get you back on track.

Begin

1 Open Help

Launch the FrontPage Help system by choosing **Help, Microsoft FrontPage Help** from the menu bar or by pressing **F1**. The **Microsoft FrontPage Help** window opens.

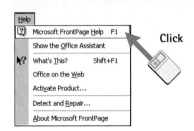

Click

2 Search Contents

Select the **Contents** tab and look through the list of *headings* (the labels next to the closed book icons) in the left pane until you find one related to your problem. Expand a heading by double-clicking its book icon.

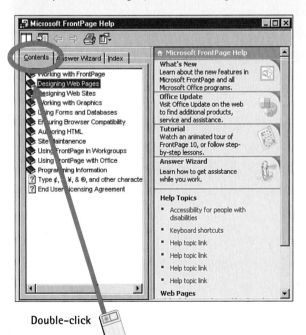

Double-click

3 Select a Topic

From the expanded subject list in the left pane, select a *topic* (the label next to the page icon with the question mark) by clicking it. A help page for that topic appears in the right pane.

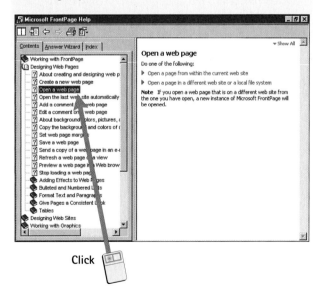

Click

4 Search the Index

If the topic you're looking for doesn't appear in the **Contents** tab, try running a search. Click the **Index** tab to get started.

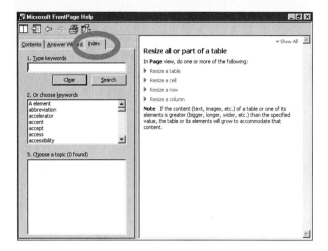

5 Run a Keyword Search

Type a word that relates to your problem in the **Type keywords** field. You also can select a keyword from the list in the **Or choose keywords** list. Click the **Search** button. If you make a mistake typing, click the **Clear** button and try again.

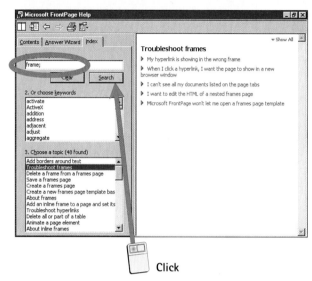

Click

6 Choose Your Topic

The results of your search are displayed in the **Choose a topic** pane. Select a heading to view the help page for that topic.

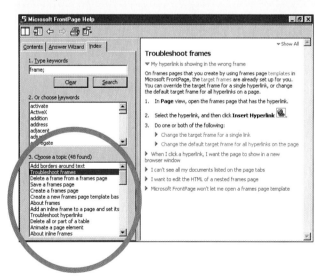

7 Quick Search

FrontPage 2002 offers a helpful new time-saver: You can search for an answer without first opening the **Help** menu. Click in the **Ask A Question** field in the Standard toolbar, type your question, and press the **Enter** key. A series of potential answers pops up. Select one of the options to open the help file on that issue. You can access previously run searches by clicking the **down arrow** next to the **Ask A Question** box.

Click

End

How to Get Help from the Answer Wizard

The **Answer Wizard** is probably the friendliest and most efficient way to find help in FrontPage. The wizard asks you to submit questions in plain English rather than using keywords or navigating through a list of topics. Although you can type a full question, entering a few words related to your problem works just as well.

Begin

1 Open Help

From the menu bar, select **Help, Microsoft FrontPage Help.**

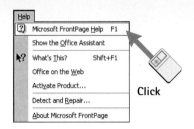

Click

2 Choose the Answer Wizard

In the **Microsoft FrontPage Help** window, click the **Answer Wizard** tab.

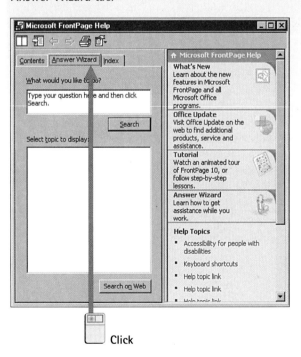

Click

3 Ask a Question

In the **What would you like to do** pane, type a few words that target the help topic you're looking for and click the **Search** button. The results of the search appear in the **Select topic to display** pane. Select the topic that most closely matches the area you want help with.

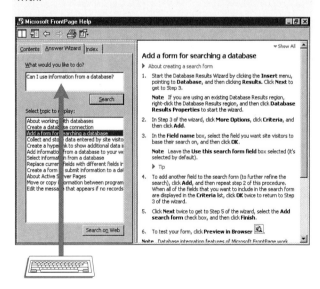

4 See More Information

Some topics require more detail than can be displayed at one time. The help pages for these broad topics have arrows that expand and collapse additional information. Click the arrow icon or the link to display a full explanation.

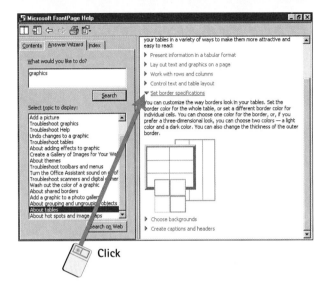

Click

6 Close Help

Exit the Help system by clicking the **Close** box in the upper-right corner of the help window.

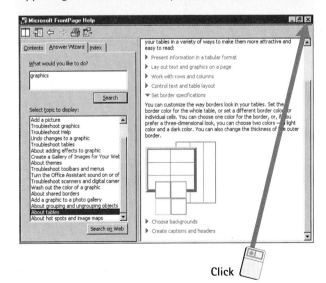

Click

5 Print Help Topics

If you run across a help page you think you'll want to refer to later, make a hard copy. Click the **Print** icon in the Standard toolbar to display the **Print Topics** dialog box. You can choose to print just the current topic (the text in the right pane) or all the related topics in the current heading. Select the desired option and click the **OK** button to begin printing.

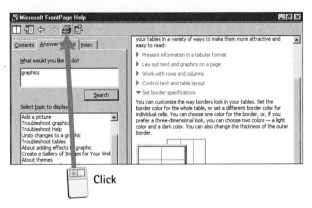

Click

How-To Hints

What's This?

FrontPage has a sort of built-in glossary that quickly describes the function of toolbar buttons and menu commands. Select **Help, What's This?** from the menu bar and then click the button or menu you want to learn more about. A small window pops up, describing the feature you clicked.

Office Assistance

The Office Assistant is an animated character—by default, a paper clip—that acts as a friendly face to the **Answer Wizard**. Select **Help, Show the Office Assistant.** Click the assistant, type a question as you would with the **Answer Wizard**, then press the **Enter** key to see a list of answers. If you prefer to use the more traditional **Help** menus, right-click the Office Assistant, choose **Options**, and then deselect the **Use the Office Assistant** check box at top of the pop-up menu. You can hide the Office Assistant at any time by right-clicking its icon and choosing **Hide**.

End

How to Use the Task Pane

The **Task Pane** helps you quickly locate features you often use, such as opening a page you recently edited or creating a new page. The pane can also help you search for files anywhere on your system. But wait, there's more. The Task Pane can even make the standard Windows **Clipboard** more useful.

Begin

1 Open the Task Pane

Your **Task Pane** may already be open. If it is not, select **View, Task Pane** to get started. At the top of the Task Pane is a list of the pages you've opened recently; following that list is a list of commands for starting new pages from scratch, pages from your Web, or template pages. Click a command to get started editing. For example, choose **Blank Page** to open an empty Web page.

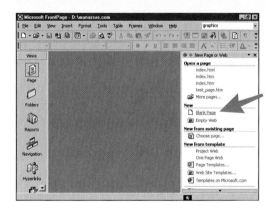

2 Switch the View

Click the **Other Task Panes** button (it looks like a downward-pointing arrow at the top of the **Task Pane**). From the short menu that appears, choose **Clipboard** to change the view of the **Task Pane** to show the contents of the Windows Clipboard.

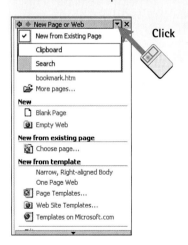

Click

3 Manage the Clipboard

The **Clipboard** pane lets you manage multiple items you copy. Enter some text onto your new blank page. Then highlight the text and press **Ctrl+C** (or choose **Edit, Copy**) to add the text to the Clipboard. When an item is in the Clipboard, you select the item from the **Clipboard** pane, and FrontPage will paste it into a document at the current insertion point. If you don't like the result, press **Ctrl+Z** to undo.

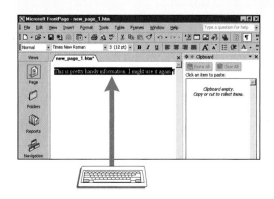

4 Search for Files

Click the **Other Task Panes** button in the **Task Pane** and choose **Search** to change to the **Search** pane. In this view, you can search for files or for words inside the files anywhere on your hard drive or in a specific Web site.

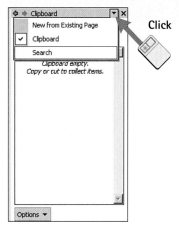

Click

5 Enter a Search Term

Type the word or words you're looking for in the **Search text** field. You can enter the name of a file you want to open or some text on one of your pages. If you want to search everywhere on your hard drive, click the **Search** button. If you want to limit the search, click the **down arrows** in the **Other Search Options** area and enable the appropriate check boxes to specify where to search on your system and what types of files to find. When you're done, click the **Search** button.

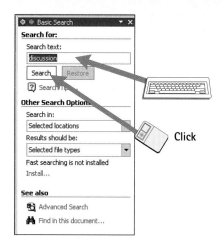

Click

6 Open a Page

When the search is complete, FrontPage displays a list of files that meet the search criteria. Select a file to open it. To run another search, click the **Modify** button. When you're finished, you can hide the pane by choosing **View, Task Pane** again.

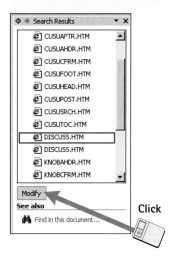

Click

How-To Hints

Make Pane Disappear

The **Task Pane** can sometimes cut down on your available workspace. You can tell FrontPage whether it should show the Task Pane when you start editing a page. Select **View, Task Pane**. The box marked **Show at startup** is selected by default. Click the box to deselect it, and the **Task Pane** won't open by itself.

End

Task

(1) How to Create a New Web Page **20**

(2) How to Create a New Web Site **22**

(3) How to Use Page View Tabs **24**

(4) How to Choose and Apply a Theme **26**

(5) How to Modify a Theme **28**

(6) How to Choose a Browser for Preview **32**

(7) How to Preview a Page **34**

(8) How to Save and Name a Page **36**

(9) How to Close and Retrieve Pages **38**

PART 2

Creating Pages

*N*ow that you've had a chance to look over the FrontPage interface, it's time to get down to some serious site building. The tasks in this part of the book show you how to create *pages*, the building blocks of your new Web site.

Intimidated by an empty page? No problem. FrontPage acts as a personal design consultant, offering suggestions for your site's colors and creating matching graphics. FrontPage calls this collection of design elements a *theme*. Applying a theme takes just a few clicks of the mouse.

As you pick and choose the elements for your pages, FrontPage creates the necessary HTML code in the background. You can focus on making great-looking pages, not on fussing with code.

After laying out a few sample pages, you'll learn how to preview them. By checking your pages in a browser before publishing those pages on the Internet, you can be rest assured that your visitors will see the same thing you do. ●

1

How to Create a New Web Page

You start creating your new Web site by opening a blank page or choosing from a list of premade pages provided by FrontPage. These premade sample pages are called *templates*.

Begin

1 Choose Page View

Start FrontPage in the usual way (see Part 1, "Getting Started with FrontPage 2002," for help). When the program displays the FrontPage window, you're ready to begin: From the **Views bar,** click the **Page** button to put the program in **Page** view, or editing mode.

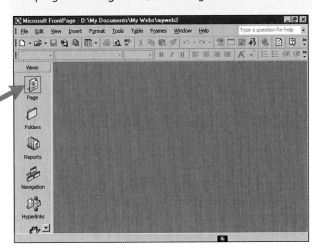

Click

2 Start from Scratch

To create a blank page in a flash, click the **New Page** button on the Standard toolbar or press **Ctrl+N.** A new blank page appears in the FrontPage window.

Click

3 Choose a Template

In the mood for a page that's a little more flashy? From the Standard toolbar, click the downward-pointing arrow next to the **New Page** button and choose **Page.** The **Page Templates** dialog box opens, displaying a list of templates from which you can choose.

Click

4 Preview Templates

On the **General** tab in the **Page Templates** dialog box, click a template icon to examine a preview of a page and a short description of its contents. Continue selecting and previewing templates until you find the one that's closest to the format of the page you want to create. (For this example, I selected **Narrow, Left-aligned Body.**) Click **OK.**

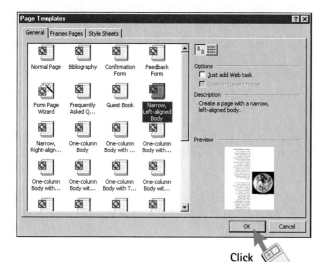

Click

5 View the Page

After you select a template, FrontPage opens a new page that contains boilerplate text and images. Highlight and replace the text with your own content. For details about text editing, see Part 3, "Working with Text." Part 5, "Working with Graphics," covers importing and managing images.

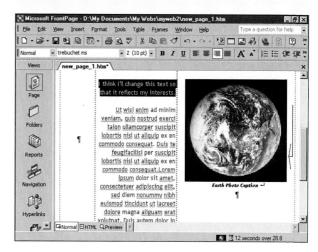

6 Close the Page

When you're done making changes to the new page, click the **Close** box in the upper-right corner of the **Page** window.

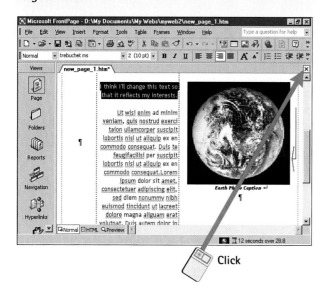

Click

How-To Hints

Which Close Box?

Note that the basic FrontPage screen has more than one window (as is true for most other Office applications); it has the application window and the document window. You close the document window by clicking the **Close** box under the toolbars (the Close box is highlighted when you point to it). You close the application by clicking the **Close** box in the upper-right corner of the topmost title bar.

End

How to Create a New Web Site

When you need just a few simple pages, you may not want to create an entire site, or what FrontPage calls a *Web*. But if you plan to work with more than one page, creating a new Web helps FrontPage keep track of the elements of your site. When you create a new Web site, you can choose from a list of collections of pages that contain sample graphics and linked pages. When you're in a rush, these Webs can be real lifesavers. The **Corporate Presence** and **Personal Web** options are great ways to create a site in a flash.

Begin

1 Start a New Web

Choose **File**, **New**, **Page or Web**. This opens the New Page or Web Task Pane.

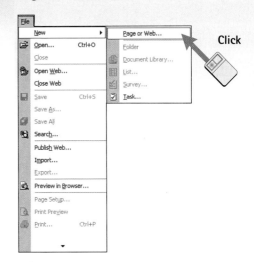

2 View the Templates

You can create a new Web site using templates, just as you did in Task 1 of this part. From the **New Page or Web** Task Pane, choose **Web Site Templates**.

3 Choose a Web

From the list of types of Web site templates that appears, FrontPage selects **One Page Web** by default. Check out the **Description** area to see what you'll get when you choose a particular Web site template. For this example, select the **Personal Web** option. You can select any option except **Import Web Wizard** (this option helps you bring into FrontPage a site that you've already created with another program). Importing existing sites is covered in Part 7, "Working with Webs."

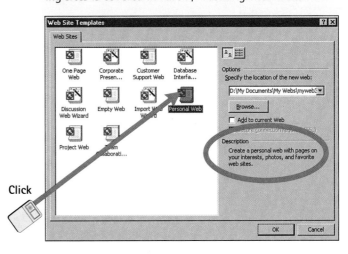

4 Name Your Web Site

At the end of the pathname in the **Specify the location of the new web** box, type a descriptive name for your new Web site (for example, alter the pathname to read **C:\My Webs\myWebname**) and click **OK**. FrontPage creates the files and folders it needs and then opens the new Web.

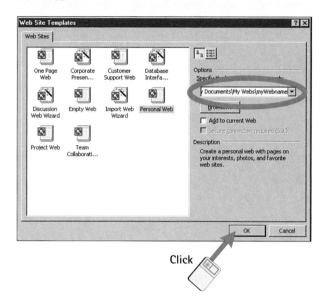

Click

5 Open Your Home Page

To see your home page, first click the **Folders** button in the **Views** bar. Your *home page*—the first page visitors see when they view your site—is named **index.htm**. Double-click the **index.htm** filename in the **Folders** view to open that page in the right pane.

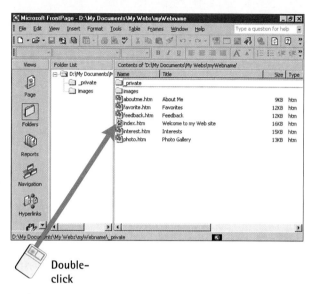

Double-click

6 Preview the Web Site

To see how the Web will look in a browser, change to **Preview** mode. At the bottom of the right pane, click the **Preview** tab. You'll learn more about the **Preview** tab in the next task, "How to Use Page View Tabs." When you finish admiring your work, choose **File, Close Web**. If you are ready to put your site on the Web, check out Part 11, "Preparing to Publish."

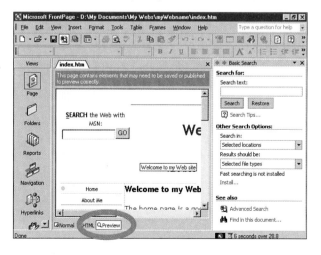

How-To Hints

Introducing Templates, Themes, and Webs

Here are some terms you'll need to keep things straight: A *template* is a predesigned Web page or collection of pages you can customize. Templates include a basic layout, font styles, and sample graphics. You will see a list of templates when you click **File, New,** then choose **Empty Web** from the **New Page or Web** Task Pane. A *theme* is a collection of fonts, colors, and graphics you can apply to a single page or to every page in a Web site. You can even apply a theme to a template to make it conform to the look of your other pages. *Web* is FrontPage lingo for a collection of Web page files.

End

How to Use Page View Tabs

In the dark ages of Web publishing, you created a page in a text editor and then opened the page in a browser to make sure that everything displayed correctly. FrontPage lets you preview a page without opening another program. Just use the handy tabs at the bottom of the editing window.

Begin

1 Choose Page View

From the **Views bar**, click the **Page** button to put the program in **Page** view, which is really *editing mode*.

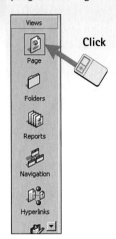

Click

2 Select File, Open

Each Web site can contain multiple Web page files. To work with a Web page file, you must first open the page: Select **File, Open** from the menu bar.

Click

3 Select a Page

From the **Open File** dialog box, select the page file you want to open. In this example, we selected the **photo.htm** file (the Photo Album page) from the personal Web site we created in Task 2. Click the **Open** button.

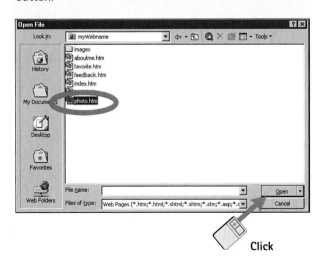

Click

4 Select the Normal Tab

In Page view, the **Normal** tab is selected by default. Click the **Normal** tab when you want to assemble and edit pages.

5 Switch to HTML Tab

Click the **HTML** tab to see the *source code*—the text a Web browser reads to display pages. FrontPage generates the source code for you, so you don't have to use the **HTML** tab unless you want to see what's going on behind the scenes.

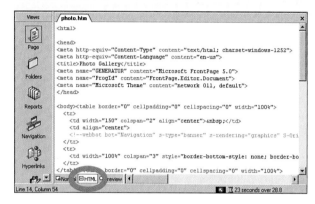

6 Choose the Preview Tab

Click the **Preview** tab to see what your pages will look like in a browser. To show pages in **Preview** mode, FrontPage requires Microsoft's Internet Explorer browser. If Internet Explorer is not installed, the **Preview** tab does not appear.

How-To Hints

Download Internet Explorer

Because **Preview** mode requires Internet Explorer, you can obtain the latest version of the browser at this site: **www.microsoft.com/windows/ie**. Internet Explorer is bundled with Windows 98/2000/Me, so if you use any of those operating systems, you should be all set. To preview pages using another browser, see Task 6, "How to Choose a Browser for Preview," later in this part.

Jump Between Modes

As you work on pages, you can switch quickly between tabs by pressing **Ctrl+Page Up** or **Ctrl+Page Down**.

View Tags in Normal Mode

For those who know a little HTML, FrontPage enables you to see HTML source code without leaving the word processor–like feel of **Normal** mode. Instead of clicking the **HTML** tab and viewing a page full of HTML source code, try selecting **View, Reveal Tags**. HTML tags appear around your pictures, text, and other elements on your page. Select the option again to hide the tags.

End

How to Choose and Apply a Theme

Applying a theme to your pages is the easiest way to create a sharp-looking Web site. The preset colors and graphics of a theme make your pages look organized and professional. You can pick a theme at any time while building your site. And you can change your mind later with a few clicks. If you decide to pick a new theme for your site, FrontPage updates all your pages automatically.

Begin

1 View Themes

Open the page you want to modify in **Page** view and choose **Format, Theme** from the menu bar. The **Themes** dialog box opens.

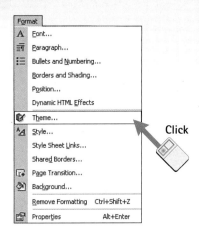

Click

2 Take Your Pick

Choose a theme from the list of themes in the **Themes** dialog box. Notice the preview in the right pane, which displays your current selection and shows you what your banners, text, and graphics will look like.

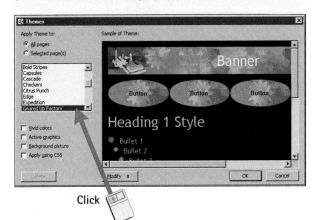

Click

3 Use Lively Colors

If you want to use more colorful fonts and back-grounds, select the **Vivid colors** option. Notice the effect this option has on the sample heading style in the preview pane.

4 Use Active Graphics

If you want the theme you have selected to use attention-grabbing graphics—including animated buttons that change when you point at them with your mouse—select the **Active graphics** option. Notice the change this option makes to the hyperlinked buttons and bullets in the preview pane.

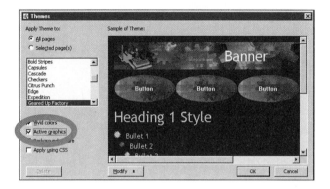

5 Use a Background Picture

To use an image instead of a solid color for the background of the page, select the **Background picture** option. Notice the default image that FrontPage uses as the background for the page. You can change the background and other page elements, as you'll see in the next task, "How to Modify a Theme."

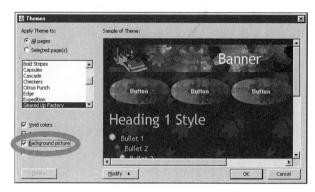

6 Use Cascading Style Sheets

You can apply a theme by creating an external document that defines page styles (a Cascading Style Sheet, or CSS) instead of changing the HTML code on each page. To do so, enable the **Apply using CSS** option. This option helps ensure compatibility among different browsers. Some older browsers do not support the entire CSS standard. Select this option if you know your visitors will be using the latest version of Netscape Navigator or Microsoft Internet Explorer (as is true on an intranet). In most cases, leave this option disabled.

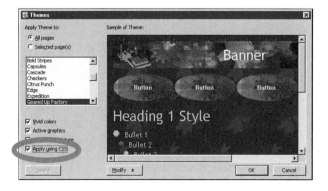

7 Apply the Theme

Click the **OK** button to select the theme and apply it to your Web page.

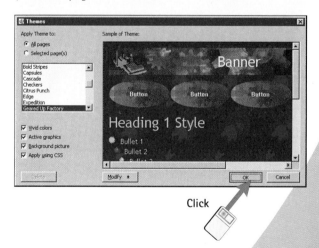

Click

End

How to Modify a Theme

One problem with themes is that everybody starts with the same ones. You spend hours developing your site—and then maybe you see the same look on somebody else's Web page. No problem. You can customize themes to reflect your sense of style. Don't like a particular color? Give it the boot. Pick your own fonts, add new graphics, and create a great-looking theme that's yours alone.

Begin

1 Open the Themes Dialog Box

With the Web (or page) you want to modify open in **Page** view, choose **Format, Theme** from the menu bar. The **Themes** dialog box opens.

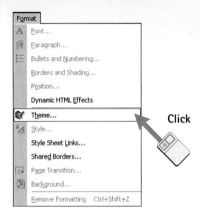

Click

2 Preview a Theme

From the list presented, choose a theme. Click the **Modify** button to begin making changes to the theme options. The dialog box changes to include several editing buttons.

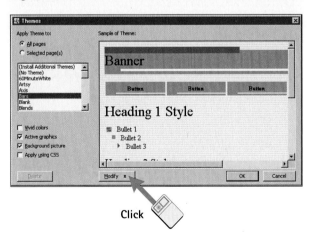

Click

3 Select Colors

To change the color scheme used by the theme, click the **Colors** button. The **Modify Theme** dialog box opens, optimized to work with color schemes.

Click

4 Preview Color Schemes

Select a color scheme by scrolling through the list. Make a selection and notice the effect your choice has on the theme's font, hyperlink, and background colors in the **Sample of Theme** pane on the right side of the dialog box.

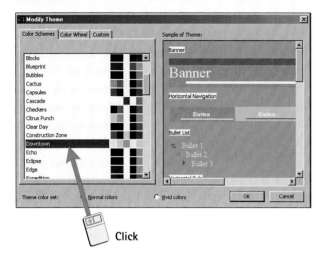

Click

5 Set Colors for Individual Elements

Click the **Custom** tab if you want to set colors for individual elements such as hyperlinks and the page background. From the **Item** drop-down list box, choose the item you want to change and then make a selection from the **Color** drop-down list. Notice the effect your choices have in the **Sample of Theme** pane on the right.

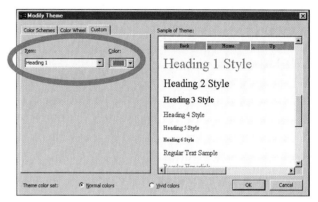

6 Choose Normal or Vivid Colors

When you decide on a color scheme, choose the **Normal colors** or **Vivid colors** option, depending on your desired level of glitz. Click the **OK** button.

Click

How-To Hints

Modified Themes Can Change the Entire Site

The changes you are making to the colors, graphics, and text of the theme can affect all the pages in the site or just selected pages within the site. Before you save the modified theme and close the **Themes** dialog box, select the appropriate **Apply Theme to** option in the top-left corner of the **Themes** dialog box. If you choose to apply the theme to a selected page, the theme affects only the current page you are viewing. If you want to apply changes to a handful of pages only (rather than to the open page or to all pages in a Web), first switch to **Folders** view and press the **Shift** key as you select the pages you want to change. Then choose **Format, Theme**.

Continued

7 Set Theme Graphics

To modify the images in your theme, click the **Graphics** button in the **Themes** dialog box. The **Modify Theme** dialog box opens, optimized to work with graphics.

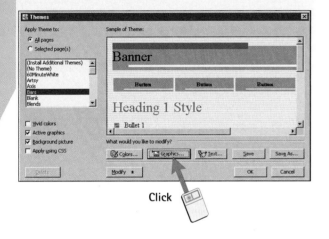

Click

8 Select an Item to Change

From the **Item** drop-down list box, choose the area that contains the graphic you want to change. For this example, I decided to change the **Banner** graphic.

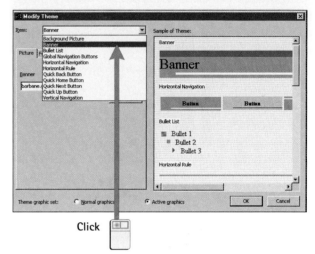

Click

9 Swap a Graphic

To replace a graphic with your own, click the **Browse** button, navigate to the file you want to use, and click **Open**. The new image you selected appears in the **Sample of Theme** preview pane.

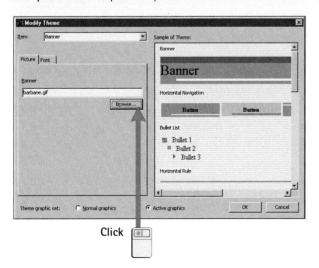

Click

10 Change Fonts Used on Graphics

You can replace the font on a graphic (such as on a banner or a button) by choosing the **Font** tab. Select the item you want to change from the **Item** list at the top of the dialog box. From the **Font** list, select the typeface and then set the style, size, and horizontal and vertical alignments. Watch the **Sample of Theme** pane to see the effect of your changes. When you're satisfied, click **OK**.

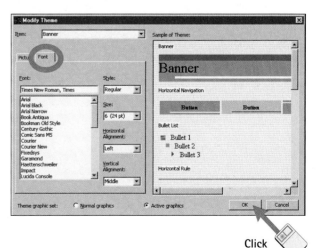

Click

11 Choose Text Styles

Click the **Text** button in the **Themes** dialog box to select your own font faces and styles for the body text and headings on your pages. Note that the changes you make with the **Text** button do not affect the text that appears on top of any graphics on the page. (You modify the text on graphics using the instructions in Step 10.)

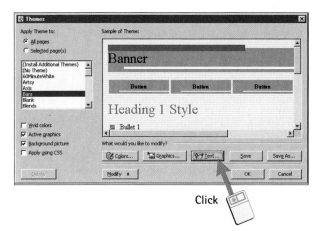

Click

12 Pick the Text Item

From the **Item** drop-down list box, select the category of text you want to change. To change the main text on the page, for example, choose **Body**. Select your font options and click **OK**.

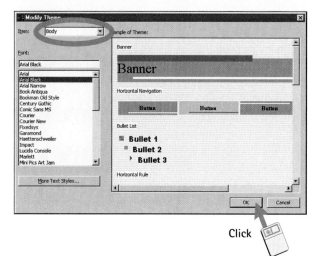

Click

13 Save the Theme

Back in the **Themes** dialog box, click the **Save** button to keep the changes to your theme. (The default themes are stored in read-only files, which can't be overwritten. FrontPage will prompt you to enter a new name for your modified theme.)

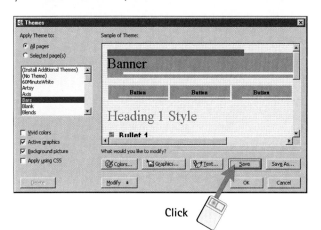

Click

14 Name the New Theme

In the **Save Theme** dialog box that opens, type a descriptive name for your theme. Click the **OK** button to close the **Save Theme** dialog box; click the **OK** button to close the **Themes** dialog box. You're done!

End

How to Choose a Browser for Preview

Before you show your site to the world, first check your pages by opening them in a browser. You can check pages with any browser installed on your PC. All you have to do is tell FrontPage which one you want to use. After you select your preferred browser, FrontPage uses that browser until you change it.

Begin

1 Launch Browser Preview

With the page file you want to view in the new browser open in **Page** view, choose **File, Preview in Browser** from the menu bar. The **Preview in Browser** dialog box opens.

Click

2 Add a Browser

If you have Internet Explorer or Netscape Navigator installed on your hard drive, FrontPage should display it in the **Browser** list. If you don't see the browser you want to use, click the **Add** button.

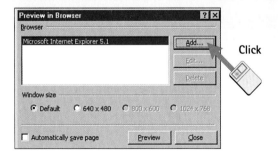

Click

3 Name Your Browser

The **Add Browser** dialog box appears. Type the name of the browser you want to use. (Note that the name you type here is the name you use to refer to the browser; it is not necessarily the browser's "official" name.)

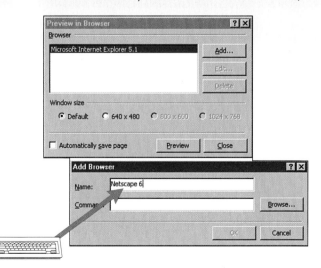

4 Find the Browser

Click the **Browse** button. Now you'll look for the browser application's file on your hard drive.

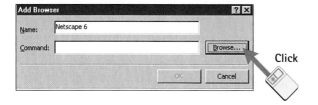

Click

5 Select the Browser

Navigate to the location of the browser you want to add. Most programs appear in the **Program Files** folder of your root drive (for example, **C:\Program Files\Netscape\Netscape 6\netscp6.exe**). Select the browser application and then click the **Open** button.

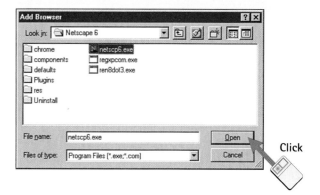

Click

6 Save Your Changes

Check to make sure that the proper browser is selected in the **Add Browser** dialog box and click **OK**. Then click the **Close** button to close the **Preview in Browser** dialog box.

Click

How-To Hints

Browser Check, Please

FrontPage's **Preview** mode requires the Internet Explorer browser. You can obtain the latest version of the IE browser at **www.microsoft.com/windows/ie**.

You can download the Netscape Navigator browser from **www.netscape.com**.

End

How to Preview a Page

A small mistake can cause big problems when visitors arrive at your freshly uploaded site. Previewing your pages as you build lets you catch problems early and test several designs before committing to one. In the preceding task, you learned how to set up any browser on your system to preview pages. FrontPage also offers an *internal browser* that lets you check out pages without opening another program. This task discusses both ways to preview a page.

1 Use the Internal Browser

Open the page you want to preview in **Page** view. Click the **Preview** tab. The **Preview** feature requires Internet Explorer 3.0 or later. If you don't have Explorer installed on your hard drive, you won't see this tab. Instead, try the next step to view your page in an external browser.

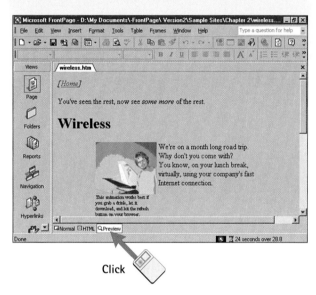

Click

2 Preview in Another Browser

To preview the page file in a browser other than Internet Explorer, choose **File, Preview in Browser**. If you don't see the browser you're looking for, refer to the preceding task, "How to Choose a Browser for Preview," for details on locating the browser you want to use.

Click

3 Select a Browser

In the **Preview in Browser** dialog box, choose the browser you want to use to preview the page.

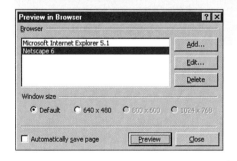

4 Pick a Resolution

Because visitors set their monitors to different screen resolutions, you can see how your page looks at several resolution settings. In the **Window size** area of the dialog box, select a resolution. Note that you can't pick a resolution higher than your current screen resolution.

5 Save Pages Before Preview

You must save your pages before you can preview them in an external browser. To save time, select the **Automatically save page** option. Otherwise, a dialog box will prompt you to save your page each time you preview.

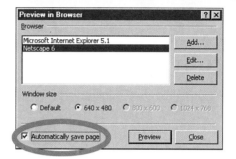

6 Choose Preview

Click the **Preview** button to launch your selected browser and open the current page.

Click

How-To Hints

Browser Differences

Beyond checking for simple display quirks, there are other reasons to view your pages in multiple browsers before publishing. Some features in FrontPage are not available to users of Netscape Navigator. For example, the Scrolling Marquee feature, which displays text moving across the page like a ticker tape, appears as static text to a Netscape user. The best way to find potential problems is to check your pages with both Internet Explorer and Netscape Navigator. If you think visitors to your Web will be using one of the handful of other browsers available (such as the well-designed Opera browser), check your site using that browser, as well.

End

How to Save and Name a Page

A program crash can mean hours of lost work. To avoid the fate of reckless page builders who let it ride and lose it all, get in the habit of saving your work often.

Begin

1 Save the Page

With the page file you have been working on open in any view, choose **File, Save** from the menu bar.

Click

2 Enter a Name

The first time you save a file, the **Save As** dialog box appears. Type a short, descriptive name in the **File name** box. It's a good idea to type all filenames in lowercase letters for consistency. You don't have to type the **.htm** extension—FrontPage adds it for you.

3 Enter a Page Title

When you save files in FrontPage, you also have the option of setting the *page title*. The title appears at the top left of your visitor's browser window, in the same bar as the **Close** box. To add a descriptive title to your page, click **Change title**.

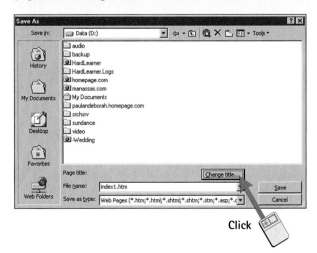

Click

4 Enter a Title

In the **Set Page Title** dialog box, type a new, descriptive title and click **OK**.

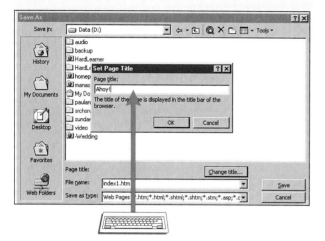

5 Save Changes

Back in the **Save As** dialog box, click the **Save** button to save the page with the filename and page title you have specified.

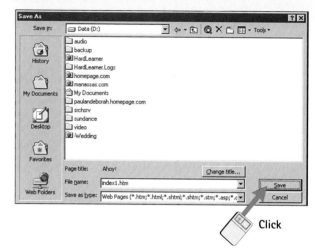

Click

6 Save Embedded Files

If you have recently added images, sound, or other objects to the page, the **Save Embedded Files** dialog box appears. By default, FrontPage saves embedded files in the same folder as the page. For now, click **OK** to keep all your files in the same place. (There's more on the **Save Embedded Files** dialog box in Part 7, "Working with Webs.")

Click

How-To Hints

Save As

After saving a file the first time, the **File, Save** command works without opening the **Save As** dialog box. To save a *copy* of the page you are working on, choose **File, Save As** and give the page a different name, following the steps in this task.

Keep It Simple

When you type a filename, avoid special characters such as the asterisk or dollar sign. Also avoid using spaces because many Web servers do not allow them.

About Titles

The **Change title** option in the **Save As** dialog box gives you a chance to describe your page to visitors. Here's another good reason to create clear page titles: Search engines use them to describe your site to prospective visitors.

End

TASK

9

How to Close and Retrieve Pages

When you finish creating a stunning layout, it's time to knock off for the day. In FrontPage, you close files as you do with any Windows software. Thankfully, FrontPage keeps track of recently used files, so opening them again won't mean searching for them all over your hard drive.

Begin

1 Close Your Work

To close an open file, click the **Close** box (the button marked with a **x**) in the **Page** window. Alternatively, press **Ctrl+F4**.

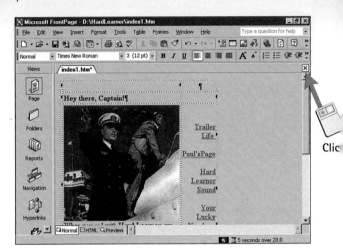

Click

2 Open a Recently Used Page

To open a page you have recently worked on, choose **File, Recent Files** from the menu bar. Select the page from the list of recently edited files that appears.

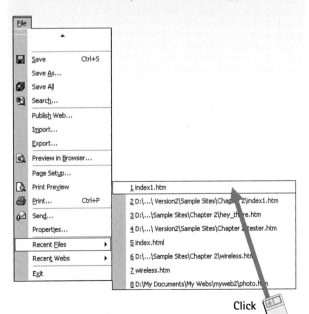

Click

3 Open an Older Page

FrontPage displays up to eight recently used pages in its **Recent Files** list. If the page you want to open doesn't appear in the list, choose **File, Open**. The **Open File** dialog box appears.

Click

4 Find Your File

FrontPage creates a folder called **My Webs** in the **My Documents** folder on your computer; by default, this is where it stores your page files and Webs. If you can't find the file you're looking for, look here.

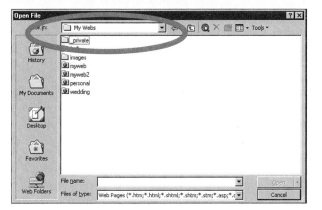

5 Select the Page

Continue opening folders until you find the page file you want to open. Select it and click the **Open** button.

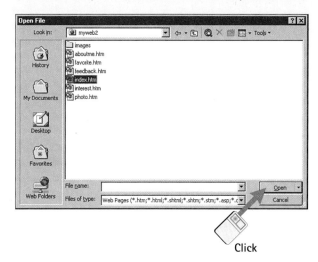

Click

How-To Hints

Open Multiple Pages

You can open multiple pages into **Page** view, although you will see only one page at a time. To open a page, select **File, Open**, navigate to the page, and click **Open**. Repeat to open additional page files. To switch from one page to another, click its name tab (you'll see the name tabs just above the page you're working on). Alternatively, choose **Window** from the menu bar to display a list of currently open pages and then select a page to view it.

End

Task

1 How to Enter Text **42**

2 How to Pull Text from an Existing File **44**

3 How to Format Text **46**

4 How to Change the Style of a Paragraph **48**

5 How to Align and Indent Text **50**

6 How to Create Lists **52**

7 How to Make a Collapsible Outline **54**

8 How to Spell Check a Page **56**

9 How to Use and Edit WordArt **58**

Working with Text

*I*n the first two parts of this book, you learned how to create simple pages. Now it's time to get your message across. In this part, I'll show you how to add text to a page and give it punch.

FrontPage uses word processor–style buttons and menus to make your transition to Web publishing fairly painless. These tools help you create eye-catching text, organized neatly on the page.

And it's easy to import text from documents you have already created—without losing the original formatting. That said, it's also simple enough to dump all the formatting and make a document look like all the rest of the text in your site, which is a pretty good idea.

Because text can get—well—a little boring, you'll also find out how to insert WordArt, a handy feature that produces text in colors and shapes that you can easily resize. *Onward.* •

How to Enter Text

Great layouts start with attractive text. To get your feet wet in working with text, this task helps you learn to type a few lines onto a page properly. As you continue through the tasks in this part, you'll learn how to spruce up your text by adding color and cool effects such as highlighting.

Begin

1 Choose Page View

To begin editing an open page, click the **Page** button in the **Views bar**. If you don't already have a page open, click the **New Page** button on the Standard toolbar. Alternatively, press **Ctrl+N** to open a new blank page.

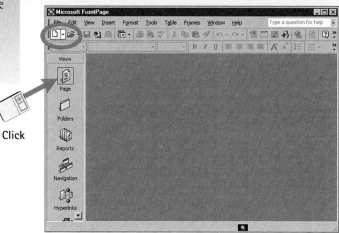

Click

2 Choose Your Starting Point

When you're working with a blank, new page, FrontPage places the insertion point at the top of the page; the text you type appears there. Go ahead and type some text. If you are starting with a page that already has text, click to select your insertion point and then start typing.

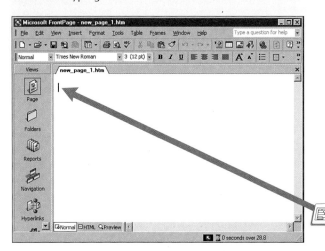

3 Show All

To see the formatting marks on your page, click the **Show All** button on the Standard toolbar. (The button icon looks like a paragraph mark.) Notice that pressing the **Enter** key produces end-of-line markers (the paragraph marks and broken arrows that mark forced line breaks).

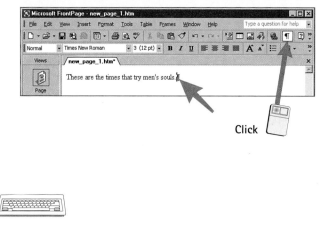

Click

4 Start a New Line

Press the **Enter** key to begin a new paragraph. To start a new line of text in the same paragraph, press **Shift+Enter**, which forces a line break (called a *soft return*).

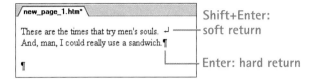

Shift+Enter: soft return

Enter: hard return

5 Fix a Mistake

Make a mistake while you're typing? Click the **Undo** button in the Standard toolbar (or press **Ctrl+Z**) to reverse your last action. Click the **Redo** button (or press **Ctrl+Y**) to reverse the **Undo** command.

Undo   Redo

6 Use Multiple Undo

Next to the **Undo** and **Redo** buttons are down arrows. Click the arrow next to **Undo** to see your last 30 actions in sequence. Click the arrow next to **Redo** to see your last 30 undos. Select from either list to jump back to the selected action. But keep in mind that you'll reverse *every action* in the list above the one you choose. And note that some actions can't be undone, such as saving a file.

Click

How-To Hints

Move and Copy Text

As your document grows, you might have to reposition paragraphs. First, highlight the text you want to move. Then press **Ctrl+X** to cut the text, or **Ctrl+C** to copy it. Position the mouse pointer where you want to paste the text and press **Ctrl+V**. You can also use the **Cut**, **Copy**, and **Paste** buttons on the **Formatting** toolbar. After you paste the text, you'll see the **Paste Options** button; click the button and choose **Keep Text Only** to remove the formatting of the text.

Find and Replace on a Page

If you want to find but not replace a word, select **Edit**, **Find** (or press **Ctrl+F**). Type the word you're looking for and click **Find Next**. To find and replace a word, select **Edit**, **Replace** (or press **Ctrl+H**).

End

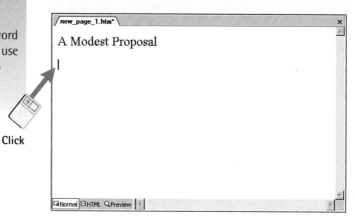

How to Pull Text from an Existing File

Suppose that your office wants to publish existing word processing documents on the Web. No problem. Just use the **Insert File** command to import existing files into FrontPage without fuss or muss.

Begin

1 Select an Insertion Point

Click a blank area on the page where you want to insert the text from your file. If you are starting with a blank page, the text will be inserted at the top of the page. Note that wherever the insertion point is, that's where the text will be inserted.

Click

2 Get the Text File

Choose **Insert, File** from the menu bar. The **Select File** dialog box opens.

Click

3 Choose the File

From the **Files of type** drop-down list, choose the option that identifies the type of file you want to import. You might want to import a text-only file, for example, like those created in Notepad. If so, select **Text Files (*.txt)**. If you want to import a Word file, select the **Word 97-2000 (*.doc)** option. Navigate to the document you want to insert in your Web page and click **Open**.

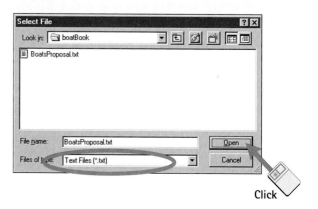

Click

4 Choose Your Conversion Options

If you selected a word processing file, FrontPage automatically retains the formatting of the original document. But if you selected a text file, the **Convert Text** dialog box appears. (A text file contains unformatted text. It might have been created in a text editor such as Notepad that does not save formatting such as bold and italics, or it may have been created by a word processor and saved in text-only format—**.txt.**) Choose the option that best suits the document you are importing and click **OK**.

Click

5 Move Selected Text

You might want to move parts of the text you've inserted to a new area of the page. To do so, highlight the text you want to move and drag it to its new location.

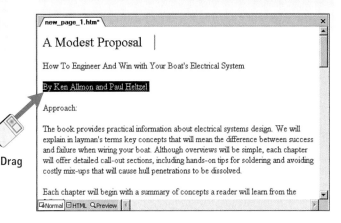

Drag

6 Clean Up the File

When you first import a file, your text may display extra line returns and font styles and sizes you might not want. To remove any undesirable formatting, select the text you want to "unformat" and choose **Format**, **Remove Formatting** (or press **Ctrl+Shift+Z**).

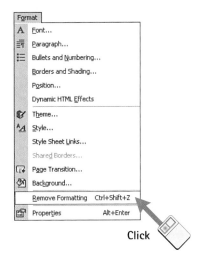

Click

How-To Hints

File Conversion Shortcut

You might find it easier to cut and paste selected information from another Windows application rather than inserting the entire file. To do so, open the text file in the program in which it was created, select the text you want, and copy it. Switch to FrontPage and paste the text on the page you are working on.

Conversion Choices

The **Convert Text** dialog box has several options you can select when importing a text file. By default, the text in the document is converted to individual, formatted paragraphs. You can select **One formatted paragraph** (all text appears as a single paragraph), **Normal paragraphs** (to use FrontPage's default text style), or **Normal paragraphs with line breaks** (to preserve line endings by adding line breaks at the end of each line). If you are importing existing text-based Web pages, select the **Treat as HTML** option.

How to Format Text

Web pages should reflect your sense of style, and FrontPage gives you more ways to lay out your text than you'll likely ever need. Most of those options are available right from the **Formatting** toolbar. If you don't see the **Formatting** toolbar on your screen, choose **View, Toolbars, Formatting** to display it.

Begin

1 Select Text

Open the page you want to work with in **Page** view. Highlight the text you want to format.

2 Choose a Font and Font Size

From the **Font** list in the **Formatting** toolbar, select a typeface. Resize text by selecting from the **Font Size** list.

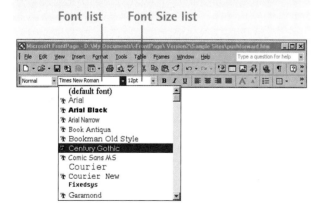

3 Emphasize Text

Click the **Bold, Italic,** or **Underline** button in the **Formatting** toolbar to apply any or all of these attributes to the selected text. Use the underline attribute sparingly because most visitors to your Web site will associate underlining with hyperlinked text.

4 See More Font Options

Choose **Format, Font** to display the **Font** dialog box, from which you can select many additional, less common, formatting options. To expand or decrease the space between the letters in the selected text (this action is typically called *kerning*), click the **Character Spacing** tab. Condense the space between characters when you have to squeeze text into a small space. Expand the space between characters to grab a visitor's attention.

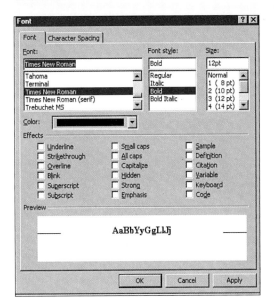

5 Change Text Color

Draw your visitor's eyes by adding a dash of color to your text. Select the text you want to color and click the **Toolbar Options** button at the right end of the Formatting toolbar. Now select the down arrow next to the **Font Color** button (a capital, underlined *A*). Select a color from the palette that appears. Notice that the **Font Color** button color changes to match your choice. The color you pick is applied to the selected text each time you click the **Font Color** button. Note that you might not have to first select the **Toolbar Options** button to find the **Font Color** button; FrontPage moves more frequently used buttons to the main area of the toolbar.

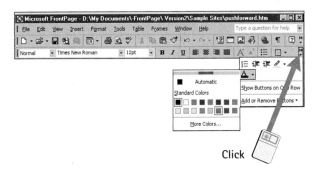

Click

6 Use a Highlight Color

You can highlight important text to draw attention to it, much as you use a highlighting marker on paper. Use this formatting technique sparingly, though. To select a highlight color, click the arrow next to the **Highlight** button on the **Formatting** toolbar and choose a color from the palette. To remove highlighting, select the highlighted text, click the down arrow again, and select the **Automatic** option.

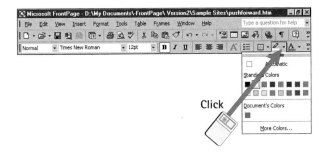

Click

How-To Hints

About Color

Consider your color choices carefully. Subtle colors are usually best and help avoid confusion. For example, many visitors expect blue text to be hyperlinked text.

Set Default Color

To set the default text color for a page, choose **Format, Background**. Make a color selection from the **Text** drop-down list. If you use a theme, the default text color is automatically selected by the theme.

End

How to Change the Style of a Paragraph

In the dark days of Web publishing, we typed HTML code (or *tags*) to separate things such as plain text from bold headings. Now, you can just click a menu selection, and FrontPage takes care of the rest. This task explains how to select headings and use the **Format Painter** tool to apply a style to paragraphs.

Begin

1 Select Paragraph

Highlight the text you want to format. If you want to format more than one paragraph, select all that you want to change. You don't have to select all the text in a paragraph to format it; select any portion to apply the formatting to the entire paragraph. Note that a paragraph is terminated by a paragraph mark, which you create by pressing **Enter**. A *line break*, created when you press **Shift+Enter**, is within a paragraph.

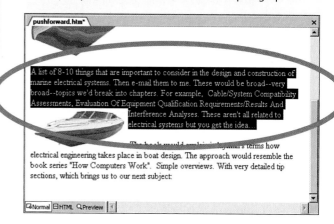

2 Set Paragraph Spacing

Select **Format, Paragraph** to open the **Paragraph** dialog box. Here you can indent paragraphs and set the spacing between lines and paragraphs. A **Preview** box shows you the result of your choices. Click **OK** to close the dialog box and apply your changes to the selected paragraph.

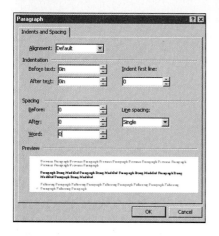

3 Choose a Heading

Headings are useful for labeling a page or section. Headings range from size 1 to size 6; a smaller number means a more important and larger heading. Heading 1 is often used as the main title on a page. Smaller headings usually act as subheads. In the **Formatting** toolbar, open the **Style** list box and choose a heading. To revert to plain text, select **Normal**.

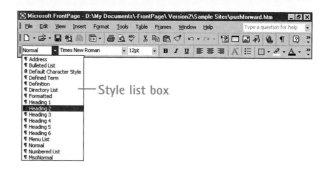

Style list box

4 Use the Format Painter

If you want to copy the format of one paragraph to another paragraph quickly, start by selecting the paragraph (or a portion of the paragraph) from which you want to copy the formatting (see the How-To Hints for more information).

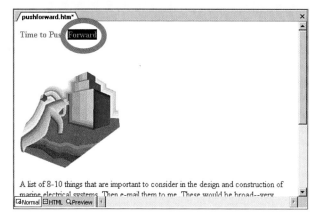

5 Copy Formatting

Single-click the **Format Painter** button in the Standard toolbar if you plan to apply formatting to just one word or paragraph. If you want to apply the format to more than one paragraph, double-click the **Format Painter** button.

Click

6 Apply Formatting

Highlight the target paragraph. When you finish highlighting, the formatting you selected in Step 4 will apply to the text you've just selected. Pretty neat, eh? Note that the **Format Painter** tool can copy hyperlinks as well as formatting. (For more on hyperlinks, see Part 4, "Connecting Files with Hyperlinks.") If you double-clicked the **Format Painter** button to apply formatting to multiple paragraphs, go back and click the button again to turn it off.

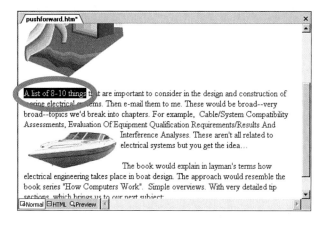

How-To Hints

Select What to Format?

When using the **Format Painter** tool, the formatting information copied depends on how much of the paragraph you highlight. Highlight a word, and the formatting for just that word is copied (for instance, italicized text). Highlight the entire paragraph, and the paragraph formatting (say, the line spacing) is also copied.

End

How to Align and Indent Text

In most cases, your page will look best with text aligned to the left margin, but you might need to change the alignment to suit special projects (such as a centered invitation). More frequently, you'll want to indent paragraphs. Indentation helps organize your page, especially when you are creating outlines and lists.

Begin

1 Select Text

Highlight the text you want to change. Note that indents and alignments apply to entire paragraphs, even if you select only a part of a paragraph.

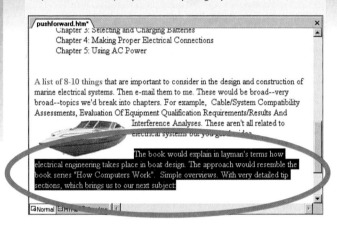

2 Choose Alignment

From the **Formatting** toolbar, click **Align Left**, **Center**, or **Align Right**. The selected text moves to the desired alignment.

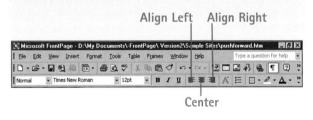

Align Left   Align Right

Center

3 Set Indentation

To quickly adjust the position of indents from the left margin, first click the **Toolbar Options** button at the right end of the **Formatting** toolbar. Then click the **Increase Indent** button. Click the **Decrease Indent** button to move the paragraph back toward the left margin.

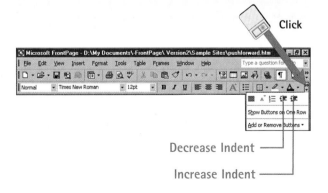

Click

Decrease Indent

Increase Indent

4 Increase Indentation

Click the **Increase Indent** button multiple times to push the paragraph farther to the right. Click the **Decrease Indent** button to reduce the indentation.

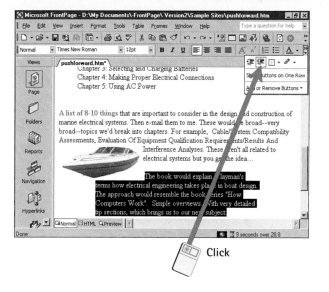

Click

5 Fine-Tune Indentation

To adjust the indentation of a paragraph (in inches), choose **Format, Paragraph**. The **Paragraph** dialog box appears. Make your selections in the **Indentation** area, and you'll see the effects of your changes in the **Preview** area at the bottom of the dialog box.

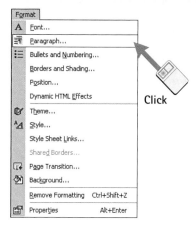

Click

6 Set Left and Right Indents

Set the indent for the left side of the paragraph by typing a number in the **Before text** box. Type a number in the **After text** box to adjust the indent on the right side of the paragraph. You can also increase the first line indentation here. Click **OK** to close the dialog box and apply the indents to the selected text.

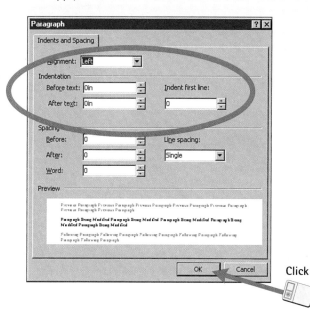

Click

How-To Hints

Set Line Spacing

If you'd like to change the spacing between lines, switch **to Page** view and select the text you want to format. Then choose **Format, Paragraph**. In the **Spacing** area of the **Paragraph** dialog box that appears, you can set the **Spacing Before** and **After** options; you can also set the spacing between words, in pixels. However, setting the spacing between words has no visible effect. FrontPage does add an HTML tag to space the words, but many browsers don't recognize this tag.

End

How to Create Lists

You can attract attention to a list of items in your text by adding *bullets*—those little solid dots or other characters that precede entries in the list. If you want to organize entries that have a set sequence order, numbered lists can help. You can create most bulleted and numbered lists using buttons on the **Formatting** toolbar. This task makes use of the **Bullets** button, but the **Numbering** button works the same way.

Begin

1 Choose Your Starting Point

Position the cursor on the page where you want your bulleted or numbered list to begin.

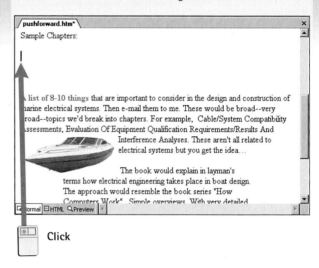

Click

2 Create a List from Scratch

Click the **Bullets** button on the Formatting toolbar. Type the first entry in your list and press **Enter**. A new bullet is created at the beginning of each new line. This example uses plain bullets, but if your page uses a theme, a graphical bullet is displayed. See Part 2, "Creating Pages," for more on applying themes.

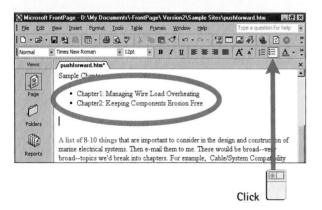

Click

3 Add Bullets to Existing Text

If you already have text on the page that you want to turn into a bulleted list, select the text and click the **Bullets** button.

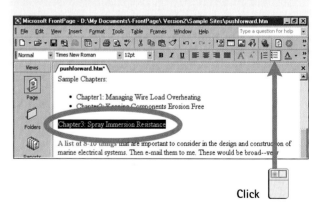

Click

4 Select Other Options

You might want to format your list with numbers or letters instead of bullets. To do so, select **Format, Bullets and Numbering** to display the **List Properties** dialog box. (To create a simple numbered list, just click the **Numbering** button in the **Formatting** toolbar.)

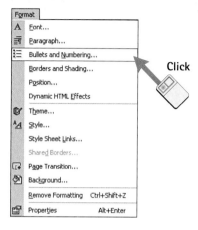

Click

5 Select Numbering Options

In the **List Properties** dialog box, click the **Numbers** tab. Make a choice from the number and letter styles available. Select a number from the **Start at** box if you want your list to start with a number other than 1.

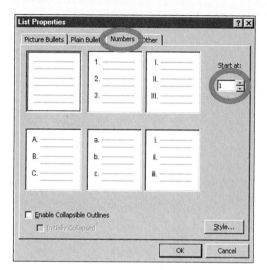

6 Use a Picture Bullet

You can use any picture you like for a bullet—just make sure that the image is small. In the **List Properties** dialog box, click the **Picture Bullets** tab and select the **Specify picture** option. Click **Browse**, navigate to the image file you want to use for a bullet, and click **OK** twice.

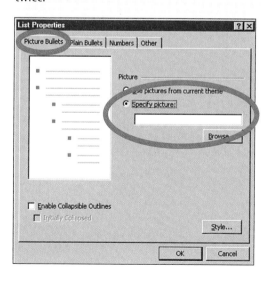

How-To Hints

Remove Bullets

To remove bullets from a list, select the list text. Then click the **Bullets** or **Numbering** button in the **Formatting** toolbar.

Create Sublists

In some cases, your list may have several levels (as is the case with an outline). You can create sublists (or "nested" lists) by selecting the items you want to nest and clicking the **Increase Indent** button twice. Note that you can use different styles of bullets in sublists: Select the nested items and choose **Format, Bullets and Numbering**; use the **List Properties** dialog box to specify your preferences.

End

Task7

How to Make a Collapsible Outline

Lists are a great way to set off important information, and collapsible outlines increase the impact of the lists. When you have lists with multiple levels, you can use a collapsible outline to display just the subject headings of the list. When a visitor clicks a heading, the rest of the text pops onto the page. (Note that to see collapsible outlines in action, you must be using the Microsoft Internet Explorer browser, version 4.0 or higher.)

Begin

1 Start Your List

Click the **Bullets** button in the **Formatting** toolbar. Then create a set of headings. In this example, chapter names serve as the headings. Under these headings, add some text. (We'll indent this text later and then tell FrontPage to hide it until the heading is clicked.) Press **Enter** after each line. (If your list already exists, simply highlight it and click the **Bullets** button from the toolbar.)

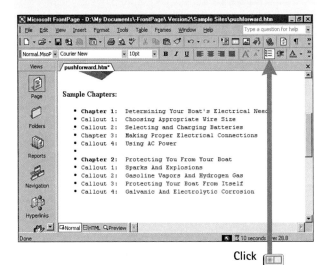

Click

How-To Hints

Make Your List Obvious

Keep in mind that if you choose to make your list initially collapsed (as explained in Step 3), visitors might not know that the list can expand. Make sure to add a bit of text that points out the collapsible list to visitors. In this example, the text **Sample Chapters** could be augmented by text such as **Click a heading to see an expanded list of contents.**

2 Choose List Properties

Select your list heading (in this case, the line that says **Chapter 1**) and choose **Format, Bullets and Numbering**. The **Bullets and Numbering** dialog box appears. Choose a list style from the **Numbers** tab or one of the **Bullets** tabs. For example, if you want to use numbers for heads and letters for subheads, click the **Numbers** tab and make a selection.

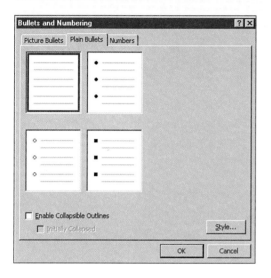

3 Enable the Outline

Enable the **Enable Collapsible Outlines** check box. If you want the nested items to be collapsed until you click them, enable the **Initially Collapsed** check box. Click the **OK** button to close the dialog box.

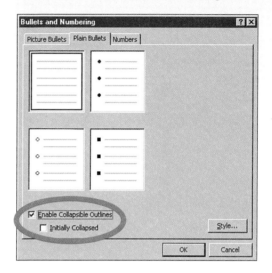

4 Choose the Sublist

Now you have to tell FrontPage which items to hide in the outline. Select the list items to collapse and click the **Increase Indent** button in the **Formatting** toolbar twice. Repeat this step for each nested list in the outline.

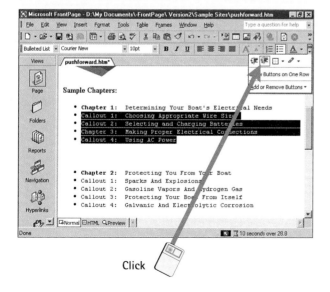

Click

5 Preview the Outline

To check out your collapsible list, save the document and click the **Preview** tab. Then click a heading to see it expand. Click it again to hide the list contents.

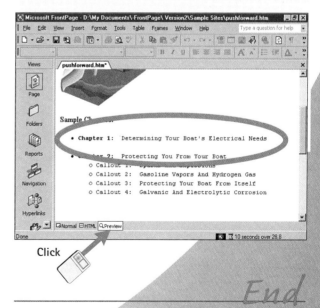

Click

End

How to Spell Check a Page

By default, FrontPage checks spelling in the background as you type. Potential errors appear with a wavy red underline. This feature saves you the trouble of running the standard spell check (in which you choose to ignore or correct each potential error the checker finds). Of course, you can also run the standard spell check feature, whether or not the background spell check feature is enabled.

Begin

1 View Options

In this example, let's first turn on background spell checking (follow these same steps to turn off the feature). Choose **Tools, Page Options** from the menu bar. The **Page Options** dialog box opens.

Click

2 Start Background Spell Check

On the **General** tab, select the **Check spelling as you type** option (deselect it to turn off the feature). Click **OK**.

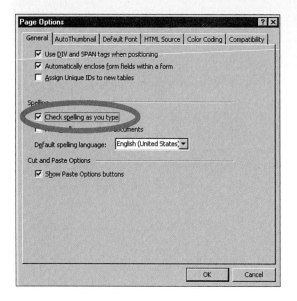

3 Check for Errors

Red squiggly lines appear on your page, pointing out potential errors. I say "potential" errors because the words FrontPage identifies as misspelled may be perfectly legitimate words; it's just that the words don't appear in FrontPage's dictionary.

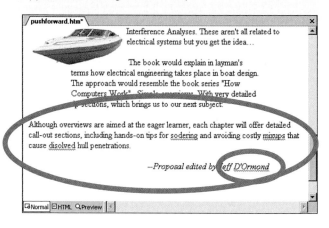

4 Take a Suggestion

To see a list of suggested corrections for an underlined word, right-click the word. To change the underlined word, select the correct spelling from the pop-up list that appears.

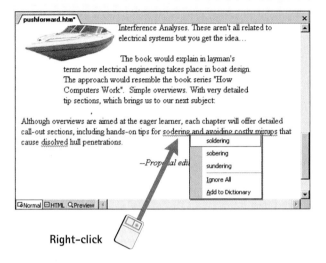

Right-click

5 Ignore a Word

If an underlined word is correct, choose **Ignore All** from the pop-up list; FrontPage will ignore all other occurrences of that word on your page. Choose **Add to Dictionary** from the pop-up list to store the word in your spelling dictionary so that it is never flagged again. The red underline disappears.

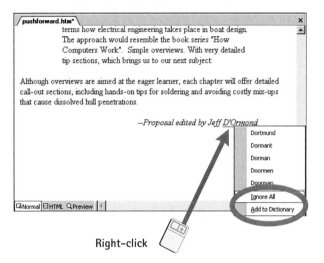

Right-click

6 Run Standard Spell Check

To run a standard spelling check, select **Tools, Spelling** (or press the **F7** key on your keyboard). The spell checker checks all the words on your page, stopping at words it does not recognize. Click **Ignore** to skip only one instance of a word; click **Ignore All** to skip all instances. If the word is misspelled, select the correct spelling from the **Suggestions** pane and click **Change** or **Change All**. If you use the word often, click the **Add** button to store the word in a custom dictionary.

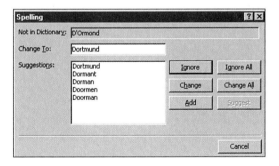

How-To Hints

Spell Check a Web

FrontPage can examine all the pages in your site for spelling errors. To see how, refer to Task 5, "How to Spell Check the Entire Site," in Part 11, "Preparing to Publish."

End

9

How to Use
and Edit WordArt

You can use FrontPage 2002's new WordArt feature to
spice up headlines and other attention-starved text.
With WordArt, you can insert a bit of text, choose a
color and pattern to fill it, and then resize and move it
on the page. This task shows you how to get started
playing with text as an image.

Begin

1 Place Your WordArt

Place the cursor on the page at the position where you
want to insert the WordArt you'll create. Choose **Insert,
Picture, WordArt** from the menu bar. The **WordArt
Gallery** window opens.

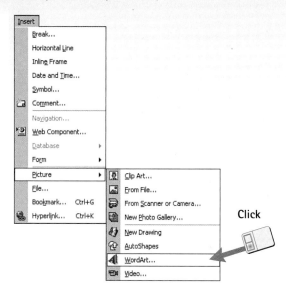

Click

2 Choose a Style

Take your pick from the fun and (*ahem*) interesting
styles that you see. Double-click the one that appeals
to you and then click **OK**.

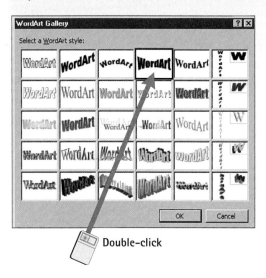

Double-click

3 Enter Your Text

FrontPage now prompts you to enter the text you want
on your page. Type it in and choose the font and size
you desire for this text from the menus at the top of
the dialog box. Click **OK**.

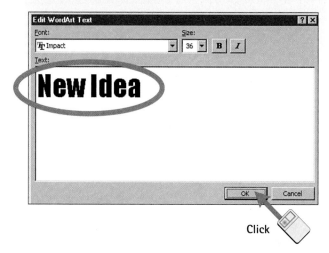

Click

4 Edit Your Art

Here's where things get interesting. Your WordArt appears on the page with a set of selection handles. Click the green circle at top and drag to rotate the WordArt. You can also grab the yellow diamond and drag to change the perspective of the text. If you don't like the effect, press **Ctrl+Z** to undo the changes.

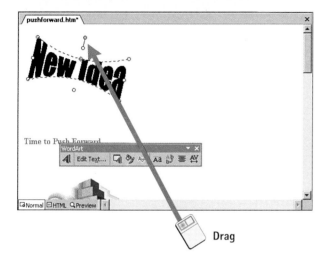

Drag

5 Resize Text

You can change the size of the WordArt by grabbing the middle handles at left or right (to resize horizontally) or the middle handles at top and bottom (to resize vertically). Drag the handles at the corners to resize the WordArt horizontally *and* vertically at the same time.

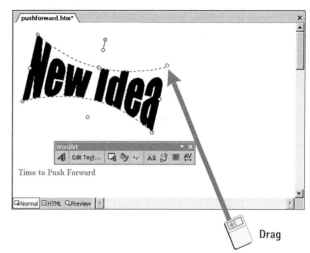

Drag

6 Use the Toolbar

If you don't see the floating WordArt toolbar, choose **View, Toolbars, WordArt** to make it appear. Hover over each button to see the name of the tool. Using the toolbar, you can change the WordArt shape, space out letters, and set the vertical and horizontal alignment. Click around to see how each tool affects the look of your WordArt. Remember that pressing **Ctrl+Z** (undo) can get you out of a jam.

How-To Hints

Select and Deselect

Note that you can't edit or position WordArt until it is selected. Just click within the WordArt to select it (the handles appear). To move the WordArt, point near the middle of the WordArt until you see a four-sided arrow, and then drag it wherever you want. Double-click the WordArt to open the **Edit WordArt Text** dialog box and the WordArt toolbar so that you can fine-tune the image.

End

Project 1

Creating a Personal Page

If you read the first few parts of this book, you now understand the basics of building a Web page. And even if you jumped ahead and have started your work in FrontPage with this project, you will learn how to create your first home page, from start to finish. To speed things up a bit, we'll start with a page that has already been created, called a *template*. To add a bit of personality, we'll choose a *theme*, change fonts and colors, and give the page a title that aptly describes its content.

Begin

1 Open a Page Template

To get started, let's look at some page designs and select one that will be simple to work with but that will serve as a good example of basic page building. Click the **down arrow** next to the **New Page** button in the Standard toolbar and choose **Page**. The **Page Templates** dialog box opens.

Click

2 Select a Page

Select a template icon to see a short description of the page it will create. A small preview window shows you what the page will look like. When you find a page that suits you, click the **OK** button. A new page opens in the FrontPage window, filled with either Latin-looking boilerplate text or instructions on how the page should be edited.

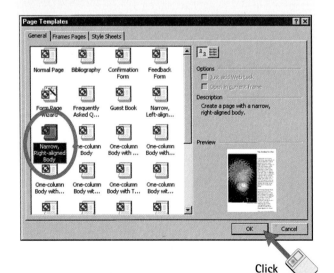

Click

3 Open the Themes Dialog Box

FrontPage themes let you choose a matching set of colors, graphics, and text and apply them all at once. To see a list of available themes, choose **Format, Theme** from the menu bar. The **Themes** dialog box opens.

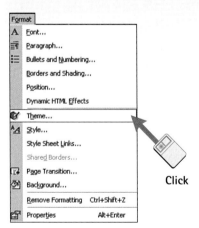

Click

4 Choose a Theme

Select a theme from the list in the left pane and preview it in the **Sample of Theme** pane on the right. If you don't find a theme you like, you can create your own by modifying the elements of an existing theme. We show you how to pick your own text styles, colors, and graphics in Task 5, "How to Modify a Theme," in Part 2, "Creating Pages."

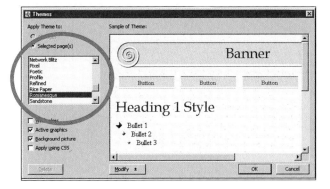

5 Set Theme Options

FrontPage provides a few quick controls that affect the look of your selected theme. Select the **Vivid colors**, **Active graphics**, and **Background picture** options to see a sample of your theme using these features. For this example, deselect the **Background picture** option to make the page less busy and load faster. Deselect any options you don't care for. When you finish, click **OK**.

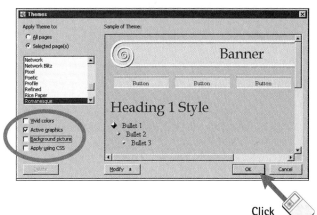

Click

6 Enter New Text

Highlight the boilerplate text that comes with the page template and replace it by typing your own text.

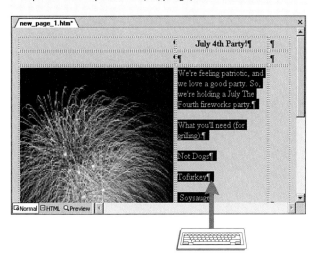

How-To Hints

How to Install More Themes

If you installed only the typical themes when you installed Microsoft Office, you can install the rest of the themes that are available on the CD-ROM: From the menu bar, choose **Format, Theme**. Then scroll to the top of the themes list (near the top left of the dialog box). Select **Install Additional Themes** from the list and click **Yes** to confirm.

In addition, many Web sites offer themes for download. A search in any major search engine should produce a list of theme-offering sites.

Continues

7 Select the Text to Format

You can change the font styles and colors of text on the page. To do so, first select the text you want to change.

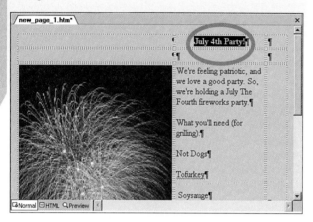

8 Change the Text Font

Choose a typeface and font style from the **Font** and **Font Size** menus on the **Formatting** toolbar.

9 Give the Text Emphasis

Click the **Bold** or **Italic** button on the **Formatting** toolbar to apply either (or both) of those emphasis formats. Use the **Underline** button only rarely; visitors tend to think that underlined text is a hyperlink to open another file.

10 Change Font Color

Change the color of the selected text by making a choice from the **Font Color** menu. Open the menu by clicking the arrow next to the **Font Color** button on the **Formatting** toolbar. To choose a custom color, click the **More Colors** option.

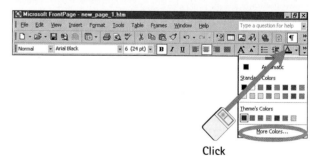

Click

11 Use the Eyedropper to Select a Color

Here's a simple way to sample a color that appears anywhere on your screen. In the **More Colors** dialog box, click the **Select** button. The mouse pointer becomes an eyedropper. Move the pointer over any image on the screen and click a color to sample it. (The eyedropper tool works anywhere on the screen where you can select a color.) Click the **OK** button to apply the color to the selected text. Selecting colors from a picture on your page is a great way to accentuate your design.

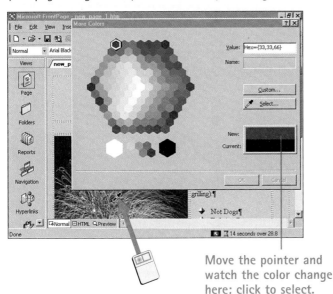

Move the pointer and watch the color change here; click to select.

12 Align Text

To change the position of text on the page, select the text and click the **Align Left**, **Center**, or **Align Right** button on the **Formatting** toolbar.

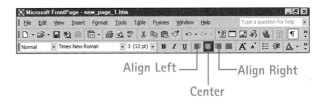

Align Left ———   ——— Align Right

Center

13 Create a List

Lists highlight important details on the page. To create a list, first select the text you want to use. On the **Formatting** toolbar, click the **Bullets** button to create a bulleted list. (The bullet characters are tiny graphics that were selected automatically in Step 4 when you chose a theme.)

14 Spell Check the Page

Before saving the page, run a quick spell check. Position the cursor at the top of the page and then click the **Spelling** button on the **Standard** toolbar.

Click

Continues

15 Ignore, Change, or Add Words

If the spelling checker finds a word it doesn't recognize, make a selection from the options offered in the **Spelling** dialog box. If the word is correct, click **Ignore** (click **Ignore All** if the word is used more than once). You can also select one of the suggestions offered and click **Change** or **Change All**. To add the word to the spelling dictionary, click **Add**. The spelling checker lets you know when it finishes scanning your document. Click **OK**.

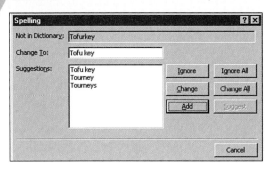

16 Save the Page

Now save the work you've done to the new page: Click the **Save** button on the **Standard** toolbar. Because the page has never been saved before, the **Save As** dialog box opens.

Click

17 Title the Page

When a visitor opens your page, the *page title* appears in his or her browser window, above the browser's menu bar. It's a good idea to title all your pages because search engines use page titles to describe your site to prospective visitors. Click the **Change title** button at the bottom of the **Save As** dialog box to set a meaningful title for your page.

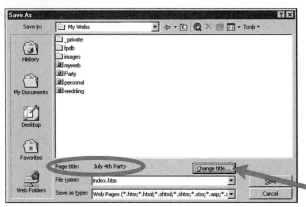

Click

18 Enter the Page Title

In the **Set Page Title** dialog box, type a few words to describe your page. By default, FrontPage uses the first few words it finds on the page. When you are satisfied with the new page title, click the **OK** button.

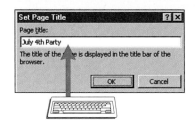

19 Set the Filename

Back in the **Save As** dialog box, type a descriptive name for the file in the **File name** box. Do not use spaces or special characters in your filename (doing so causes problems when you copy pages to a Web server). However, you *can* use the dash (-) and underscore (_) characters in filenames. Click the **Save** button.

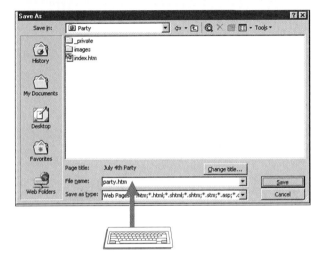

20 Save Embedded Files

The first time you save a page that includes graphics you haven't used before, you are prompted to save them. The options for saving embedded files are described in more depth in Task 4, "How to Save Embedded Files," of Part 7, "Working with Webs." For now, click the **OK** button to save any graphics files on your page.

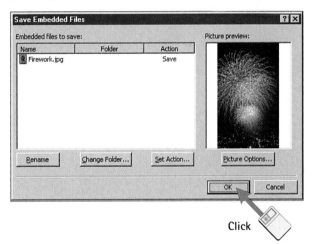

Click

21 Preview the Page

Drum roll, please. It's time to take the wraps off your first functioning Web page. To see how the page looks in the Internet Explorer browser, click the **Preview** tab. Check for obvious errors, and pat yourself on the back for a job well done. (To correct any errors, click the **Normal** tab to return to editing mode.)

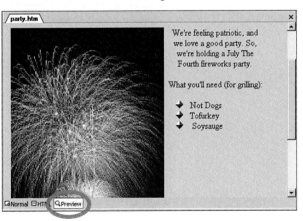

How-To Hints

Teach Old Text a New Trick

You can easily set off important text by adding a border. Just select the text you want to outline and click the down-pointing arrow next to the **Outside Borders** button on the **Formatting** toolbar. The button, a new feature in FrontPage 2002, looks like a square with dotted lines inside it. Select the border you want from the menu that appears. To remove a border, select **No Border** from the **Outside Borders** button menu.

End

Task

1 How to Use Hyperlinks View 68

2 How to Set and Edit Hyperlinks 70

3 How to Create Internal and External Hyperlinks 72

4 How to Create Bookmarks 74

5 How to Link to a Movie or Audio File 76

6 How to Change the Look of Links 78

7 How to Follow a Hyperlink 80

PART 4

Connecting Files with Hyperlinks

So far, FrontPage looks a lot like other Windows word-processing programs. But when you start working with hyperlinks, things get interesting.

You might hear hyperlinks referred to as *hotlinks* or simply as *links*. All these terms mean the same thing: an object you click to open another object. The link you click might open a Web page, download a file to your computer, or launch the appropriate program to handle files of many different types, including an e-mail client or a multimedia player.

In this part of the book, you'll discover how to create hyperlinks that connect your pages, address an e-mail message, or launch a sound or a movie. Later in the book, we'll talk about linking images and dig deeper into working with multimedia. Stay tuned.

How to Use Hyperlinks View

Let's take a look at FrontPage's **Hyperlinks** view, a visual representation of how your pages are linked together. Icons represent your pages, and lines between these icons represent the hyperlinks in your site.

Begin

1 Open a Web

Are you starting from scratch? Try opening one of the sample sites FrontPage provides such as the **Personal Web**. Click the down-pointing arrow next to the **New Page** button and then select **Web**. Select **Personal Web** and click **OK**. To open an existing Web, select **File**, **Recent Webs** and make a selection.

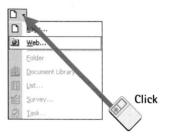

Click

2 Select Hyperlinks View

From the **Views bar**, click the **Hyperlinks** button. The selected Web opens in **Hyperlinks** view.

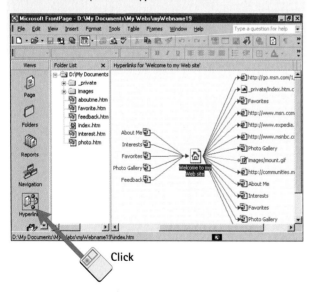

Click

3 Explore Your Links

The pages and folders in your Web appear in the **Folder List** pane (in the center of the window). To move a page to the center of the **Hyperlinks** view pane (the right pane), click its name in the **Folder List**.

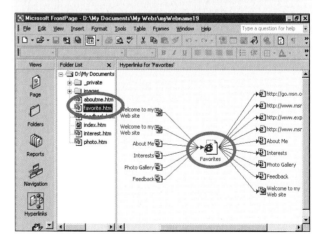

4 View Page Links

To see the links on a page without centering the page in the right pane, click the plus symbol next to the page icon in the **Hyperlinks** view pane. Make the links disappear by clicking the minus symbol.

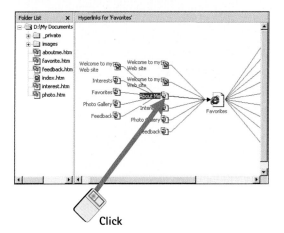

Click

5 View a Page by Title

To view pages by filename rather than by page title, right-click a blank area of the **Hyperlinks** view pane. Deselect **Show Page Titles** from the shortcut menu that appears.

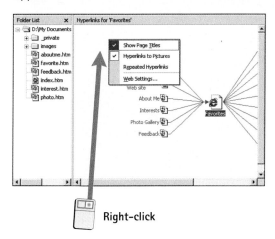

Right-click

6 View Picture Links

To see any links to graphics in **Hyperlinks** view, right-click a blank area of the view window. Select **Hyperlinks to Pictures**.

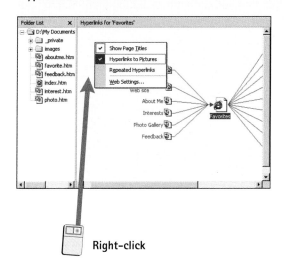

Right-click

7 Open a Page

To open a page for editing, double-click its icon in the **Folder List** or in the **Hyperlinks** view pane.

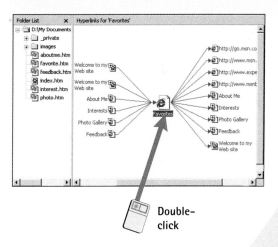

Double-click

End

How to Set and Edit Hyperlinks

Creating hyperlinks takes just a few clicks. In this task, we'll connect one page to another, but you can link a page to any type of file, including pictures and sounds. In Task 5, you'll learn how to link to movies and audio files. In Part 5, "Working with Graphics," you'll find out how to use an image as a hyperlink.

Begin

1 Open a Page

Open the page on which you want to create a hyperlink by selecting **File, Open**. In the **Open File** dialog box, select the page name you want to open and click **Open**. The page opens by default in **Page** view.

Click

2 Select Text

Highlight the text you want to use as your hyperlink. Make sure that your text clearly identifies what will happen when the visitor clicks the link. You might want to avoid hyperlinking the words *Click here*, which are overused and considered too obvious. Link to any words that pertain to more information (your bio, contact information, or other pages in your site, for instance). Keep text links short and simple, or they will be difficult to read.

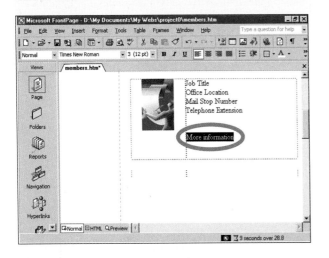

3 Create the Hyperlink

From the **Standard** toolbar, click the **Hyperlink** button. The **Insert Hyperlink** dialog box opens.

Click

4 Select a Page

From the list of existing pages in your Web, select the page you want to link to and click **OK**. Note that the **Insert Hyperlink** dialog box shows you the files in the current Web. To find a file on your system that isn't in the current Web, click the **Browse for File** button (it looks like an open folder), select the file, and click **OK**. The path to the selected file appears in the **Address** box. The address is the Web address (or URL) where your file exists (more about URLs in the next task, "How to Create Internal and External Hyperlinks").

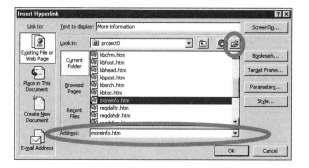

5 Check the Hyperlink

To see the hyperlink in action, click the **Preview** tab. Your hyperlink appears as it will to visitors. Click the link. When you finish admiring your work, click the **Normal** tab.

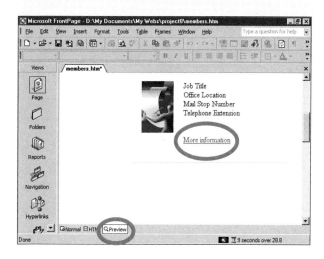

6 Edit a Hyperlink

To edit a hyperlink (that is, to direct the link to a different file), right-click the link and choose **Hyperlink Properties** from the shortcut menu. You can also open the **Edit Hyperlink** dialog box by pressing **Ctrl+K**. Repeat Step 4 to select a new page to link to.

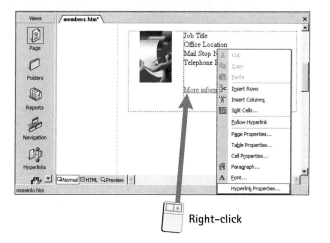

Right-click

7 Remove a Link

To remove the link, open the **Edit Hyperlink** dialog box (see Step 6) and click the **Remove Link** button.

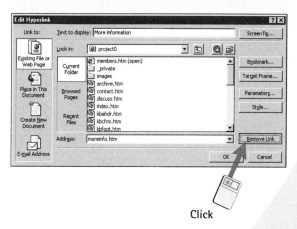

Click

End

How to Create Internal and External Hyperlinks

In addition to connecting pages within your own site, you can create links that jump to somebody else's Web page. You can also use hyperlinks to collect feedback from visitors by creating an e-mail link that fills in your address when the link is clicked. You can even create a link to a page that doesn't yet exist. All this, plus more exciting tips, in this task.

Begin

1 Select Text

Select the text you want to use as a link and then click the **Hyperlink** button from the **Standard** toolbar. The **Insert Hyperlink** dialog box appears.

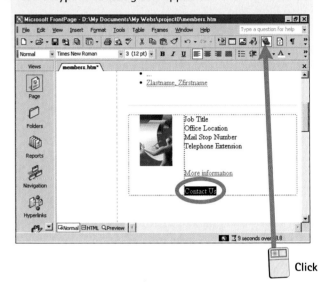

Click

2 Create an E-mail Hyperlink

To show your visitors that you want to hear from them, create a link that sends e-mail to a specified address. Click the **E-mail Address** button; the dialog box changes to include fields specifically for e-mail information. In the **E-mail address** field, type the address to which you want the message delivered. You can also type the subject of the message, for instance **Feedback** or **Home page comments**. When a visitor clicks the link, a message window launches with the address you entered. When you finish, click **OK**.

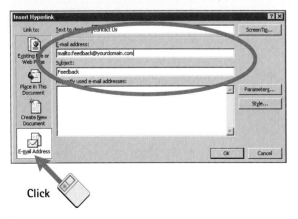

Click

3 Create a Link to a File

To link to a file on your hard drive, select **Existing File or Web Page** and then click the **Current Folder** button. To find a file on your system, click the **Look in** pop-up menu and then select the folder on your system where the file is saved. Clicking the **Browse for File** button works in a similar way to the **Look in** menu (the button looks like an open folder with an arrow over it). Notice how FrontPage smartly keeps track of pages you have recently used, whether you opened them from your hard drive or on the Web. Click the **Recent Files** button to see documents you've opened recently.

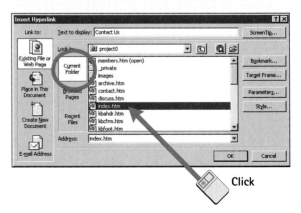

Click

4 Link to an Outside Web Site

You can create hyperlinks to outside Web sites. If you know the address of the site to which you want to link, type it in the **Address** text box in the **Insert Hyperlink** dialog box. Alternatively, click **Browsed Pages** to see a list of Web sites you've recently visited with your browser.

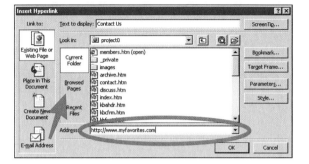

5 Select a Page with Your Browser

To use your browser to search for a particular Web site that you want to link to, click the **Browse the Web** button. Use your browser to open the page on the Web to which you want to create a link. Press **Alt+Tab** (or click the **Minimize** button in the top-right corner of your browser). FrontPage fills in the **Address** box for you, using the address of the last page you visited.

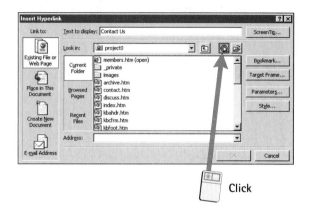

Click

6 Create a Link to a Blank Page

If you want to create a link to a blank page, click the **Create New Document** button. Enter the filename in the **Name of new document** field (FrontPage adds the **.htm** extension for you). The **Full Path** area tells you where on your hard disk the page will be saved. If that's not where you want to save the file, click the **Change** button, navigate to the folder you want, and click the **OK** button.

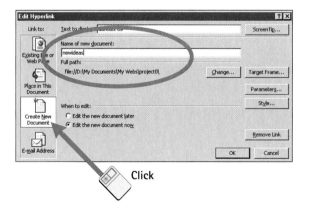

Click

How-To Hints

What's a ScreenTip?

The **ScreenTip** button in the **Insert Hyperlink** dialog box lets you add a bit of text that will appear when a site visitor points the mouse at a link (but does not yet click, an action known as *hovering*.)

Follow a Hyperlink in Page View

To quickly test your new hyperlink in **Page** view (with the **Normal** tab selected), hold the **Ctrl** key and click the link. Here's another shortcut: Right-click the link and select **Follow Hyperlink**.

End

How to Create Bookmarks

Suppose that your Aunt Sidney wants to publish her memoirs on the Web. To make her, uh, *fascinating* trials and tribulations easier to navigate, you can create links to specific markers you set on pages. For instance, you can create a link that jumps directly to her college graduation or that goes straight to her thrilling trip to Coney Island. FrontPage calls these page markers *bookmarks*. This kind of link is also commonly known as an *anchor*. No matter what you call them, these little aids help you get to the "good parts" of a lengthy article more quickly.

Begin

1 Locate Your Bookmark

Click to mark the point where you want a bookmark created. You can select a block of text or just place the cursor in front of the area you want to bookmark.

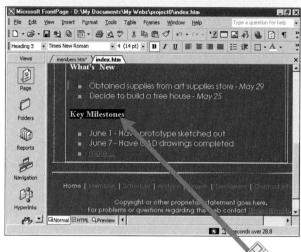

Click

2 Insert a Bookmark

From the menu bar, choose **Insert**, **Bookmark**. The **Bookmark** dialog box appears.

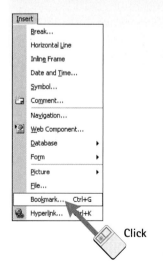

Click

3 Name the Bookmark

Type the name of your bookmark, preferably one word for wider browser support. Click **OK** to close the dialog box. The bookmark has been created.

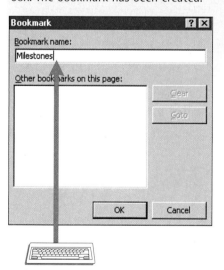

4 Create a Hyperlink

Select the text you want to convert to a hyperlink.
Right-click the text and choose **Hyperlink** from the
pop-up menu that appears (or click the **Hyperlink** button from the **Standard** toolbar). The **Insert Hyperlink**
dialog box opens.

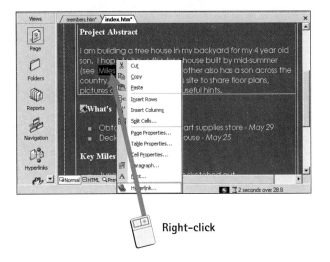

Right-click

5 Select a Bookmark

Click the **Existing File or Web Page** button and then
click the **Bookmark** button. From the list of bookmarks
that appears, choose the bookmark you named in
Step 3. In this example, it's the only bookmark on the
page. Click the **OK** button twice to save your changes
and close the open dialog boxes.

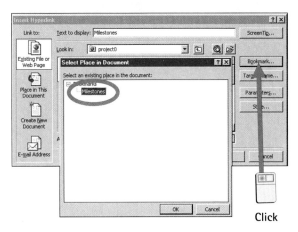

Click

6 Preview the Bookmark

Click the **Preview** tab. Click the hyperlink you created in
Steps 4 and 5 to test your new bookmark.

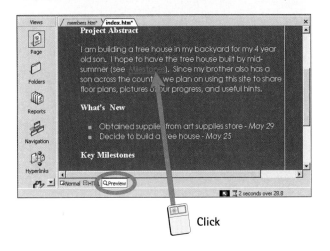

Click

How-To Hints

Back to the Top

Consider adding a bookmark to a starting point on your page. For example, in an outline, you can create an index that links to
section headings throughout the page. At the
section headings, create a link marked **Back to
Index**. When users click that link, they jump
back to the index. This commonly used trick
saves the user from scrolling.

End

How to Link to a Movie or Audio File

Every day, movie and audio files are becoming more prevalent on the Web. Faster Internet connections—including cable modems and Digital Subscriber Line (DSL) connections—let your visitors see your latest home movies or listen to files you record with your PC. That said, remember to be kind to folks with slower modem connections. Where possible, limit the size of the files you put on your site. Here's how to link to sounds and movies that show off your directing talents.

Begin

1 Create Descriptive Text

Create and highlight some text you can use as the hyperlink to the multimedia file. This text should be something descriptive. If the file you want to link to is large (as most audio and video files are), you should list the file size. That way, visitors can decide whether their modem connections can handle the file.

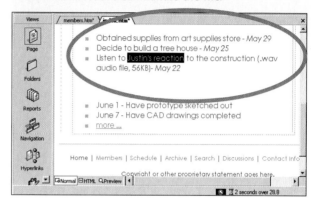

2 Add a Hyperlink

Press **Ctrl+K** (or click the **Hyperlink** button in the **Standard** toolbar). The **Insert Hyperlink** dialog box opens.

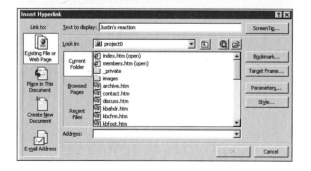

3 Select Your Multimedia File

Click **Existing File or Web Page** and then click the **Current Folder** button. If the multimedia file you want to link to is on your hard drive, click the **Look in** pop-up menu (which appears only when you click the **Current Folder** button) and navigate to the folder on your system where the file has been saved.

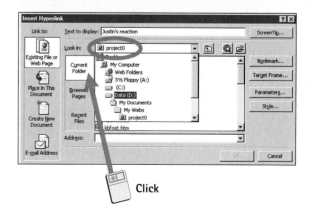

Click

4 Select the File

Double-click the video or audio file to select it. Then click the **OK** button to close the dialog box and create the link to that file. Appropriate video files for the Web include QuickTime (**.mov**), Windows Media (**.avi**), and RealVideo (**.ram**). Useful audio files include MPEG Layer 3 (**.mp3**), RealAudio (**.ra**), and Windows Wave files (**.wav**).

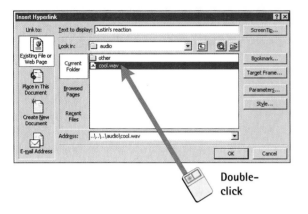

Double-click

5 Link to a File from the Web

You can create a link to an audio or video file on the Web. If you know the path to the file on the Web, type it in the **Address** box in the **Insert Hyperlink** dialog box. If you have recently opened that file with your Web browser, click the **Browsed Pages** button and select the file from the list. Click the **OK** button to create the link.

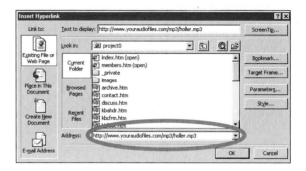

6 Preview Your Hyperlink

Click the **Preview** tab to open the file you're working on in the internal browser. Click the link; the video or audio file you specified for that link opens in the player associated with your browser. Your browser, for example, might be configured by default to open **.wav** files with Windows Media Player or to open RealAudio files with the RealPlayer.

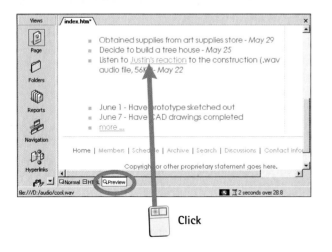

Click

How-To Hints

Insert a Video on a Page

You can add a video that will appear directly on the page, rather than linking to a video file that causes a separate window to open. See Task 1, "How to Insert a Video," in Part 8, "Adding Multimedia."

End

How to Change the Look of Links

As you surf the Web, you'll see lots of different hyper-link color schemes. With FrontPage, you can choose any colors you want for your links. A link can be in one of three stages, and each stage can have its own color. The *default hyperlink color* appears when a link hasn't yet been clicked. This is the color seen most of the time, so choose wisely. The *active hyperlink color* appears when you click a link. The *visited hyperlink color* appears after you have clicked the link.

Begin

1 Open Page Properties

The tools for selecting link colors are a bit hard to find. Select **Format, Background** to view your choices. (Alternatively, right-click a blank area of the page and select **Page Properties** from the pop-up menu.) The **Page Properties** dialog box opens.

Click

2 Set Default Link Color

Make sure that you are on the **Background** tab of the dialog box. From the **Hyperlink** drop-down list box, select the default link color.

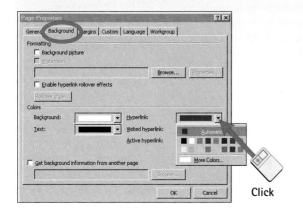

Click

3 Select Visited Link Color

From the **Visited hyperlink** drop-down list box, select a color for links that your visitor has clicked before.

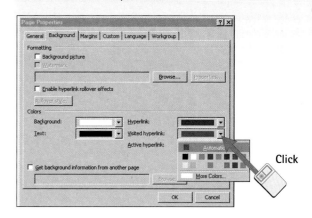

Click

4 Select Active Link Color

From the **Active hyperlink** drop-down list box, select a color for links that have just been clicked. Because this color is seen only briefly, some people leave it the same as the default hyperlink.

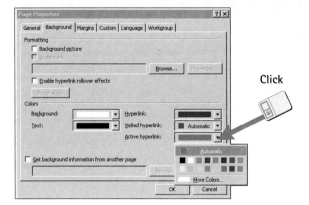

Click

5 Create a Rollover

For an especially flashy effect, try a *hyperlink rollover*. When a visitor points at a text link with the mouse, the text changes appearance. Based on your choices, the text can change color or appear bold. To apply rollover effects to all the links on your page, click the **Enable hyperlink rollover effects** check box.

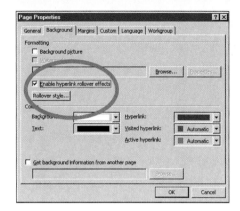

6 Select a Rollover Style

Click the **Rollover style** button to open the **Font** dialog box. Now, the fun part: Make your style choices from the options in the dialog box. Click **OK** twice to save your rollover link style changes.

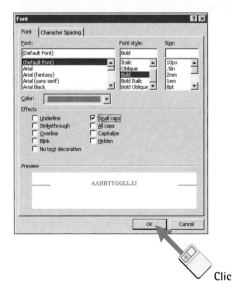

Click

How-To Hints

Colors and Themes

If you want to change hyperlink colors on a page that uses a theme, you can't use the instructions given in this task. The theme controls the colors used by the hyperlinks. To change hyperlink colors on a page controlled by a theme, see Task 5, "How to Modify a Theme," in Part 2, "Creating Pages."

End

How to Follow a Hyperlink

Nothing puts out the unwelcome mat like broken links. To keep your site in good form, check links after you create them. This task provides explanations for several ways to browse your links (that is, to check your links) before you publish a page.

Begin

1 Check Links from Page View

When editing in **Page** view (with the **Normal** tab selected), press the **Ctrl** key and click a link. Doing so opens the link in the same window as the page you were working on, ready for editing. (Alternatively, right-click the link and choose **Follow Hyperlink**.)

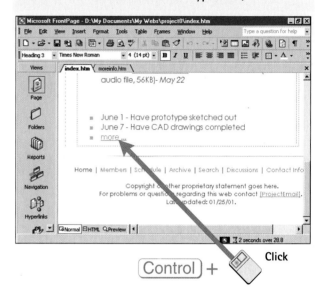

Control + Click

2 Return to the Original Page

After you follow a hyperlink to a new page, how do you get back to your original page? Choose the appropriate page name tab. You can also select the **Window** menu option and choose the page name from the list that appears.

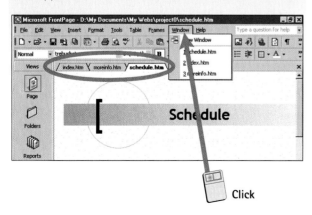

Click

3 Follow a Bookmark

To jump to a bookmark, select **Insert**, **Bookmark**. The **Bookmark** dialog box opens. Choose the desired bookmark from the list and click the **Goto** button.

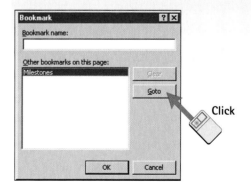

Click

4 Use the Preview Tab

In **Page** view, you can also click the **Preview** tab to test a link. The internal browser displays your page as a normal browser would. In **Preview** mode, just click a link to follow it.

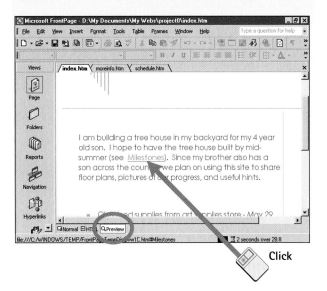

Click

5 Back to the Start

After following links, you might want to return to your original page. To do so, right-click a blank area of the page you're viewing and choose **Back**.

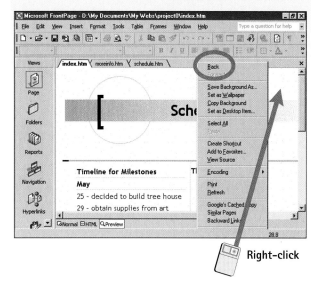

Right-click

6 Use the Normal Tab

Here's another way to return to the page from which you clicked a link: Select the **Normal** tab. You zip right back to where you started.

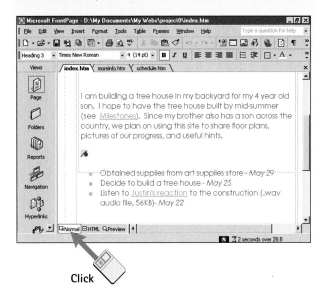

Click

How-To Hints

Preview Links

The point can't be made strongly enough how important it is to check hyperlinks. In addition to previewing links as explained in this text, you should use the FrontPage **Reports** view to do a site-wide check of your links before publishing the site. Refer to Task 4, "How to Repair and Update Links," in Part 11, "Preparing to Publish."

End

Task

1   How to Import an Image **84**

2   How to Find and Insert Clip Art **86**

3   How to Import a Scanned Image **88**

4   How to Set Picture Properties **90**

5   How to Crop Images **92**

6   How to Rotate Images **94**

7   How to Resize and Resample Images **96**

8   How to Link Graphics **98**

9   How to Adjust Brightness and Contrast **100**

10   How to Add Text to an Image **102**

11   How to Create a Transparent Image **104**

12   How to Wrap Text Around an Image **106**

13   How to Create an Imagemap **108**

14   How to Use the Drawing Toolbar **110**

Working with Graphics

*V*isitors will judge your site by its use of images. If photos and illustrations look boring, poorly exposed, or take too long to download, your audience might not come back to your site.

In this part of the book, you learn how to import and edit images. When your snapshots look too dim, you can make them brighter. You can add a bevel to lackluster graphics and create a three-dimensional effect. For links that appear humdrum, try hyperlinking images to interactive buttons. Feeling creative? You can start a brand-new graphic with the **Drawing** toolbar.

FrontPage allows you to display two image file types: GIF and JPEG. The program converts BMP and other common image file formats to these formats automatically when you import them. Most images that require fewer than 256 colors—such as text—use the GIF format. GIF files let you choose a transparent color—allowing the background of your page to show through. For photos that you want to display in thousands or millions of colors, the JPEG format is a better choice.

The real beauty of image editing in FrontPage is that you don't have to launch a separate graphics program. You can handle most basic tasks with the **Pictures** toolbar, which appears at the bottom of the FrontPage window when you select an image. ●

How to Import an Image

To start working with images, import a file from your hard drive or network. Because most Web browsers support JPEG and GIF, FrontPage automatically converts images from common formats, such as BMP and PCX, to one of the common Web formats.

Begin

1 Choose the Insertion Point

Open or create a Web page into which you want to place an imported graphic image. Click the page to position the cursor where you want the picture to appear.

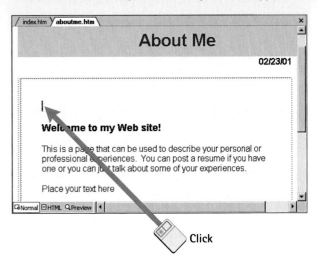

Click

2 Select an Image from Your Computer

To insert a file that exists on your local hard drive, click the **Insert Picture From File** button on the **Standard** toolbar. The **Picture** dialog box opens.

Click

3 Find the Image File

Use the **Look in** pop-up menu to select a folder on your hard drive or network.

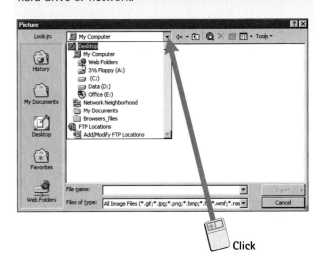

Click

4 Select the Image File

Click the image file to select it. If you choose more than one image to import, they will be placed side-by-side on your page. To choose several individual images, press and hold the **Ctrl** key as you click the image files you want to import.

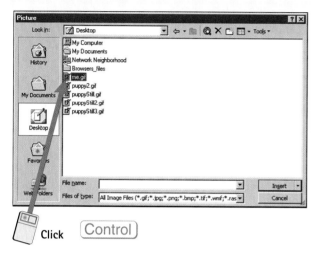

Click `Control`

5 Select All Images in a Folder

To choose all the images in a folder, press and hold the **Shift** key and click the first image file. Still holding the **Shift** key, click the last image file in the folder. All the image files between the two files you clicked are selected.

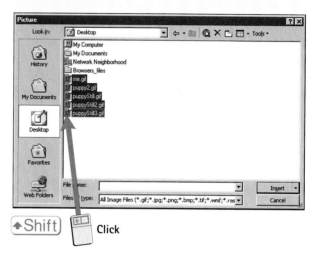

⬆Shift Click

6 Insert Your Image

After selecting an image, or collection of images, click the **Insert** button. The image or images appear on your Web page at the location you selected in Step 1.

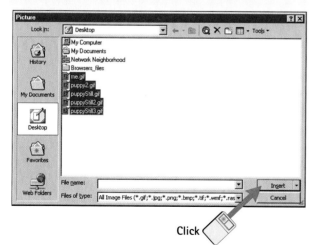

Click

How-To Hints

Copy and Paste

You can also add a graphic to a Web page by copying it from another Windows application (select the image and press **Ctrl+C**) and pasting the image into FrontPage (press **Ctrl+V**).

End

How to Find and Insert Clip Art

Your graphic skills might be few, but, with FrontPage, your options are many. Just search the collection of royalty-free images included with FrontPage (these images are called *clip art*). You'll find images for business and industry as well as personal projects such as sports and special occasions. To save you time, the collection includes Web-specific images such as banners, buttons, and backgrounds.

Begin

1 Select Area

Open or create a Web page. Click the page to position the cursor where you want the clip art to appear.

Click

2 Choose the Clip Art Command

From the menu bar, choose **Insert, Picture, Clip Art**. The **Clip Art Gallery** opens.

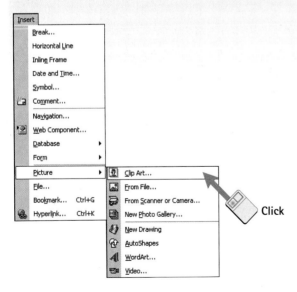

Click

3 Catalog Your Clips

The first time you attempt to insert clip art, FrontPage asks whether you want to catalog all the graphics and multimedia on your drive. Click **Now** to do so now, or skip this step by clicking **Later**. We'll skip cataloging for right now. You can choose this option later if you want to add items to the **Clip Organizer**.

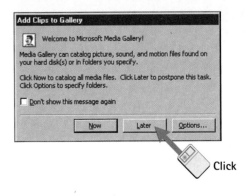

Click

4 Search for a Clip

The **Insert Clip Art Task Pane** opens. In the **Search text** box, type one or more words that describe the kind of clip art you are looking for. Press the **Enter** key or click the **Search** button to launch a search for clip art that matches your description.

Click

5 Preview an Image

After a successful search, the **Insert Clip Art Task Pane** shows images related to your search term. Some images might be difficult to see from the small version shown. To get a better look at an image, point your mouse at it, *but don't click yet.* When an arrow appears next to the image, click the arrow and choose **Preview/Properties** from the menu that appears. A larger version of that image opens, along with information about the image.

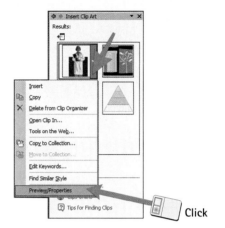

Click

6 Insert the Image

To insert a clip into your page, just click the image you want.

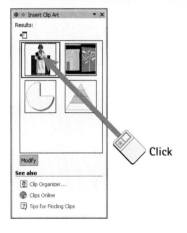

Click

How-To Hints

Search Online

Click the **Clips Online** button in the **Insert Clip Art Task Pane** to launch your Web browser and view more clip art images from which you can select at the Microsoft Web site. (Note that you might have to establish an Internet connection first.)

Find Animated Images and Sounds

You can access a collection of image clips, divided into folders, by clicking the **Clip Organizer** link at the bottom of the **Insert Clip Art Task Pane**. The **Clip Organizer** even includes some Web animations (look under **Office Collections, Web Elements, Animations**). You can preview and insert these animated images as described in Steps 5 and 6.

End

How to Import a Scanned Image

FrontPage ties in nicely with the software controls for your scanner. You can launch your scanning software and import the image without leaving FrontPage—as long as your scanner uses a TWAIN driver, as most do. Of course, your scanner or camera software must be properly installed on your computer before these instructions will work. If your digital camera doesn't use a TWAIN driver, you'll have to import the image from the camera to your hard drive using the camera's software, as explained in Step 5. Then follow the instructions in Task 1, "How to Import an Image," to put the digitized photo on your Web page.

Begin

1 Choose Insertion Point

Open the Web page into which you want to insert a scanned image. Click the page to position the cursor where you want the image to appear.

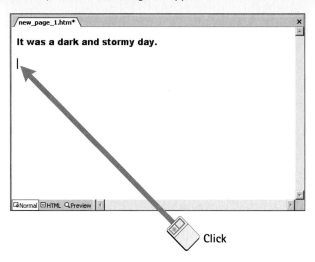

Click

2 Insert Picture

From the menu bar, choose **Insert, Picture, From Scanner or Camera**. The **Insert Picture from Scanner or Camera** dialog box opens.

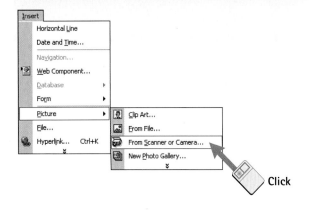

Click

3 Choose a Device

Choose the device from which you want to import the picture. If you have both a scanner and digital camera installed on your computer, for instance, click the **Device** menu and select the device you plan to use. If you have only one imaging device connected to your PC, that scanner or camera is selected by default.

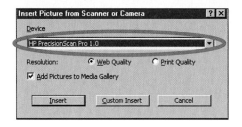

4 Choose Options

Leave the **Web Quality** option selected (the **Print Quality option** creates a larger file size). Also, you can select the **Add Pictures to Media Gallery** check box if you plan to access your photo later. If you don't plan to use the photo again, leave this option deselected.

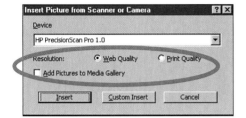

5 Use a Custom Insert

If you want to use your camera or scanner's software to import the image, click the **Custom Insert** button. Now use your device's software to make a final scan of the image and modify it before placing the image on your page. You might prefer your scanner's tools for changing the contrast and brightness of images. In most cases, you'll skip this step and let FrontPage handle the importing because the **Pictures** toolbar works well for most simple image editing tasks. This example shows the Hewlett-Packard PrecisionScan Pro software being used to crop a digitized photo before the photo is imported to FrontPage.

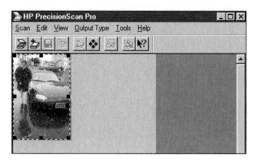

6 Acquire an Image

Assume that you don't have to do a custom insert and plan to skip Step 5. In the **Insert Picture** dialog box, click the **Insert** button. FrontPage acquires the image from your scanner or camera and places the photo on your page.

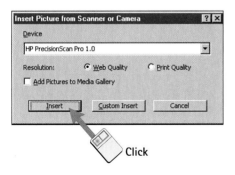

Click

7 Resize the Image

Click the photo to select it (notice that the **Pictures** toolbar appears). Drag one of the corner handles to resize the picture proportionally. When you finish resizing, click the **Resample** button on the **Pictures** toolbar to reduce the file size of the image.

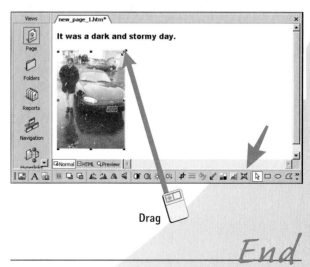

Drag

End

How to Set Picture Properties

It's a bit beyond the scope of one task to explain everything you can do with the **Picture Properties** dialog box. The important thing to understand is that you can use this tool to edit your image's appearance and position, and then you can change your mind and edit these properties again. Here's how.

Begin

1 Select an Image

Open a Web page that has an image you want to edit. Click the image to make it active for editing. Note that when you select a graphics image, the **Pictures** toolbar appears at the bottom of the FrontPage window.

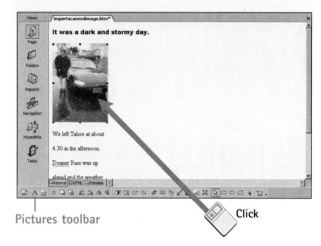

Pictures toolbar   Click

2 Choose Picture Properties

Right-click the image and select **Picture Properties** from the shortcut menu that appears. The **Picture Properties** dialog box opens.

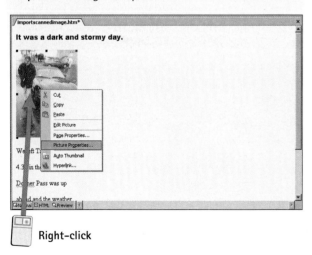

Right-click

3 Use the Appearance Tab

From the **Appearance** tab, you can set options for positioning, setting a border, and resizing the image. Choose the position of your photo, and how text will wrap around your image, by clicking the **None**, **Left**, or **Right** button. (You can also position the selected image on the page by making a selection from the **Alignment** drop-down list, which offers more selections.) If you want the image to have a border, set the thickness of the border line for the image (set it to 0 to display no border). Task 7, "How to Resize and Resample Images," looks at the tools in the **Appearance** tab used to resize images.

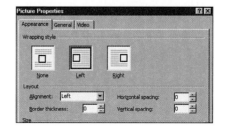

4 Select the Image Type

On the **General** tab, you can convert a graphics file from one type to another. For example, to convert a GIF file to JPEG format, select the **JPEG** radio button.

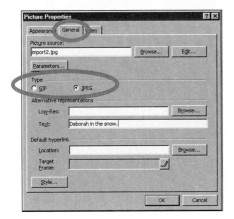

5 Set Alternative Representations

In the **Low-Res** field, you can specify a small image to display while the visitor waits for a larger, higher-quality file to download. In the **Text** field, you can supply text that will appear when a visitor holds the mouse over an image without clicking (an action known as *hovering*). This text also appears to visitors who view your pages with their browsers set to hide images.

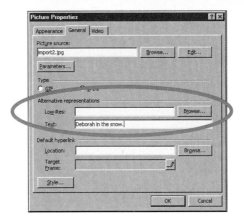

6 Set Links

If you want to hyperlink the picture to another file, you can type that file's address in the **Location** field. There's a simpler way to do this, as described in Task 8, "How to Link Graphics." Although the **Change Target Frame** button is generally used when you are working with a frames page, you can use this button to open a link in a separate browser window. Click the button and select **New Window**, and then click **OK**. Now, when a visitor clicks the link, a separate browser window launches to display the file. The page with the original link stays open.

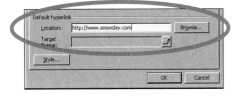

How-To Hints

Why Change Graphics File Format?

In most cases, FrontPage handles file conversions for you, so you shouldn't worry too much about it. If your image uses more than 256 colors (as most photos do), the image is saved as a JPEG. In some instances, converting a JPEG to a GIF can reduce file size, especially when you reduce the number of colors in the image. To reduce the number of colors in a GIF, check out GIF Wizard (**www.gifwizard.com**), an online service that helps you create speedy image downloads.

End

5

How to Crop Images

The FrontPage **Pictures** toolbar includes a tool for cutting unwanted areas from an image, a technique called *cropping*. You select the area you want to keep, and the rest is deleted. In addition to resizing the image and highlighting the important parts, cropping reduces download time by making the file physically smaller.

Begin

1 Select an Image

Click to select the image you want to crop. Notice that the **Pictures** toolbar appears at the bottom of the window.

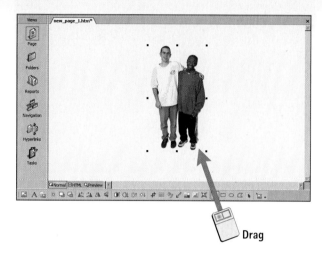

Drag

2 Select the Crop Tool

Click the **Crop** tool from the **Pictures** toolbar. A dotted box with handles appears in the center of your image.

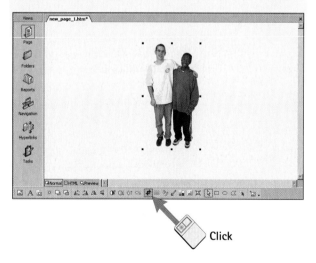

Click

3 Resize the Cropping Area

Move the mouse pointer over the outline of the dotted box until the pointer changes to a two-headed arrow. Click and drag the sides of the dotted box until the box encloses the area of the graphic you want to keep.

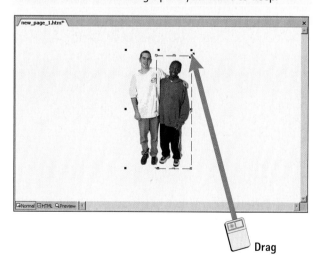

Drag

4 Start from Scratch

To create a new cropping box (that is, to scrap the work you did with any previous cropping box and start from scratch), click inside the image and drag out a new box. Use the handles to resize the box as you did in Step 3.

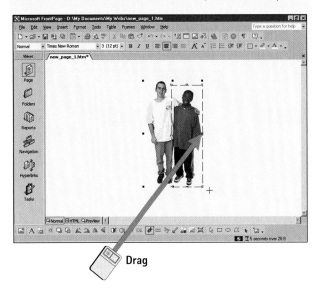

Drag

5 Select the Crop Tool Again

Click the **Crop** tool once more to finish. Notice that the image has changed: The part of the image that was outside the cropping box has been deleted.

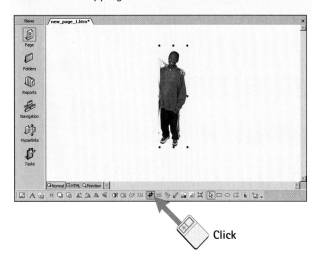

Click

6 Undo Cropping

If you accidentally crop too much of a picture, immediately press **Ctrl+Z** to "undo" the cropping. Alternatively, select the erroneously cropped picture again and click the **Restore** button on the **Pictures** toolbar.

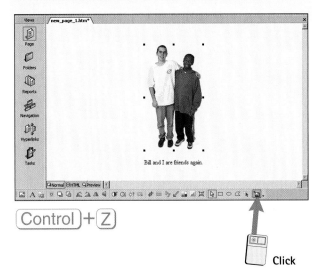

Control + Z

Click

How-To Hints

Cropping Helps Pages Load Faster

Cropping removes data from the image file, so the more you crop, the faster your now-smaller image file will load. The same is true for resizing images—as long as you click the **Resample** button on the **Pictures** toolbar. As soon as you save the page, you are prompted to save the cropped image; doing so cuts the unnecessary data from your image—and brings you kudos from your audience.

End

How to Rotate Images

The **Flip** and **Rotate** buttons on the **Pictures** toolbar let you change the orientation of images to suit your layout. When you flip an image, you create a mirror image (for example, you make a right hand into a left hand). When you rotate an image, you change the position of the image on the page.

Begin

1 Select an Image

Click an image on a Web page to select it for editing. The **Pictures** toolbar appears at the bottom of the window.

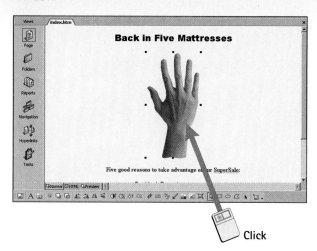

Click

2 Rotate Left

When you first import an image, it might not face the direction you want it to. No problem. To turn the image 90 degrees to the left (or counterclockwise), click the **Rotate Left** button on the **Pictures** toolbar.

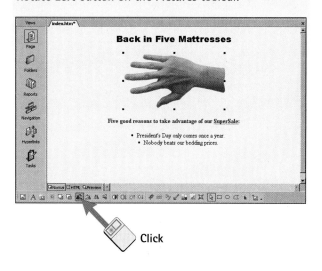

Click

3 Rotate Right

Click the **Rotate Right** button to turn the selected image 90 degrees to the right (or clockwise). If you click the **Rotate Left** button and then click the **Rotate Right** button, you effectively cancel out the changes you are making to the graphic.

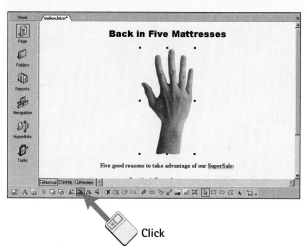

Click

4 Flip Horizontally

To create a mirror image of your graphic, click the **Flip Horizontal** button. Keep in mind though, that if your image shows text, the letters will appear backwards, as would a slide if you put it in a projector the wrong way.

Click

5 Flip Vertically

To turn your graphic upside down, click the **Flip Vertical** button.

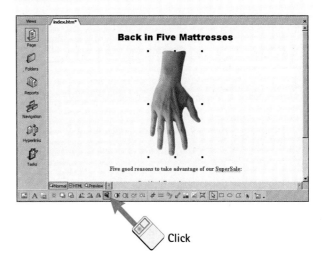

Click

How-To Hints

Save a Copy

When you close the page, the **Save Embedded Files** dialog box opens, giving you the chance to store the edited image under a different name. Doing so allows you to keep a backup copy of the original image. Suppose that you rotated an image and then resized it. If you rename the edited image and then later want to import the original image, you can.

End

How to Resize and Resample Images

You can change the size of an image in several ways. You can click and drag an image by the handles that appear when you select a picture, or you can enter a specific size in a dialog box. *Resizing* changes the appearance of the image but does not reduce the data it takes to display the file. To shrink the file's size as well as its appearance, you must *resample* the image.

Begin

1 Select the Image

Open a Web page and select the image you want to resize. The image appears selected with resizing handles along the edges of the graphic.

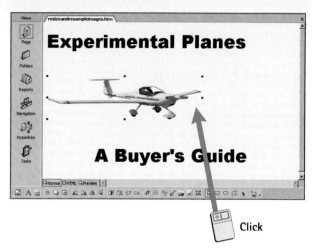

Click

2 Maintain the Aspect Ratio

Click a corner handle and drag with the mouse to resize the image while retaining the same aspect ratio (that is, to resize the image without distorting the proportions of the image).

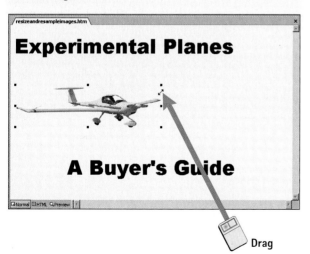

Drag

3 Resize One Side

Select a side handle and drag to adjust either the width or height of the image without affecting the other dimension.

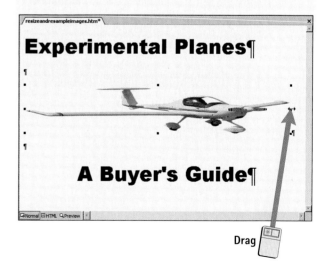

Drag

4 Select Picture Properties

You can also resize by right-clicking the image and selecting **Picture Properties** from the shortcut menu that appears. The **Picture Properties** dialog box opens.

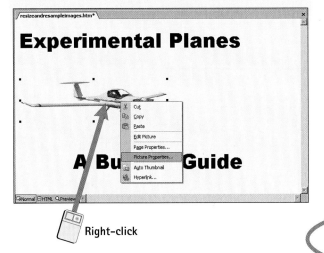

Right-click

5 Select Height and Width

The **Appearance** tab opens by default. In the **Width** and **Height** fields, enter values for those dimensions of the image. You can enter values either in pixels or in percentages of the original image's size. If you don't want to distort the image, enable the **Keep aspect ratio** check box; now when you enter one value, FrontPage automatically enters the other value so that the image isn't distorted. Click **OK** to close the dialog box and resize the image.

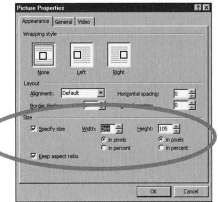

6 Resample the Image

To remove any extraneous data and reduce the file size based on changes you made to the image's size, click the **Resample** button in the **Pictures** toolbar. You might notice that the image looks sharper after resampling.

Click

How-To Hints

Create Automatic Thumbnails

A *thumbnail* is a preview of an image on the page. If you have a lot of photos to show, try using thumbnails: Select a picture and click the **Auto Thumbnail** button in the **Pictures** toolbar. A smaller version of the picture appears on your page; click the thumbnail to link to a version of the photo at its original size.

End

How to Link Graphics

Web designers often link images to other files. You can create a button that visitors click to return to your home page. Or you might want to position a picture of a mailbox on your page and then create a link that preaddresses an e-mail message to your address. Here's how.

Begin

1 Select the Picture

Open a Web page and select the picture you want to link to another file. Click the **Insert Hyperlink** button on the **Standard** toolbar. The **Insert Hyperlink** dialog box opens.

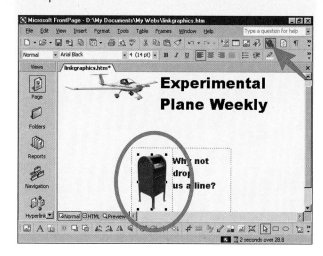

2 Type the Address

If you know the address of the file to which you want to link the graphic, type it in the **Address** box. FrontPage fills in the **http://** part of the URL for you. If you don't know the address, no problem. See the next step.

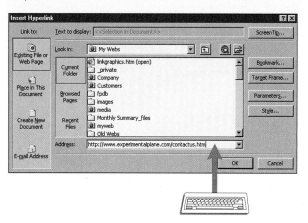

3 Browse to the Address

To set a link to an address you don't know offhand, click the **World Wide Web** button. Your Web browser launches.

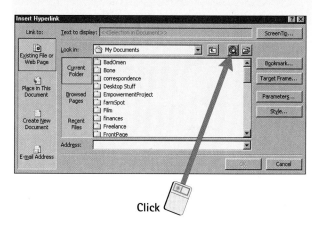

Click

4 Select the Address

Your Web browser initially displays your home page. Use the **Address** field to surf to the page you want to link to the graphic. Minimize your browser and return to the **Insert Hyperlink** dialog box. Notice that the address of the page you browsed to now appears in the **Address** field.

5 Link to a File on Your System

Here's another way to locate the file to which you want to link the graphic: In the **Insert Hyperlink** dialog box, click the **Look in** menu and select the file to which you want to link from your hard drive. When you have the file selected, click **OK**.

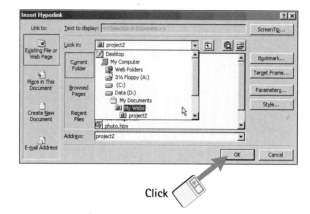

Click

6 Create a Link That Sends E-mail

If you want the link you're creating to send an e-mail message, click the **E-mail Address** button. Type the address to which you want the mail sent and click **OK**.

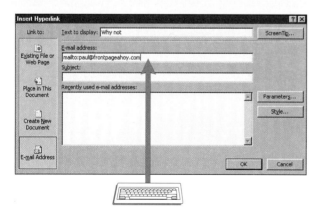

How-To Hints

Remove the Border if the Link Is Obvious

When you set a hyperlink for a graphic, a blue border automatically appears around the graphic. To delete the border, right-click the image and select **Picture Properties**. From the **Appearance** tab, set the **Border thickness** to 0 and click **OK**.

End

How to Adjust Brightness and Contrast

Some images you import need a bit of quality adjustment. For example, you can improve your picture by adjusting contrast and brightness. *Contrast* affects the difference between the lightest and the darkest areas of your picture. *Brightness* affects the overall level of light in your picture.

Begin

1 Select an Image

Open a Web page and click the image you want to edit. The **Pictures** toolbar appears at the bottom of the FrontPage window.

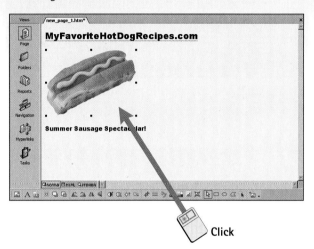

Click

2 Adjust the Contrast

Click the **More Contrast** button or the **Less Contrast** button on the **Pictures** toolbar. You can click either button multiple times to enhance the effect.

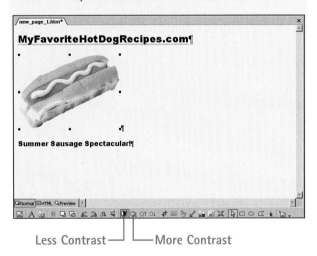

Less Contrast —— ⌐—— More Contrast

3 Adjust the Brightness

To make an image lighter or darker overall, click the **More Brightness** button or the **Less Brightness** button on the **Pictures** toolbar.

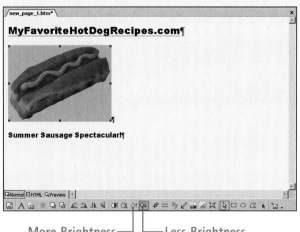

More Brightness —— ⌐—— Less Brightness

4 Wash Out a Photo

To increase brightness and reduce contrast in one operation, click the **Color** button and then choose **Wash Out**. This button is useful when you want to place text over a picture, as we do in the next task, "How to Add Text to an Image."

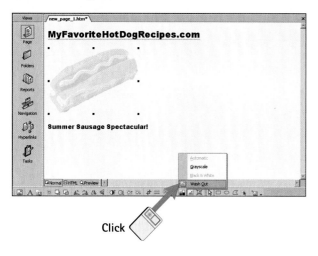

Click

5 Undo the Changes

If you want to cancel your most recent adjustment to the image, press **Ctrl+Z** (or click the **Undo** button on the **Standard** toolbar; click the arrow next to the **Undo** button and select the action you want to undo).

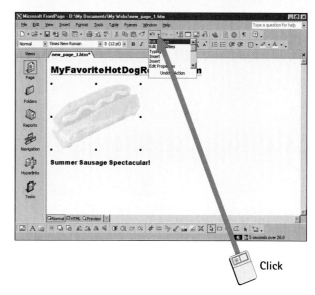

Click

6 Restore the Image

To quickly reset the image to its original state, click the **Restore** button, which removes all the effects applied since you imported or last saved the file. This button is particularly handy when you've applied multiple effects.

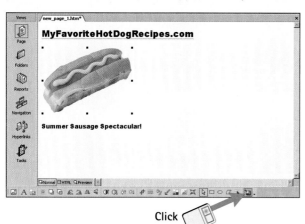

Click

How-To Hints

Take Color Out of a Picture

Here's another quick effect you can apply to images: Try converting a color picture to black and white. Just click the **Color** button and then select **Grayscale**, which converts a color photo to black and white.

End

How to Add Text to an Image

Labeling an image can be a pain. You typically open an image editor, add a layer of text over the image, and then merge the text and image into one file. Finally, you import the finished file into your Web page editor. FrontPage simplifies the process by enabling you to label images easily and to change the text and formatting whenever you want.

Begin

1 Select the Image

Click the image you want to work with to get it ready for editing. The **Pictures** toolbar appears at the bottom of the window.

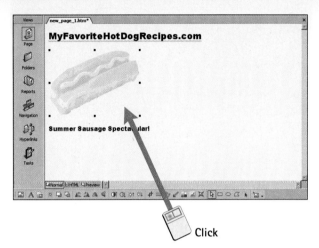

Click

2 Open a Text Box

Click the **Text** button in the **Pictures** toolbar. A text box appears on top of the selected graphic.

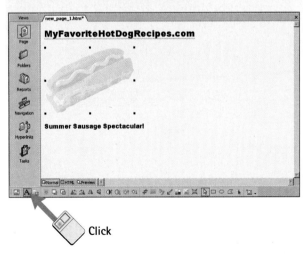

Click

3 Type a Message

Type the message you want to appear on the picture.

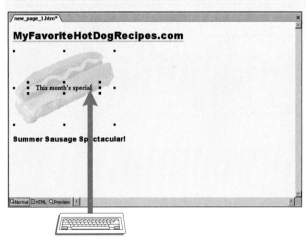

4 Change the Text Box Size

Increase or decrease the size of the text box in which you type by clicking and dragging one of the text box's handles. You can also click outside the text box, and then click and drag to reposition the text box. Note that you cannot reposition the text box off the graphic.

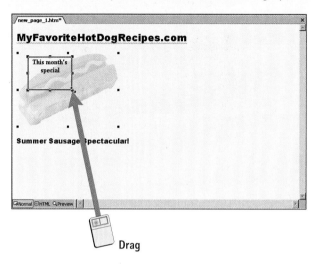

Drag

5 Change Formatting

With the text box selected, choose a **Font** and **Font Size** from the **Formatting** toolbar.

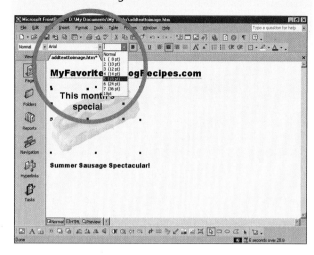

6 Select a Font Color

Choose a color for your text by making a selection from the **Font Color** menu (click the arrow next to the **Font Color** button in the **Formatting** toolbar to display the menu). Choose a light color for text that appears on top of dark pictures, and vice versa. If you use colors that don't appear in the **Standard** palette (such as those from a theme or a template), the colors from these documents appear in the **Theme** or **Document** palette. When you start with a brand-new page, you won't see these selections.

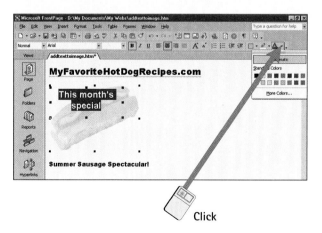

Click

7 Preview the Picture

Change to the **Preview** tab at the bottom of the FrontPage window to check out your new image (or click the **Preview in Browser** button on the **Standard** toolbar). Note that even after you close the page file, you can open it later and make changes to the text: Just click the text box to select the text and then add or delete text or change formatting as you want.

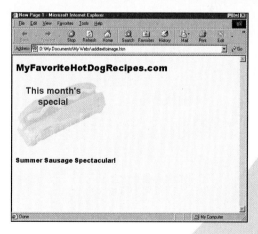

End

How to Create a Transparent Image

By setting a *transparent color* for an image, you can separate the image from its background. The **Transparent Color** tool lets you choose one color that will disappear from a picture. Doing so makes the background of your Web page show through parts of the graphic, so that the image appears to "float" on the page.

Begin

1 Select the Image

Click the image you want to edit. The **Pictures** toolbar appears at the bottom of the window.

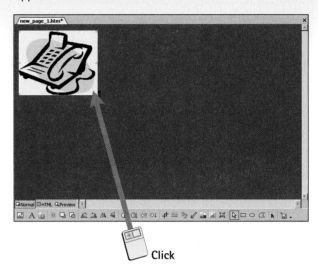

Click

2 Click the Transparent Color Button

Click the **Transparent Color** button on the **Pictures** toolbar. The pointer changes to a pencil shape with an arrow.

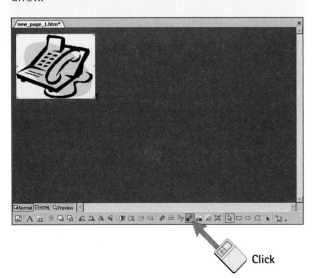

Click

3 Convert the Image to GIF

If the image has not been saved in the GIF format, you are prompted to convert the file. Note that clip art is often not in GIF format. (If your file *is* a GIF, skip to the next step.) When prompted to convert the graphic format, click **OK**. Note that converting a graphic to a GIF might increase the image's file size and therefore increase download time.

Click

4 Choose the Transparent Color

With the pencil-shaped pointer, click the color in the graphic that you want to make transparent. That color—and only that color—"disappears" everywhere in the image. In this example, we clicked the area behind the image to make the white background color disappear; now the background color of the Web page will show through.

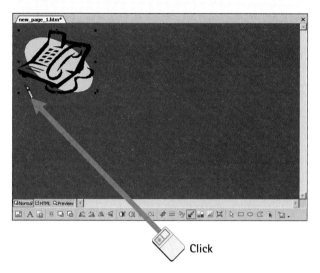

Click

5 Preview the Effect

Click the **Preview** tab to see your newly transparent image in the internal browser.

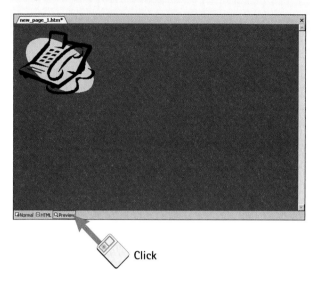

Click

6 Remove Transparency

If you don't like the transparent effect, you can remove it. Click the **Undo** button on the **Standard** toolbar. You can also press **Ctrl+Z** to undo the last effect you applied.

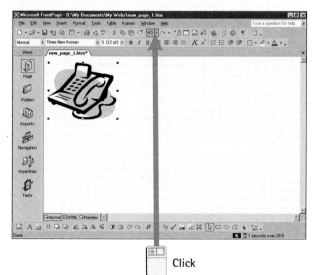

Click

How-To Hints

Add a Beveled Edge

To give your images a bit more depth, add a beveled edge. Many folks use this trick to make pictures appear like buttons. In fact, perhaps too many people use this trick, so use it sparingly. Select the image you want to edit and then click the **Bevel** button on the **Pictures** toolbar.

End

How to Wrap Text Around an Image

Aligning images lets you create professional-looking layouts that neatly mix text and graphics. With FrontPage, you can flow text around images and specify the amount of spacing between page elements.

Begin

1 Select the Image

Click to select the image you want to align. The **Pictures** toolbar appears at the bottom of the window.

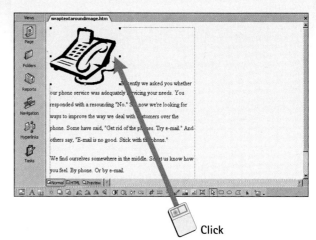

Click

2 Align the Image

From the **Formatting** toolbar, click **Align Left** or **Align Right**. Click **Align Left** to place the picture at left, with text flowing around it on the right. Click **Align Right** to push the image to the right and flow text on the left. To completely surround the image with text, click and drag the image until you see an insertion marker. Release the mouse when you think the text will fully wrap around the image. Keep experimenting until it looks right.

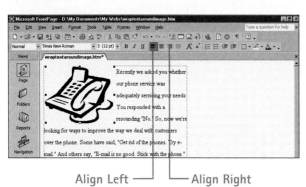

Align Left ——— —— Align Right

3 Choose Picture Properties

For more alignment options, right-click the image and choose **Picture Properties** from the shortcut menu. The **Picture Properties** dialog box opens.

Right-click

4 Use the Appearance Tab

On the **Appearance** tab, click the arrow next to the **Alignment** drop-down list box to see more options. In addition to the **Left**, **Right**, and **Center** options (which are also found on the **Formatting** toolbar), you can select vertical alignment.

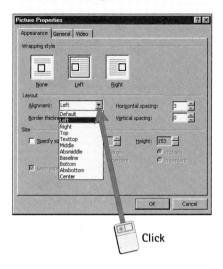

Click

5 Set Horizontal Spacing

In the **Horizontal Spacing** field, enter a number (in pixels) that specifies the amount of whitespace on the left and right sides of the picture. Usually, whitespace of 3 to 5 pixels makes an attractive text offset.

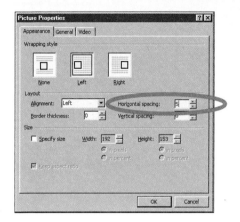

6 Set Vertical Spacing

Enter a number in the **Vertical Spacing** field to add space to the top and bottom of the picture. Again, whitespace of 3 to 5 pixels is sufficient. Click **OK** to save the changes and see the effect on your image.

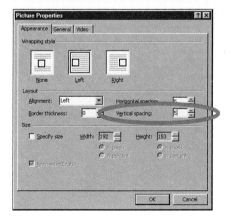

How-To Hints

Other Alignment Options

Most of the choices available in the **Alignment** drop-down list box in the **Picture Properties** dialog box vary the alignment of the selected graphic only slightly. You might find it easier to align elements using tables, as discussed in Part 6, "Creating the Page Layout."

End

How to Create an Imagemap

After finishing your first imagemap, you'll feel like a real Web publisher. *Imagemaps* take a standard graphic and add a bit of information that lets you hyperlink areas of the image to any file you like—to pages in your site, other graphics, you name it. Just draw the areas you want visitors to click, add a URL to that area, and you're set. The hyperlinked areas you draw (also called *hotspots)* are visible only in editing mode. Visitors won't see them.

Begin

1 Select the Picture

Click the graphic you want to convert to an imagemap. The **Pictures** toolbar appears at the bottom of the FrontPage window. You can create rectangular, circular, or polygonal hotspots on your graphic, as described in Steps 2, 3, and 4.

Click

2 Create a Rectangular Hotspot

To create a rectangular hotspot, click the **Rectangular Hotspot** button on the **Pictures** toolbar. Click the image and drag the box until it covers the area you want to make into a hotspot. Skip to Step 5.

Drag

3 Create a Circular Hotspot

To create a circular hotspot, click the **Circular Hotspot** button on the **Pictures** toolbar. Click the image and drag the circle until it covers the area you want to make into a hotspot. Skip to Step 5.

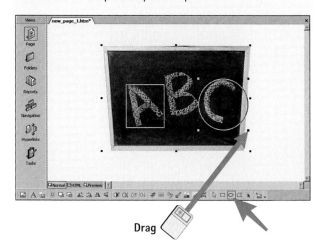

Drag

4 Create a Polygonal Hotspot

For odd-shaped areas, click the **Polygonal Hotspot** button. On the graphic, click once for each point in the shape; a straight line appears between each two consecutive points. To finish outlining the area, click the starting point again (or double-click to tell FrontPage you've finished selecting the hotspot area).

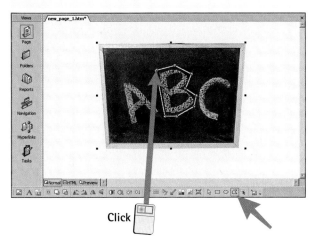

Click

5 Enter a Web Address

When you release the mouse after creating any of the three hotspot shapes, the **Insert Hyperlink** dialog box opens. Create a link to a Web page, a file, or an e-mail address. (For more information, see Part 4, "Connecting Files with Hyperlinks.") When you're done, click **OK**.

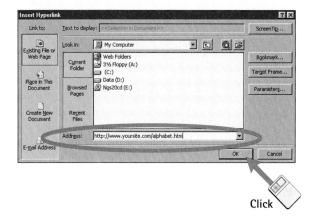

Click

6 Remove a Hotspot

To remove a hotspot, first click the **Highlight Hotspots** button on the **Pictures** toolbar. The graphic image disappears, leaving only the outlines of the hotspots visible. (To make the image reappear, click the **Highlight Hotspots** button again.) Select the hotspot you want to remove and press the **Delete** key. The hotspot and its link to another file are gone.

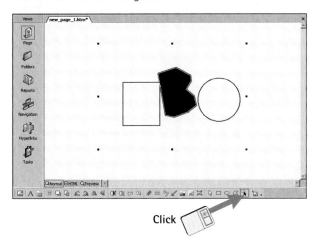

Click

How-To Hints

More About Imagemaps

Imagemaps are particularly useful when you need to create a handful of links such as the navigational icons for your site. Keep in mind, however, that some people browse with images turned off to speed up the browsing process. Make sure that you duplicate with text links any important links you create on an imagemap.

End

How to Use the Drawing Toolbar

If you can't find just the right image, you can create your own. FrontPage 2002 includes some simple-to-use yet sophisticated tools for creating shapes and lines. You can give your drawings a three-dimensional look or add a drop-shadow to make them stand out on your page. All this, plus more handy instructions for using the **Drawing** toolbar are coming right up.

Begin

1 Open the Drawing Toolbar

To start your new creation, choose **View**, **Toolbars**, **Drawing**. The **Drawing** toolbar appears at the bottom of the screen.

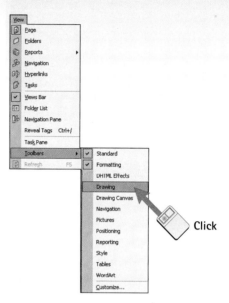

Click

2 Create a Shape

Let's start with a simple shape. From the **Drawing** toolbar, choose **AutoShapes**, **Basic Shapes**, and make a selection from the pictorial menu of shapes that appears. For this example, I'll use a **Regular Pentagon**. Click a point on the page and drag the mouse pointer; when you release the mouse button, the shape appears.

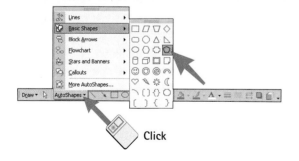

Click

3 Fill the Shape

Now add some color to the drawing. We can paint the shape by clicking the down arrow next to the **Fill Color** button. Select a color, or choose **Fill Effects** and choose a gradient, texture, pattern, or picture to fill the shape. You can add color to the outside line of the shape by clicking the arrow next to the **Line Color** button.

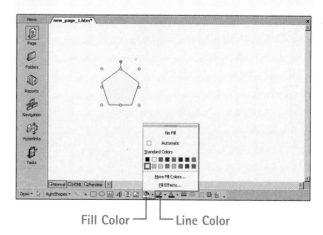

Fill Color — └ Line Color

4 Make an Object Three-Dimensional

Now let's give the shape some depth. With the drawing selected, click the **3D Style** button in the **Drawing** toolbar. Choose the 3D effect that best fits the perspective you want to achieve.

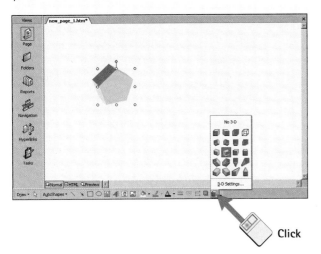

Click

5 Add a Shadow

You can add depth to an object in a more subtle way by adding a shadow. Click the **Shadow Style** button and choose a style of shadow that suits the shape you're creating.

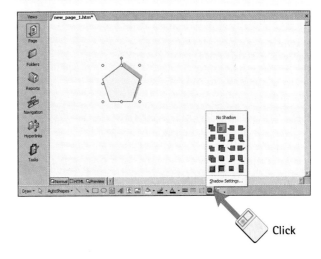

Click

6 Edit an Object's Shape

You can click an object's handle and drag to expand or reduce the size of the object. Click the green handle at the top and drag to rotate the image on the page.

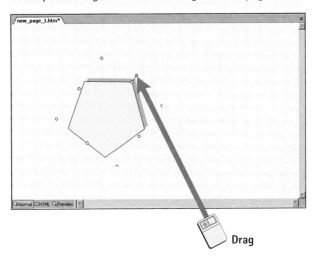

Drag

7 Add a Text Box

Text boxes are useful when you want to precisely position a block of text on the page. They can also be helpful when you want several blocks of text to be positioned around your page, each with its own formatting. Click the **Text Box** button on the **Drawing** toolbar and drag to create a text box. Enter some text in the box. You can choose the text color from the **Font Color** button in the **Drawing** toolbar. Click and drag a text box handle to resize it.

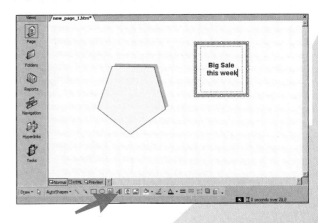

End

Task

1 **How to Choose and Modify Backgrounds 114**

2 **How to Sample a Custom Color 116**

3 **How to Align Elements with Tables 118**

4 **How to Merge and Split Table Cells 122**

5 **How to Add and Remove Rows and Columns 124**

6 **How to Change Table Borders 126**

7 **How to Change a Table Background 128**

8 **How to Insert and Customize Horizontal Lines 130**

9 **How to Build Pages with Frames 132**

10 **How to Modify or Delete Frame Borders 136**

11 **How to Set Links in Frames 138**

12 **How to Insert an Inline Frame 140**

13 **How to Position Elements Precisely 142**

PART 6

Creating the Page Layout

*S*o far, creating a site with FrontPage has been pretty basic. Now let's shake things up a bit. By using a few handy layout tricks, you can take more control over the look and feel of your pages. In this part, you find out how to weld your individual page elements into a cohesive whole. It's really quite simple.

We start by looking at ways to customize backgrounds and colors. Then we consider *tables*, a handy way to organize text and graphics by placing them in rows and columns. As you become more comfortable with your page layouts, you might want to incorporate *frames*, a way to view multiple pages in a single browser window. Finally, we look at *absolute positioning*, a cool way to place page elements precisely—and even layer them on top of each other. ●

How to Choose and Modify Backgrounds

Although FrontPage themes help you choose your entire Web site's look—including colors, fonts, and graphics—you can change individual elements on a single page. For instance, a well-chosen background can enhance your company's contact page or the family section of your personal site. You can choose from a set of colors FrontPage provides or choose a picture from your hard drive—FrontPage converts the image file to the correct format. If you decide to use an image, the picture is repeated (or *tiled*) to fill the background.

Begin

1 Pick Your Background

Start by choosing **Format**, **Background** from the menu bar. The **Page Properties** dialog box opens to the **Background** tab.

Click

2 Choose a Color

Click the **Background** drop-down list and select the color you want to use for the background of the current page. Don't see the color you're looking for in the drop-down list? Click **More Colors** to open the **More Colors** dialog box.

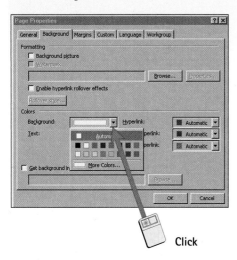

Click

3 Use the Color Palette

In the **More Colors** dialog box, move the mouse over the color palette to point to the color you want; watch the **Current** box to verify the color you select. (See Task 2, "How to Sample a Custom Color," for information about creating a custom color.) Click **OK** when the desired color is selected.

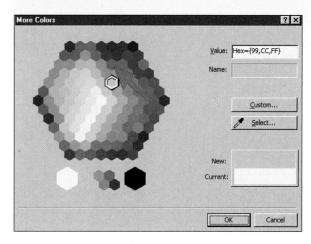

4 Choose a Picture

If you want to use an image as the background for your page, select the **Background picture** option in the **Page Properties** dialog box. Click the **Browse** button, navigate to the image file you want to use, and click **Open**.

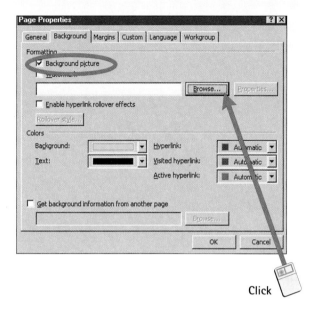

Click

5 Choose Text Colors

The **Background** tab includes options for changing the color of text on the page. Click the **Text** drop-down arrow and choose a default color for text on the page. You can also set the color of hyperlinks, as discussed in Part 4, "Connecting Files with Hyperlinks."

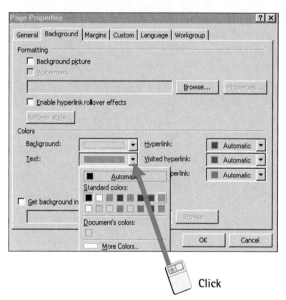

Click

6 Use an Existing Background

If you want to use a background you've already selected for another page in the current Web, select the **Get background information from another page** option. Click the **Browse** button to navigate to the page that has the background you want to use. Select the page and choose **OK**.

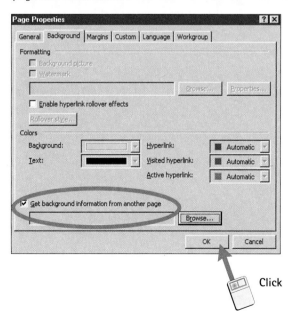

Click

How-To Hints

Keep Your Background Steady

Because the background scrolls as your visitor moves down the page, you might want to click the **Watermark** option, which holds your image in place as your visitors scroll.

Set the Background for a Theme

If you want to replace the default background for all the pages in your site, change the theme background. From the menu bar, choose **Format, Theme**. Select a theme and then click the **Modify** button. Click the **Graphics** button and then choose **Browse** to navigate to the image you want to use. You'll find more on modifying themes in Part 2, "Creating Pages."

End

How to Sample a Custom Color

What to do when the mauve color in your company logo is nowhere to be found in the FrontPage Color menu? Try creating a custom color. You can open the **Custom Color** menu anywhere you can select a color (such as when you change font, hyperlink, or background colors). In this example, we want to make the color of a headline the same as a color in the company logo, so we'll sample the color from a picture opened in FrontPage.

Begin

1 Select the Text to Match

To match text to a color in an image on the screen, select the text you want to color (in this case, the word *Accordions*).

2 Select Font Color

Click the arrow next to the **Font Color** button in the **Formatting** toolbar. A drop-down menu opens.

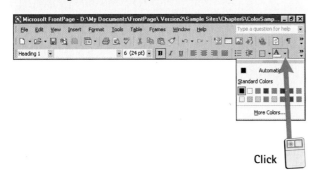

Click

3 Choose More Colors

From the menu that appears, choose **More Colors**. The **More Colors** dialog box opens.

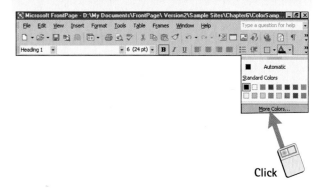

Click

4 Position the Windows

Position the **More Colors** dialog box so that you can see the color you want to sample in the area behind the dialog box. In this example, I want to sample a color used in the image of the accordion to apply to the text *Accordions*. If you want to sample a color from an image in another program, make sure that the other program's window is open, and the image you want to sample is displayed.

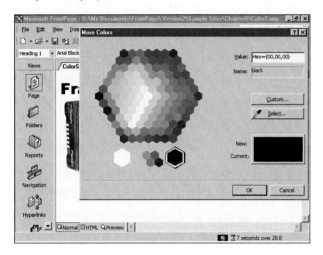

5 Open the Eyedropper

To pick a color that appears on the screen behind the dialog box, click the **Select** button. The mouse pointer changes to an eyedropper. (If you have to click another button before you select a color, click **Select** again to change the mouse pointer back.)

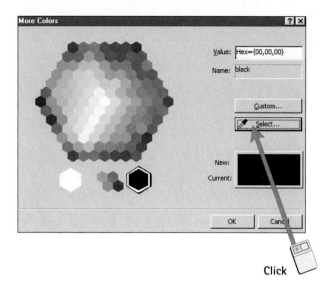

Click

6 Select a Color

Move the eyedropper anywhere on the screen. Notice that the **New** box changes to reflect the color the mouse is currently sampling. You can sample colors from menu bars, images, other buttons—anything on the screen. Position the mouse over the color you want to sample and click to select that color. Click **OK** to close the **More Colors** dialog box. The selected text now appears in the chosen color.

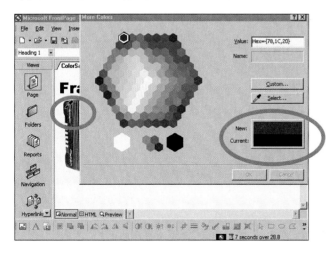

7 Choose the Color Again

To use the sampled custom color again, select the text you want to color, open the **Font Color** menu, and choose the appropriate color from the palette under **Document Colors**.

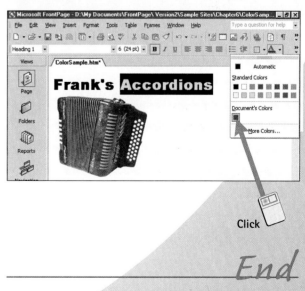

Click

End

How to Align Elements with Tables

Tables help you control your page layouts. If you work with Microsoft Word or Excel, you probably already know how to insert tables and manage cells. Just tell FrontPage how many rows and columns you want, insert your page elements, and your page looks smart and professional. This task creates a simple table and then adds both text and graphics to the table cells. Later tasks explain how to change tables to fit your needs and make them more attractive by adding colors to cells and customizing table borders.

Begin

1 Insert a Table

Open the page on which you want to insert the table. Choose **Table**, **Insert**, **Table**. The **Insert Table** dialog box opens.

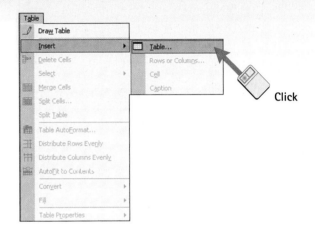

Click

2 Set Rows and Columns

In the **Rows** and **Columns** text boxes, type the number of rows and columns you want the table to contain.

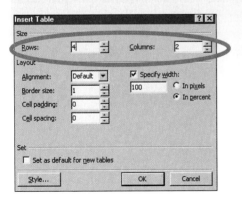

3 Align the Table

Before placing your table on the page, you can make layout choices. Click the down arrow next to the **Alignment** text box and make a selection to position the table on the page.

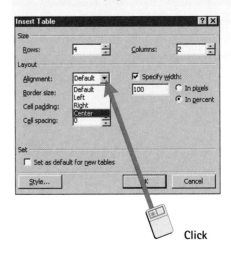

Click

4 Set Border Options

If you specify a border size of **0**, the border around the table is invisible in a browser (but you will see a dotted line that represents the border in **Page** view). Generally, invisible borders or borders of no more than 2 pixels are preferable and more professional looking than wider borders.

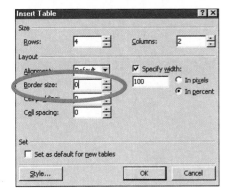

5 Set Cell Padding and Cell Spacing

Type a number in the **Cell padding** text box to set a buffer of whitespace around the text or image in a cell. The value in the **Cell spacing** box determines the number of pixels between cells.

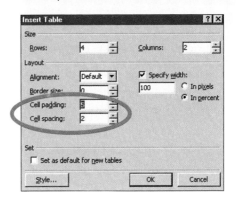

6 Set Table Width

The **Specify Width** option is selected by default. You can select either the **In pixels** or **In percent** option to specify the width of a table. Selecting **In percent** sets the table's size in proportion to the visitor's open browser window. (A table set to 100% can be used to organize the entire page.) If you plan to make more tables with the properties you have set, select **Set as default for new tables**. When you finish making changes, click **OK** to save your settings.

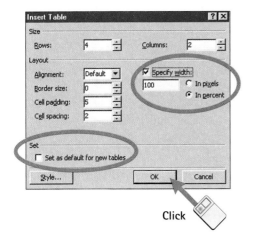

Click

How-To Hints

Dynamic Table Resizing

When you set your table width as a percentage of the browser window (as in Step 6), the visitor decides how wide your tables are. If the browser is open wide, the table expands. When the visitor decides to reduce the size of a window, the table contracts, and its contents can become jumbled. To avoid this, set the table size to a specific number of pixels.

Continues

7 Insert Text

Click to position the insertion point in the cell where you want to add text. Type some text in the cell. Press **Enter** to start a new paragraph in the cell; press **Shift+Enter** to start a new line without creating a new paragraph. You can also use keyboard shortcuts to make navigating the table easier: To jump to the cell on the right, press **Tab**. Press **Shift+Tab** to jump one cell to the left.

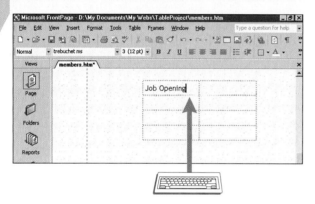

8 Insert a Picture

Position the insertion point in the cell in which you want to place an image or picture. Click the **Insert Picture from File** button in the **Standard** toolbar, navigate to your image, and double-click to place it in the table.

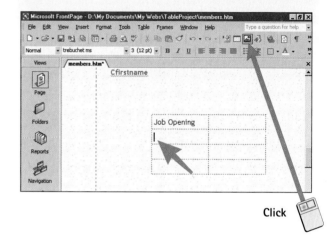

Click

9 Set Vertical Alignment

Many table-building tools are found on the **Tables** toolbar; display it by selecting **View, Toolbars, Tables**. You can change the vertical alignment of elements within a cell. Select the element you want to modify, and then click the **Align Top**, **Center Vertically**, or **Align Bottom** button in the **Tables** toolbar.

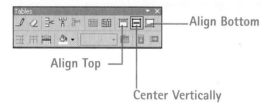

Align Bottom

Align Top

Center Vertically

10 Resize the Table by Dragging

To expand or reduce the size of the table, position the mouse pointer over the edge of a cell until the pointer changes to a double-headed arrow. Drag to adjust the size of a row or column.

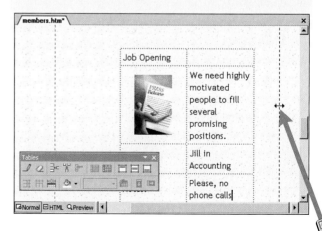

Drag

11 Draw the Table

To insert a new table quickly, click the **Draw Table** button on the **Tables** toolbar. The pointer changes to a pencil. Drag to create the table outline. You can add more rows or columns simply by drawing them (dragging the table border) where you want them to appear.

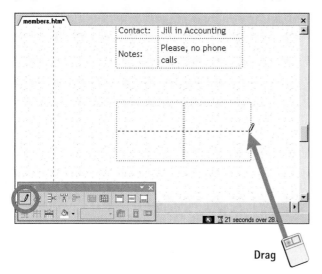

Drag

12 Erase a Cell

If you make a mistake and want to remove a row or column, try the **Eraser** tool. Click the **Eraser** button in the **Tables** toolbar and drag over a cell border to make it disappear.

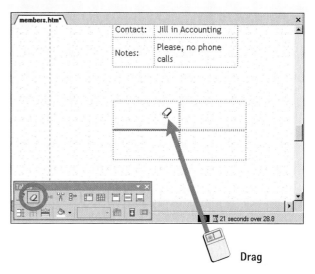

Drag

13 Use the Insert Table Button

Perhaps the fastest way to start a new table is by making a selection from the **Insert Table** button on the **Standard** toolbar. First, place the cursor where you want the new table to appear. Click the **Insert Table** button and drag across the drop-down menu that appears to highlight the number of rows and columns you want the table to have. When you release the mouse, the table appears on the page.

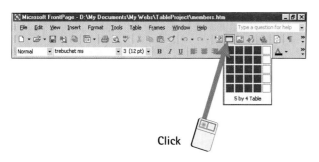

Click

How-To Hints

Change Size and Color

To resize the table so that it matches the size of your table elements, click the table to select it and then click the **AutoFit to Contents** button on the **Tables** toolbar. The Autofit button is just to the left of the **Fill Color** button (which looks like an overturning paint bucket). To change the color of cells in your table, select the cells, click the **Fill Color** button, and choose a color. Moving one button to the right, you can make a selection from the **Table AutoFormat Combo** button menu, which lets you choose a color and layout scheme for your entire table without having to edit the look of each individual cell.

End

How to Merge and Split Table Cells

Dad always said, "Measure twice and cut once." But with tables, you can jump in headfirst and make changes later. As your table grows, you might have to combine (*merge*) and divide (*split*) cells to get the table to look the way you want it to look.

Begin

1 Display the Tables Toolbar

Open the page that contains the table you want to modify. Display the **Tables** toolbar by selecting **View, Toolbars, Tables**.

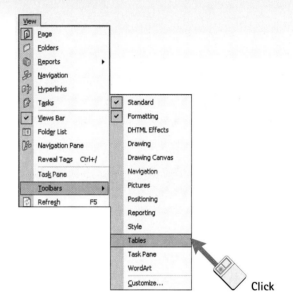

Click

2 Split a Cell

To divide one cell into two, click to position the mouse pointer in the cell you want to split. Click the **Split Cells** button on the **Tables** toolbar. Alternatively, right-click the selected cell and choose **Split Cells** from the context menu that pops up. The **Split Cells** dialog box appears.

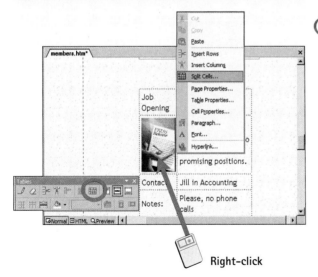

Right-click

3 Choose Rows or Columns

Select either the **Split into columns** or the **Split into rows** option. (Note that both of these options affect just the selected cell; you don't add rows or columns to the entire table, just to the selected cell.)

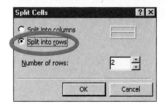

4 Enter the Number of Columns or Rows

Enter the number of rows or columns you want to split the cell into. (Note that the **Number of** text box changes to read **rows** or **columns**, depending on the option you select.) Click **OK** to split the cell as specified.

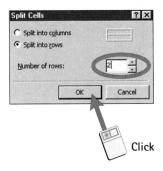

Click

5 Select Cells

To merge cells (that is, to combine multiple cells into a single cell), use the mouse to select at least two adjacent cells.

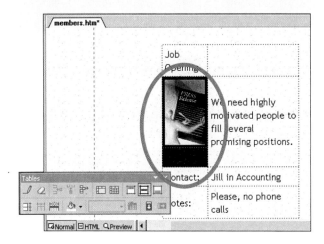

6 Merge Cells

Right-click the selected cells and choose **Merge Cells** from the context menu. Alternatively, click the **Merge Cells** button on the **Tables** toolbar. *Voilà!* The selected cells merge into a single cell.

Right-click

How-To Hints

Quick Table Trick

A quick way to tidy up a table is to select adjacent rows and then choose **Table, Distribute Rows Evenly**. (You also can choose **Table, Distribute Columns Evenly**.) Your table resizes to the same height and width in every cell. Because this feature can dramatically adjust the spacing of your table, press **Ctrl+Z** (Undo) if you're not happy with the redistribution of rows or columns.

End

How to Add and Remove Rows and Columns

When your house needs an extra bedroom, you hire a contractor. When your table needs more room, you can always add new rows and columns (and it won't take two months and cause a migraine). If you're careful, you can add on to your table without disrupting your text and graphics.

Begin

1 Display the Tables Toolbar

Open the page that contains the table you want to modify. Display the **Tables** toolbar by selecting **View**, **Toolbars, Tables**.

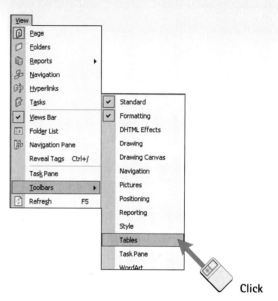

Click

2 Insert Rows

Place the insertion point in the cell *below* where you want to add a row (the new row is inserted *above* the insertion point). Click the **Insert Rows** button on the **Tables** toolbar. To insert multiple rows, click the button again. You can also right-click the selected cell and choose **Insert Rows** from the context menu.

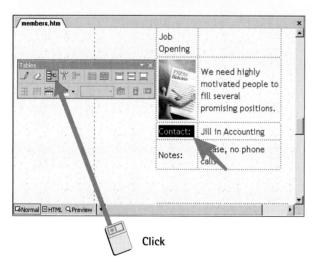

Click

3 Insert Columns

Place the insertion point in the cell *to the left of* where you want to insert a column (the new column is inserted *to the left of* the insertion point). Click the **Insert Columns** button on the **Tables** toolbar. Click the button several times to insert multiple columns.

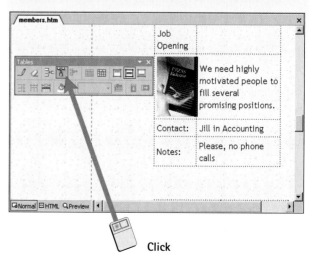

Click

4 Select Cells to Delete

To delete cells, drag the mouse to select the cells of the row or column you want to remove. Note that just the cells you select will be deleted, not the entire row or column; your table can develop some "ragged edges" if you insert and delete many cells.

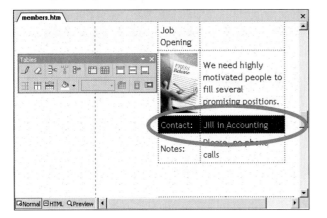

5 Delete Cells

Click the **Delete Cells** button on the **Tables** toolbar. Alternatively, right-click the selected cells and select **Delete Cells** from the context menu. The selected cells are gone!

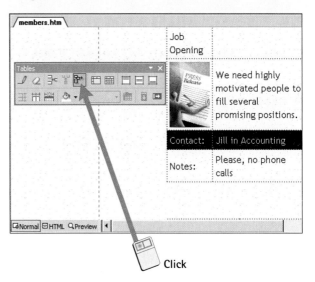

Click

How-To Hints

More Adding and Deleting

When the **Tables** toolbar isn't handy, you can insert rows by choosing **Table, Insert, Rows or Columns**. Similarly, you can delete cells by selecting **Table, Delete Cells**.

Add a Caption

You can add a caption to your caption by positioning the insertion point in the table and selecting **Table, Insert, Caption**. By default, the caption appears *above* the table. To send the caption to the bottom of the table, right-click the caption and select **Caption Properties** from the context menu. Choose **Bottom of Table** and click **OK**.

End

How to Change Table Borders

Flexibility is a table's middle name. You can set the size of a table *border* (the box around the table), and you can also change the border's color. In fact, you can pick a border color for the entire table or choose two colors—one for the inside border and one for the outside border—to create a three-dimensional effect.

Begin

1 Select the Table

Position the insertion point in the table to select the table for editing.

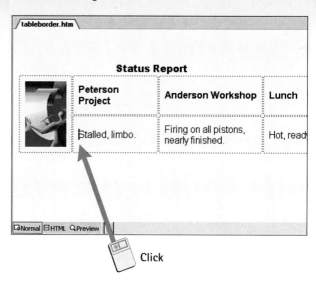

Click

2 Open Table Properties

Right-click the table and choose **Table Properties** from the context menu. The **Table Properties** dialog box opens.

Right-click

3 Set Border Size

In the **Borders** area, type a number in the **Size** text box to set the width of the border lines in pixels. For colored borders, you must specify a border of at least 1 pixel, or you won't be able to see your color choices.

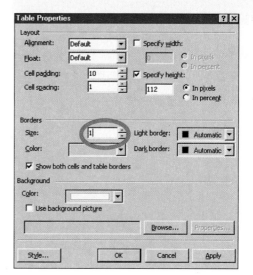

4 Choose Colors

Make a selection from the **Color** menu to choose one color for the entire table border. Create a two-color border by making selections from the **Light Border** and **Dark Border** menus. When you finish, click **OK**. Keep in mind that if you use a theme for your page, these colors are set automatically.

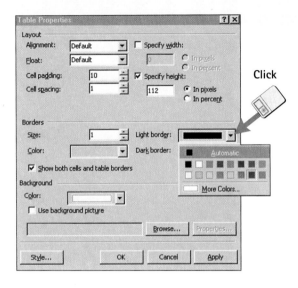

Click

5 Change Cell Borders

You can also change the border of individual cells. Click to position the insertion point inside the cell whose borders you want to change.

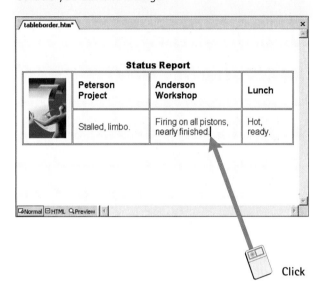

Click

6 Select Cell Properties

Right-click the selected cell and choose **Cell Properties** from the context menu. The **Cell Properties** dialog box appears, looking very similar to the **Table Properties** dialog box you saw in Step 3.

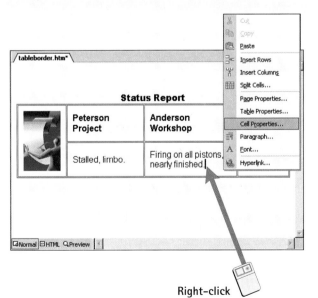

Right-click

7 Change Borders

In the **Borders** area, the color menus work the same as those for the table borders did in Step 4. Make a selection from the **Color** menu for a single-color cell border. Choose from the **Light Border** and **Dark Border** menus for a two-color border. When you finish, click **OK**.

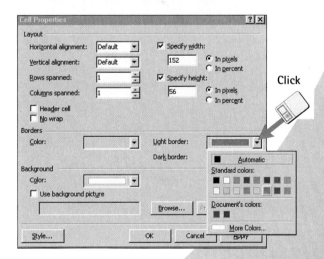

Click

End

How to Change a Table Background

To make your tables eye-catching—and easier to read—choose background colors for individual cells. You can also set a single background color for the entire table.

Begin

1 Select a Table

Click in (or highlight) the table to select it.

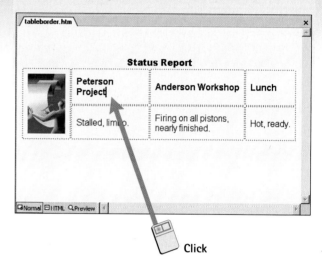

Click

2 Change a Table Background

Right-click the table and choose **Table Properties**. The **Table Properties** dialog box opens.

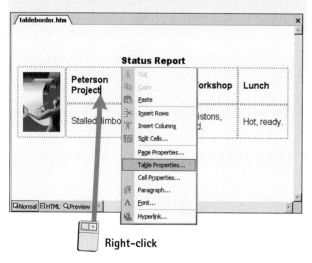

Right-click

3 Select Background Color

In the **Background** area, make a selection from the **Color** drop-down menu.

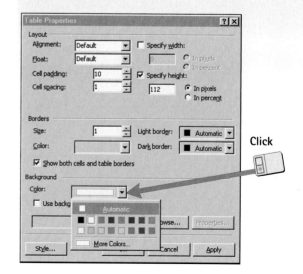

Click

$\mathcal{4}$ Select Background Picture

To use a picture as the table background instead of a color, select the **Use background picture** check box. Click the **Browse** button and navigate to select the picture file you want to use. Note that if your table is larger than the background picture, the picture will be tiled to fill the table area.

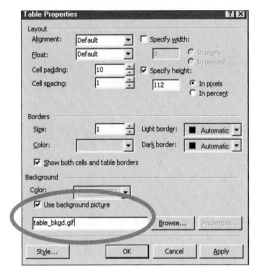

$\mathcal{5}$ Save Settings

When you finish making changes, click the **OK** button to close the **Table Properties** dialog box. Your image should appear in the table's background, as seen here.

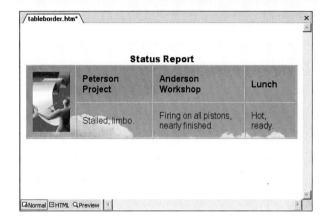

$\mathcal{6}$ Change a Cell Background

You can also change the background for individual cells. Right-click a cell (or select several cells) and choose **Cell Properties** from the context menu. The **Cell Properties** dialog box opens.

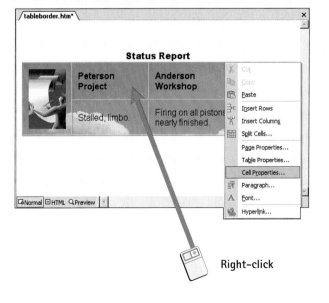

Right-click

$\mathcal{7}$ Set Background Color or Picture

Choose a background color or picture for the selected cells in the same way that you selected a background color or picture for the entire table in Steps 3 and 4. Click **OK** when you finish.

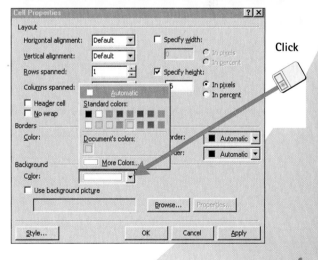

Click

End

How to Insert and Customize Horizontal Lines

Horizontal lines (also called *horizontal rules*) are pretty much self-explanatory. You might already know that horizontal lines, used sparingly, can help keep your page tidy and organized. What you might not know is that you can tailor horizontal lines to fit the look of your page.

Begin

1 Insert Horizontal Line

Open the page on which you want to insert horizontal lines. Click to position the insertion point. From the menu bar, choose **Insert, Horizontal Line**. A default line appears on the page.

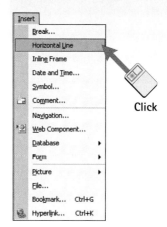

Click

2 Open Horizontal Line Properties

Double-click the line to open the **Horizontal Line Properties** dialog box.

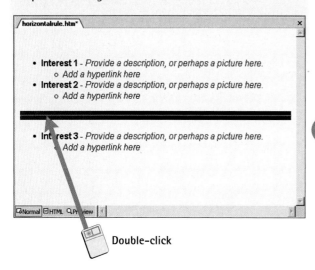

Double-click

3 Set Width and Height

If you're not using a theme for the page, you can type a value in the **Width** text box. Select a radio button to specify whether the line width is measured in pixels or as a percentage of an open browser window. Then type a value in the **Height** text box; the height of the line is measured in pixels.

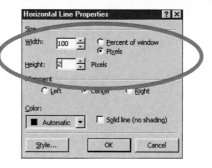

4 Set the Alignment

If you're using a theme for your page, alignment is the only line property you can set. Click the **Left**, **Center**, or **Right** radio button to change the alignment of the rule.

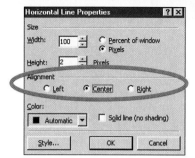

5 Choose the Line Color

If you're not using a theme for the page, you can specify a color for the line. Click the **Color** menu and make a selection from the drop-down menu.

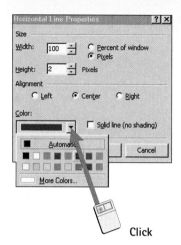

Click

6 Choose Solid Line

Many times, it's preferable to use a solid line rather than the default 3D shading that accompanies a horizontal line. Select the **Solid line** check box to remove the shading from the line.

7 Save the Settings

To save your settings and preview the horizontal line on the page, click **OK**.

How-To Hints

Changing the Properties of a Themed Line

If you use a theme, your horizontal line options are limited (as noted in this task). However, you *can* pick your own graphic to serve as the horizontal line. Choose **Format**, **Theme**; in the **Themes** dialog box, click the **Modify** button. Then click the **Graphics** button. From the **Item** drop-down list, select **Horizontal Rule**. Click the **Browse** button and navigate to the image file you want to use for the horizontal line. Select the file and click **OK**. Click **Open** and then **OK** to save your changes and to close the **Modify Theme** and **Themes** dialog boxes.

End

How to Build Pages with Frames

A *frames page* displays the contents of several pages in one browser window. Web designers often use frames as navigation elements, although you need a frames-capable browser to view them. In this example, you create a page with two frames. When you click a link in one frame, the contents of the page are displayed in the other frame.

Begin

1 Open New Page

From the **Standard** toolbar, click the down-pointing arrow next to the **New Page** button and choose **Page** from the drop-down menu that appears. The **Page Templates** dialog box opens.

Click

2 View Frames Pages Templates

To see a list of template options specifically designed to include frames pages, click the **Frames Pages** tab.

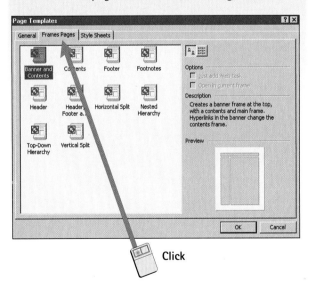

Click

3 Choose a Template

Select a template and view a description of it on the right side of the dialog box. In this example, I chose one of the most straightforward templates: **Contents**. Click **OK**. The new page opens, displaying two areas (the frames) and several buttons.

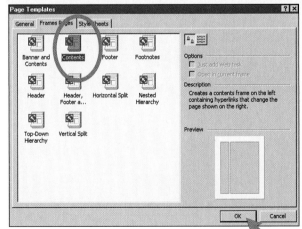

Click

4 Create a Blank Page

Click the **New Page** button in the left pane to open a blank page in the left frame. The new page opens and is ready for editing. Note that you can resize the frame by dragging the bar between the frames. In this example, I'll add some text in the frame that I'll use as an index. To link text in one frame so that it launches a page in another frame, see Task 11, "How to Set Links in Frames."

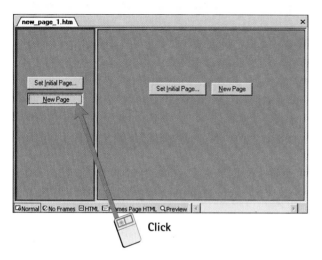

Click

5 Set Initial Page

You can use the initial page to welcome visitors and describe how your frames page works. To show an existing page in the frame, click the **Set Initial Page** button. The **Insert Hyperlink** dialog box opens.

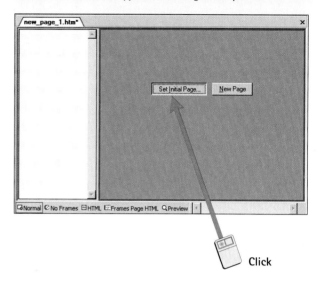

Click

6 Select Page

Use the **Current Folder** pane to browse through the directory structure of the current Web; use the buttons to the right of the **Look in** menu to select files outside of the current Web. Browse to the page you want to display, select it, and click **OK**. The selected page opens in the frame on the right.

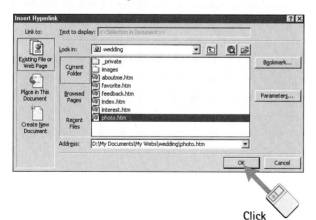

Click

How-To Hints

Frames–Capable Browsers

Most browsers, including Netscape Navigator, Microsoft's Internet Explorer and WebTV, and the smaller Opera browser support frames. However, a small part of the Web population still uses older browsers without frames support or text-based browsers that might not display your information correctly if you use frames. To see what visitors will get if their browsers do not support frames, click the **No Frames** tab in **Page** view. You can edit the message you see there if you want.

Continues

7 Set Frame Properties

To see the page options for the left frame, right-click the page in the left frame and choose **Frame Properties**. The **Frame Properties** dialog box opens.

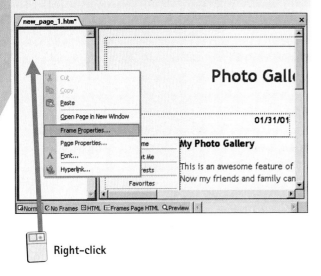

Right-click

8 Change the Frame Name

The **Name** text box shows a default name, which is set when you choose a template. This name refers to the *frame* (not to the page inside the frame). You can change the name here, but, in most cases, the default name will work just fine.

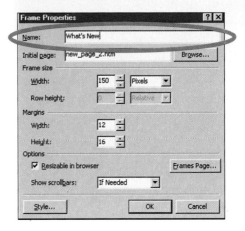

9 Set Frame Size

You can set the current frame size relative to the other frames in the page by a percentage of the page width or by a specific width in pixels.

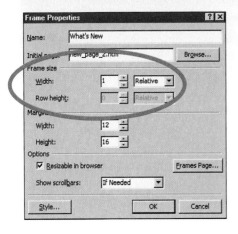

10 Set Frame Margins

You can set the amount of horizontal and vertical indentation within a frame by entering values (in pixels) in the **Margins Width** and **Height** text boxes.

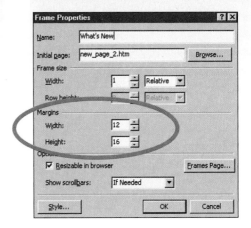

11 Save Frames Settings

Save the changes you've made to the settings by clicking the **OK** button.

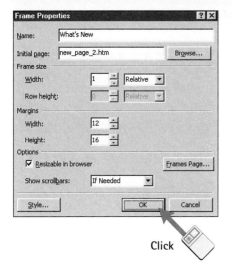

Click

12 Set the No-Frames Message

Some older browsers do not support frames. You might want to customize the message FrontPage displays for visitors with these older browsers. It's also helpful to include a link to an alternative version of the page that does not use frames. Click the **No Frames** tab in **Page** view and make your changes to the text.

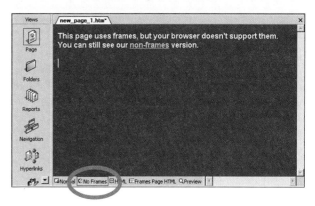

How-To Hints

Choose Wisely

Frames pages are a pet peeve of many Web surfers, especially when frames are used excessively. Frames are best used for special purposes—such as a demonstration of a new concept. Avoid creating too many frames on one page—at most, three or four. An entire site created with frames can be difficult to manage and harder still for users to navigate. Check out sites on the Web that use frames effectively, and borrow ideas from the sites you like.

Split and Delete Frames

You can split a frame into two separate frames by choosing **Frames, Split Frames**. To remove a frame altogether, select the frame and choose **Frames, Delete Frame**.

How to Modify or Delete Frame Borders

After you create a frames page, you can customize the frames settings. You might want to hide the frame borders (for instance, if you decide that the borders interfere with your goal for a clean design). You can also space out frames and decide whether visitors can scroll down a frames page.

Begin

1 Open Frame Properties

Open the frames page you want to modify. Right-click anywhere on the page you want to edit and choose **Frame Properties** from the context menu. The **Frame Properties** dialog box opens.

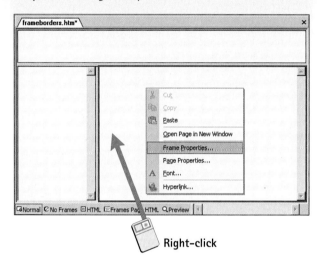

Right-click

2 Set Resizable in Browser

The **Resizable in browser** option lets you set whether visitors will be able to click a frame border and drag to resize it. The box is checked by default.

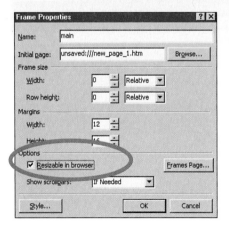

3 Set Scrolling Options

Specify whether visitors can scroll through the page. Make a selection from the **Show scrollbars** drop-down menu. Choose **If Needed** if you want a scrollbar to appear when content overruns the size of the frame. Choose **Never** if you don't want the page to scroll (for instance, on a page with a logo) or **Always** if you want the visitor to always have the option of scrolling (good for long text documents).

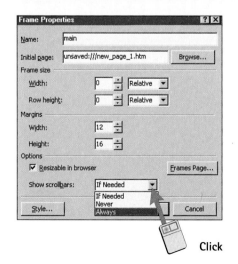

Click

4 Open Page Properties

You can set some options specifically for the frames on the page. Click the **Frames Page** button to open the **Page Properties** dialog box.

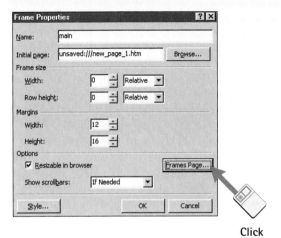

Click

5 Set Frames Spacing

Type a value in the **Frame Spacing** text box. This value sets the space (in pixels) that appears between all frames on the page.

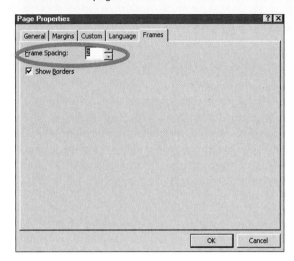

6 Show Borders

The **Show Borders** option is selected by default. Deselect this option if you want borders to be invisible. When you are done, click **OK** twice to close both dialog boxes and review the results of your changes on the page.

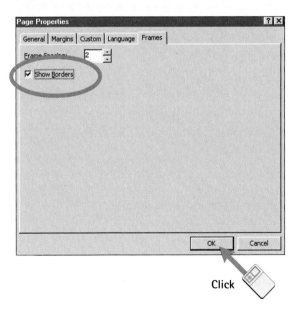

Click

How-To Hints

Frame Making

Frames are useful for creating site navigation tools, such as a list of hyperlinks in a left pane that, when clicked, displays the contents of a page in a right pane. The problem for your visitors is that frames can be hard to bookmark. Some visitors might find the information they want several pages into your Web site. But when they bookmark the site, they return to your home page. (Some browsers are smart enough to show the correct set of frames, but many will revert to the home page.) Keep this in mind when you design your site and use frames only when you consider them necessary.

End

How to Set Links in Frames

When you open a frames page template, any hyperlinks you create are set to appear in a certain frame. The frame where a linked page opens is called the *target frame*. You can change this setting to make the linked page open in another frame. You can also set the link so that it opens the page in a separate browser window.

Begin

1 Select Text

Open the page that contains the frames and the text for which you want to create a link. Highlight the text you want to link.

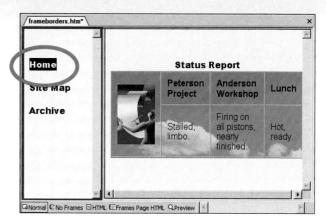

2 Set Hyperlink

Click the **Insert Hyperlink** button on the **Standard** toolbar to open the **Insert Hyperlink** dialog box. Alternatively, you can right-click the selected text and choose **Hyperlink** from the context menu.

Click

3 Choose a Page

To designate the page to which you want to link the selected text, select a file from your system, or enter the Web address in the **Address** box. In this example, I am linking the text **Home** in the left frame to the home page I've created for the site.

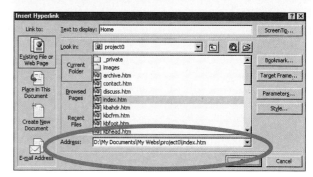

4 Change the Target Frame

To select the frame in which the hyperlinked page will appear, click the **Target Frame** button. The **Target Frame** dialog box opens.

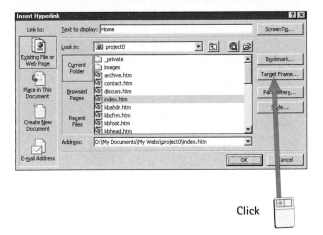

Click

5 Choose the Target Frame

The **Current frames page** area shows a preview of the current frames page. Click the frame in which you want the linked page to appear. Typically, you do not select the same frame in which the link text (the text you selected in Step 1) appears.

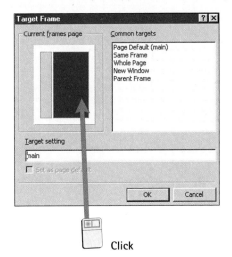

Click

6 Set as Default

If you want the page you selected to be the default for all links, select the **Set as page default** option. Click **OK** twice to save your settings in the **Target Frame** dialog box and the **Insert Hyperlink** dialog box.

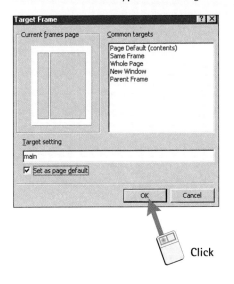

Click

How-To Hints

Set Target to New Window

You can also set the target frame so that your hyperlink opens in a new browser window. In the **Target Frame** dialog box, select the **New Window** option from the **Common targets** list.

End

How to Insert an Inline Frame

Inline frames are new to FrontPage 2002. This feature allows you to place a frame within a new or existing page. You can use an inline frame to display dynamic information that can change without affecting the rest of the page. Inline frames can also be used to link to somebody else's page right within your page (that is, without opening another browser window). This practice is typically frowned on unless you have the other site's permission. But, if you do, go for it!

Begin

1 Set the Insertion Point

Click a point on your page to choose where your inline frame will appear. Then choose **Insert, Inline Frame** from the menu bar. A new frame appears on the existing page.

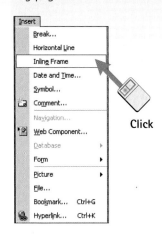

Click

2 Use a Blank Page

To start the new frame off as a blank page, click the **New Page** button in the new frame. You can now start typing into the frame area. Keep in mind that this is a separate page that you must save in addition to the page on which you started working.

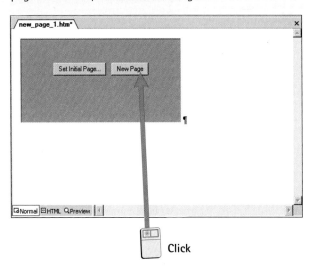

Click

3 Use an Existing Page

If you'd like to use an existing page in the new inline frame, click the **Set Initial Page** button. The **Insert Hyperlink** dialog box opens. Type a URL or select a page from your computer or network, and click **OK**.

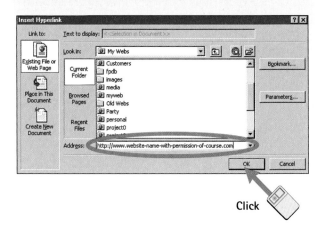

Click

4 Select the Inline Frame

Move the mouse pointer over the inline frame until the white arrow pointer appears. Click to select the inline frame. Handles appear around the edges of the frame.

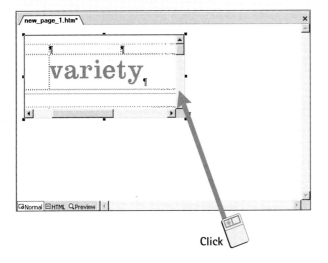

Click

5 Make Changes to Frame Properties

From the menu bar, choose **Format, Properties.** In the **Inline Frame Properties** dialog box that opens, you can set margins (in pixels) to provide white space around the frame page to make the page appear neater. You can also deselect the **Show border** check box, which is typically a good way to keep the page design clean. You also can resize the frame in this dialog box, but it is usually easier to resize the frame by dragging the frame handles (as we do in the next step). When you finish making changes, click **OK.**

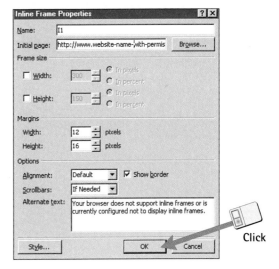

Click

6 Resize the Frame

As you did in Step 4, select the inline frame to make the handles appear. Drag a middle handle to make the frame taller or wider. Drag a corner handle to resize the frame proportionally.

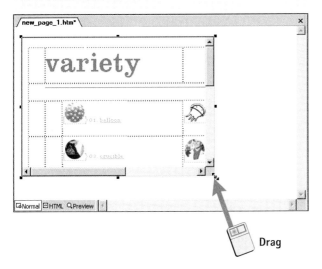

Drag

How-To Hints

Open in New Window

If you want to edit the contents of an inline frame in a new window, first right-click inside the inline frame. From the context menu that appears, choose **Open Page in New Window.** Now you can edit the contents of the frame more easily.

Compatibility Concern

Before you make wide use of inline frames in your Web site, consider that viewing inline frames requires Netscape Navigator 6 or later or Microsoft Internet Explorer 4 or later.

End

TASK *13*

How to Position Elements Precisely

Until recently, arranging text and graphics exactly where you wanted them took some head scratching. Unfortunately, creating exact layouts with tables, while effective, can be time consuming. If you know that your visitors will be viewing your site with specific, current browsers—for instance, on an intranet at your office—consider using *absolute positioning*. Browsers such as Microsoft Internet Explorer and Netscape Navigator (versions 4.0 and above) support absolute positioning. Even when visitors adjust their browsers' windows, absolutely positioned elements stay exactly where you placed them.

Begin

1 Display the Positioning Toolbar

Open the page on which you want to position elements absolutely. Select **View**, **Toolbars**, **Positioning**. The **Positioning** toolbar appears on the page. Move the toolbar to a convenient place on the page.

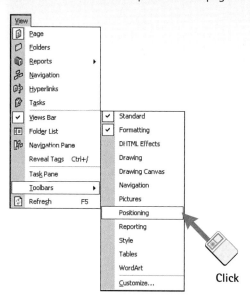

Click

2 Select the Page Element

Select the graphic or text you want to position. In this example, I selected the headline text, but you could also click the picture to select it for positioning.

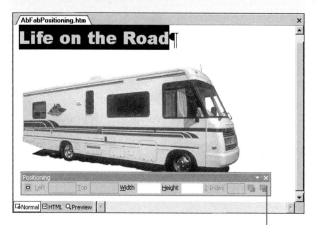

Positioning toolbar

3 Click Position Absolutely

Click the **Position Absolutely** button on the **Positioning** toolbar. A set of handles appears around the element you selected. The **Left** and **Top** boxes on the **Positioning** toolbar display the position of the object in relation to the top-left corner of the page.

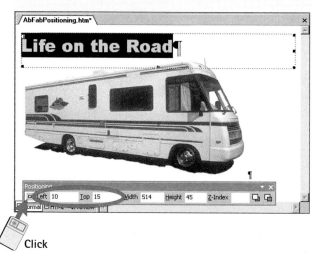

Click

142   PART 6: CREATING THE PAGE LAYOUT

4 Place the Image

Move the mouse over the selected element; the pointer changes to a four-headed arrow. Drag the object to where you want it on the page. Notice that the **Left** and **Top** values in the **Positioning** toolbar change to reflect the element's new position on the page.

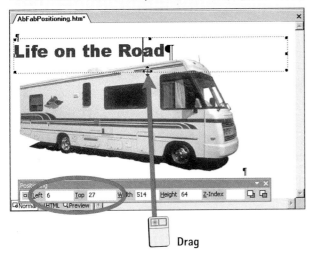

Drag

5 Select Bring Forward

You can lay an object on top of another object and then click the **Bring Forward** button on the **Positioning** toolbar. The **Z-Index** box on the **Positioning** toolbar shows the position of the selected element in terms of layers (whether the object is in front of or behind the main text layer; the main text layer is layer 0). A positive number indicates that the object is in front of the main text layer; a negative number means that the object is behind the main text layer.

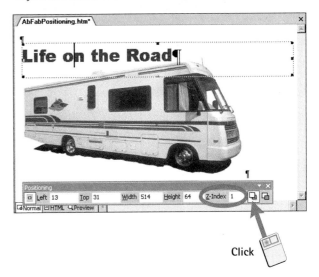

Click

6 Select Send Backward

Click the **Send Backward** button on the **Positioning** toolbar to position the selected element behind another page element, such as text. To see how the page looks in a browser, click the **Preview** tab (the page might appear slightly differently than it does in the **Normal** tab).

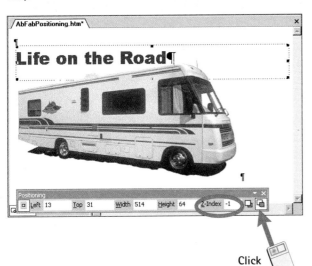

Click

How-To Hints

Tables or Absolute Positioning?

In most cases, you don't know what browsers your visitors will be using, so you can't be sure that absolute positioning will result in a neat, legible page. If you can't predict which browser will be used to view the page, you should stick with tables to align the elements on your page. Of course, you won't be able to layer elements on top of each other with tables, but your visitors will be able to see your content— which, in my humble opinion, is a pretty important design goal.

End

Task

1 How to Work with a Predesigned Site **146**

2 How to Save and Retrieve Web Sites **148**

3 How to Import an Existing Web Site **150**

4 How to Use Folders View **152**

5 How to Add and Remove Pages **154**

6 How to Create a New Page from an Existing Page **156**

7 How to Move or Copy Pages **158**

8 How to Find and Replace Text in a Site **160**

9 How to Use Navigation View **162**

10 How to Create Shared Borders **164**

11 How to Automate Navigation **166**

12 How to Insert a Page Banner **170**

13 How to Use Tasks View **172**

PART 7

Working with Webs

*F*rontPage calls the collection of pages, pictures, and other elements that make up your site a *Web*. Although you can publish pages without creating a Web, you lose some of what FrontPage does best—managing the structure of your site.

Whether you import Web pages you created with another program or start from scratch, FrontPage adds certain elements to make your life easier. The program tracks your changes so that you can move documents or add new ones without having to update each page by hand to reflect those changes. If you want to add a bit of updated news on your site, for example, FrontPage makes it as simple to add this text to one page as it is to add it to 100. You can remove it just as easily. In addition, creating a Web lets you automate the navigation of your site. Navigation elements—such as text or buttons that can be clicked to jump from one page to another—make your site easier for visitors to browse.

Because managing a Web can be overwhelming, FrontPage offers a **Tasks** view that lets you organize the jobs that have to be accomplished before you publish the Web. If you work with a group of people, you can even assign the less exciting tasks (such as running the marketing copy by the boss) to somebody else. And isn't that what teamwork is all about?

How to Work with a Predesigned Site

When you have to create a site in a hurry, try using one of the predesigned Webs included with FrontPage. Your choices range from a simple one-page Web to fully fleshed-out corporate and personal Webs that include graphics and hyperlinks.

Begin

1 Open the Web

Click the **down-pointing arrow** next to the **New Page** button. Select **Web**. The **Web Site Templates** dialog box opens, showing a list of predesigned Webs (also called Web *templates*) and wizards that can take you step by step through the basic Web-building process.

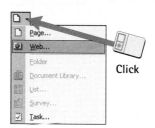

Click

2 Choose a Web

Select the type of Web you want to create from the **Web Sites** list. When you select an item from the list, a description of the template or wizard appears on the right side of the dialog box.

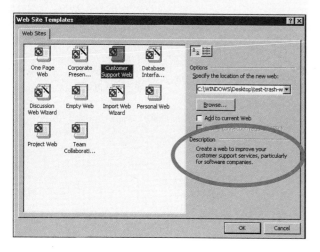

3 Enter a Location and Name

In the **Specify the location of the new web** field, type a name for the site you are going to create. If you don't want the Web stored in the location shown, enter a new one. You might want to keep your Webs in the **My Documents** folder or on your root drive. I prefer to keep my Webs on my second hard drive, under **D:\My Documents\My Webs**. When you have entered the location and name, click **OK** to create the specified Web. You can later change the Web name by selecting **Tools**, **Web Settings** and entering the new name in the **Web name** text box.

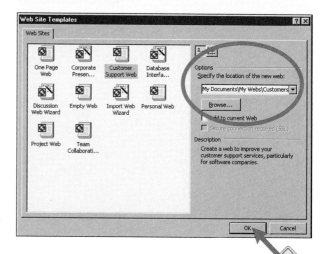

Click

4 Switch to Folders View

Click the **Folders** icon in the **Views** bar to see a list of all the pages, graphics, and other elements of the new Web in **Folders** view. Already, FrontPage has done quite a bit of work for you!

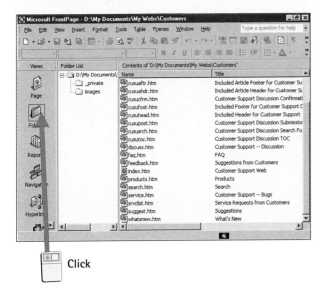

Click

5 Open the Pages to Edit

You can double-click any page in the list in **Folders** view to open it in **Page** view so that you can begin the editing process. Remember that the **index.htm** file is the default "home page" of the site; you might want to start your work with this page.

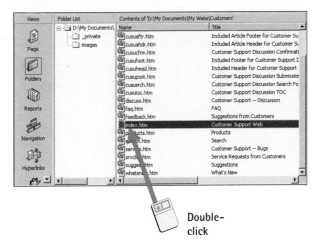

Double-click

6 Begin Editing

The selected page opens in **Page** view. From this page, you can click existing links to jump to other pages and explore the framework of the Web that FrontPage has created for you. Edit the elements on individual pages and refer to the tasks in earlier parts of this book for help.

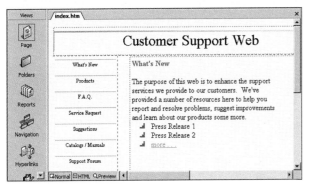

How-To Hints

Create a New Web

If you don't see a predesigned Web that interests you in the **Web Site Templates** dialog box, it's easy to start a new Web from scratch. Just open the **Web Site Templates** dialog box as you did in Step 1, and select **One Page Web** or **Empty Web** (a Web with no pages). Click **OK** and start editing your personal Web.

Delete a Web

To delete a Web that you're working on, change to **Folders** view. Right-click the top-level folder for your Web and choose **Delete**. Be careful, though—you can't bring a Web back after you've deleted it.

End

How to Save and Retrieve Web Sites

Opening and closing existing Webs is simple. FrontPage keeps track of recently used Webs so that you can easily retrieve the Webs you've been working on. You can also open more than one site at a time.

Begin

1 Open a Recently Used Web

Select **File, Recent Webs**. The submenu that appears lists several of the Web sites you have worked on recently. Make a selection, and that Web opens. Click the **Folders** button in the **Views bar** to view all the files in your Web.

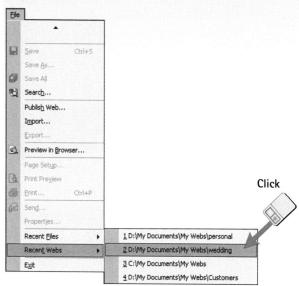

Click

2 Open a Web You Haven't Used Recently

If the Web you want to open doesn't appear in the **Recent Webs** submenu in Step 1, choose **File, Open Web** instead. The **Open Web** dialog box appears.

Click

3 Enter the Web Name

If you know the name of the Web you want to open, type the name in the **Web name** box in the dialog box (for instance, **C:\My Documents\My Webs\Personal**). If you don't want to type the complete pathname of the Web, go to Step 4.

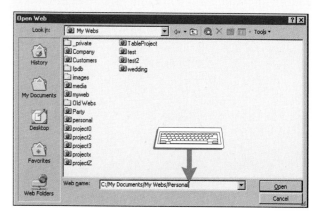

4 Select the Web

To navigate to your Web, click the arrow next to the **Look in** drop-down list box and browse to the folder that contains the Web you want to open.

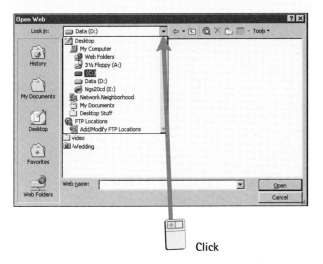

Click

5 Click Open

After you select the Web folder you want to open, click the **Open** button. The selected Web opens. You can switch to **Folders** view to view your files.

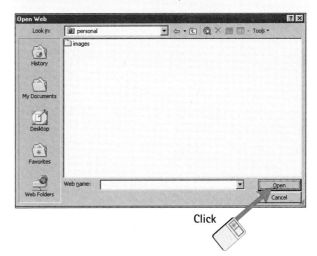

Click

6 Close the Web

When you finish working, save your Web by choosing the **Save** button on the **Standard** toolbar. Close the Web by selecting **File, Close Web**. When prompted, click **OK** if you want to save changes to any pages you have changed.

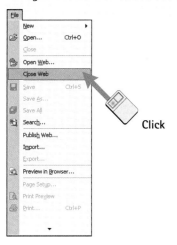

Click

How-To Hints

Where's Your Web?

When you choose the **File, Open Web** command or pick a site from the **Recent Webs** list, you're simply opening a folder. A small globe icon appears on your Web folders to differentiate them from other folders on your hard drive. By default, Web folders are stored on your root drive, in the **My Webs** folder created when you installed FrontPage.

End

How to Import an Existing Web Site

FrontPage rather deftly handles Web pages created in other programs. The program offers a wizard that steps you through the process of importing a "foreign" site into FrontPage—whether that site is on the World Wide Web or is stored on your hard drive. You can even tell the wizard how much space to allow when importing the site or import just the graphics or text from the site.

Begin

1 Start the File Import

If you have any FrontPage Webs open, close them (choose **File, Close Web**). Start the import by selecting **File, Import**. The **Web Site Templates** dialog box opens with the **Import Web Wizard** option selected by default. Note that, if you plan to import a site that resides on the Web, you should first establish your Internet connection.

Click

2 Name the Site

In the **Specify the location of the new web** text box, type a name (and change the directory path, if necessary) for the Web that will be created when you import your files. (A new folder on your hard drive will be created with the name you type here.) Type a name you'll easily remember—it won't appear when you publish it. Then click **OK**. The next screen of the wizard opens.

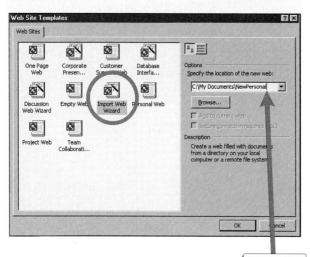

3 Select the Web Site

Select whether the site should be imported from the local computer or network or if it exists on the World Wide Web. If you select the **Local** option, the **Browse** button appears.

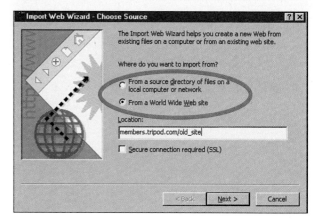

4 Enter Location

If you are importing a Web site from the World Wide Web, type the URL of the site in the **Location** field. (Note that you don't have to type the **http://** part of the address.) If you are importing a local site, click the **Browse** button and select the site on your local hard drive or network. Click **Next** to go to the next wizard screen.

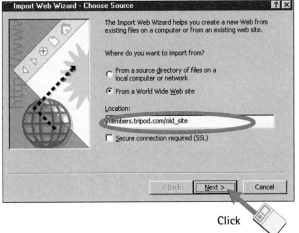

Click

5 Set Options

Choose from the options presented by the wizard. (See the How-To Hints if you're not sure what to choose.) Click **Next**.

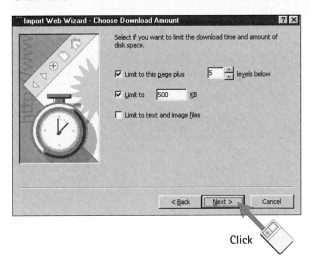

Click

6 Finish

When the last screen of the wizard appears, click **Finish** to import your Web. When the wizard finishes with the import process, the Web opens in FrontPage with the name you specified in Step 2.

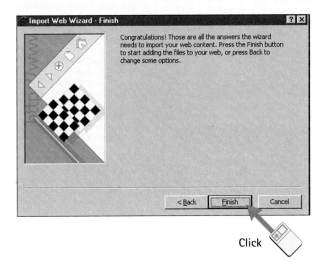

Click

How-To Hints

Wizard Import Options

The **Import Web Wizard** takes its cues from the location you specified in Step 4. If you entered a site (**www.mysite.com**) rather than a page name (**www.mysite.com/index.html**), you'll download the home page as well as the number of levels of linked pages you choose in the wizard's **Choose Download Amount** dialog box. If you want to download an entire site without regard to size, deselect all the option check boxes. You might have to do so when importing a site to a new computer, for instance. You can select the **Limit to** check box and enter a number in kilobytes so that the site does not take up unwieldy amounts of space on your hard drive. However, this option makes it hard to predict what pages will be left behind when the limit is hit. To finish, click **Next**.

End

How to Use Folders View

Most of your time building pages is spent switching from **Page** view to **Folders** view. In **Folders** view, you see the files in your site in a Windows Explorer–like window. From this view, you can launch pages, create new folders, and sort your files.

Begin

1 Switch to Folders View

With a Web open in FrontPage, click the **Folders** button in the **Views bar** to switch to **Folders** view.

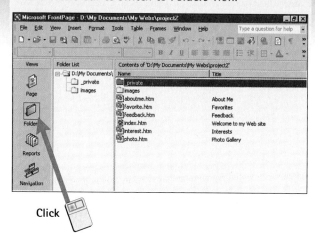

Click

2 Create a New Folder

To create a new folder, select **File**, **New**, **Folder**. Alternatively, right-click a blank area of the pane and choose **New Folder** from the context menu. To create a subfolder, select a folder to open and then perform this step.

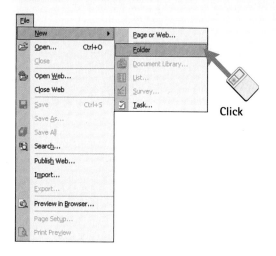

Click

3 Name (or Rename) Filename or Page Title

Click a filename under the **Name** or **Title** column. Click again, and FrontPage highlights the name and makes it ready for editing. Begin typing to rename the file. Press **Enter** to finish.

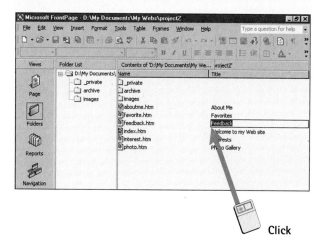

Click

4 Sort Files

Click a column name (listed in the gray bars at the top of the right pane) to re-sort the list of files in your site. Click again to sort the files in ascending or descending order (filenames will appear in numeric or reverse numeric order, for instance). Press a letter key on your keyboard to jump to the first file that begins with the letter you type.

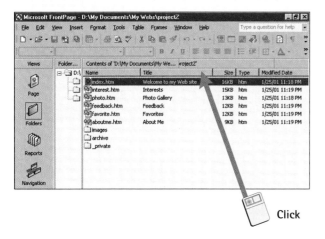

Click

5 Set File Summary

You can add a comment to any file. You might want to leave a comment, for instance, if you work with a group and want to pass on changes you've made to the site. Right-click a file and choose **Properties** from the context menu. The **Properties** dialog box opens.

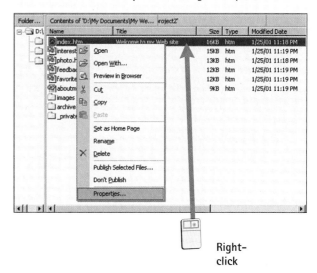

Right-click

6 Set Summary Info

Select the **Summary** tab and type a message in the **Comments** field. Click **OK** when you're finished.

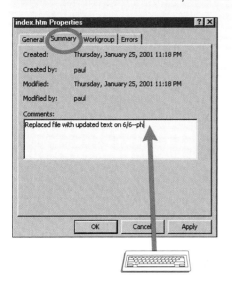

How-To Hints

Click Options

You can see a list of your Web's folders without leaving the view from which you are working. Select **View, Folder List**. With the **Folder List** pane open, you can manage pages just as you would in **Folders** view. Select **View, Folder List** again to make the additional pane disappear.

End

How to Add and Remove Pages

Managing pages in your Web is a day-to-day task. If you are familiar with Windows Explorer, you'll have no trouble adding and removing pages in a FrontPage Web.

Begin

1 Open Folder List

Open the Web you want to work with. To see the files in your Web, open the **Folder List** by selecting **View, Folder List**. Alternatively, switch to **Folders** view from any other view by clicking the **Folders** button in the **Views bar**.

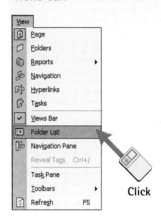

Click

2 Create a New Page

Click the **down-pointing arrow** next to the **New Page** button in the **Standard** toolbar and choose **Page**. (You can also open an empty page by right-clicking a blank area in the **Folder List** and choose **New, Page** from the context menu.) The **Page Templates** dialog box opens.

Click

3 Select Page

Select the type of page you want to insert in the Web. When you select a page, a description appears on the right side of the dialog box. Click **OK** when you have selected the desired type of page.

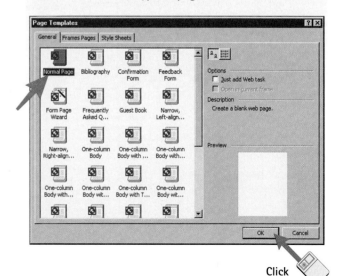

Click

4 Import a Page

You also can import an existing page from another Web site located on your local hard disk or network or on the Internet. Select **File, Import** to open the **Import** dialog box. (Note that if you see the **Web Site Templates** dialog box instead of the **Import** dialog box, you have not first opened a Web as instructed to do in Step 1. You must open a Web before performing this step.)

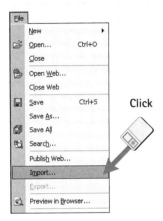

Click

5 Select a File

Click the **Add File** button; when the **Add File to Import List** dialog box opens, select the local file you want to import and click **Open**. Back in the **Import** dialog box, click **OK**. If you want to import a page from the Internet, click **From Web**; the **Import Web Wizard** launches (see Task 3, "How to Import an Existing Web Site," in this part for more information).

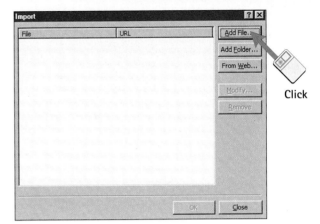

Click

6 Delete a Page

To delete a page from your Web, select its filename in the **Folder List**. (Remember that page files have the extension **.htm**.) You can select multiple page files by pressing **Shift** as you click multiple files. Press the **Delete** key on your keyboard to delete the selected page files from your Web. When prompted, confirm that you want to delete the listed file or files.

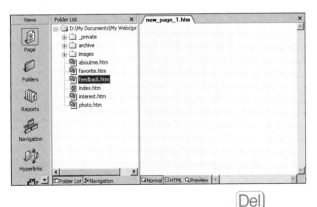

Del

How-To Hints

Fix Broken Links

Keep in mind that any links to a page you delete will no longer work. You should remove all links to the deleted page: Select **View, Reports, Problems, Broken Hyperlinks** to view a list of broken links. Task 4 in Part 11, "Preparing to Publish," explains how to repair and update links.

About Themes

Files (pages) you add to your Web take on the appearance of any theme you have applied— whether you create a new page or import an existing page.

End

How to Create a New Page from an Existing Page

What's the fastest way to start a new page? Well, if you want the new page to look like some other page in your site, try opening an existing page and editing it. FrontPage 2002 has cleverly included a feature that lets you do just that—without worrying about accidentally saving the edited file over your original file. Here's how to get started.

Begin

1 Choose File, New Page or Web

Open the FrontPage Web that contains the original page (the one you want to copy to create the new page). From the menu bar, select **File, New, Page or Web**. The Task Pane opens.

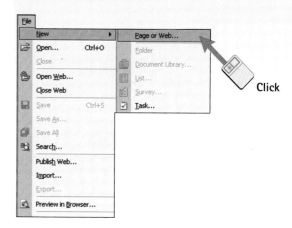

Click

2 Choose Page

In the Task Pane, under **New from existing page**, select **Choose page**. The New from Existing Page dialog box opens.

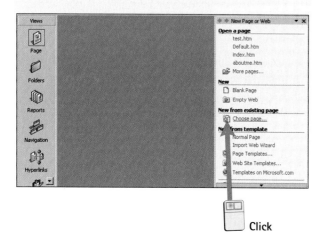

Click

3 Navigate to Page

Now let's see, where did we save that perfectly designed HTML document? Use the **Look in** pop-up menu to navigate to the page on your hard drive or network.

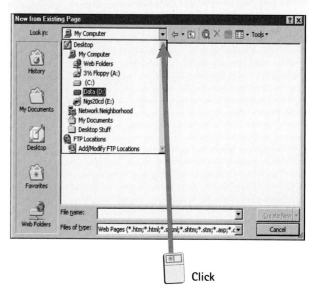

Click

4 Choose the Folder

When you find the folder (the Web) in which the page you're looking for is saved, select the folder and click the **Open** button. The folder opens.

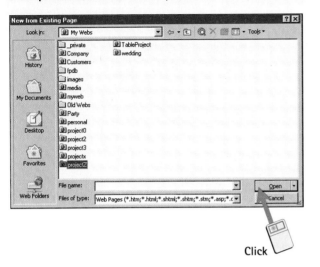

Click

5 Select the Page

Select the page you want to base the new page on. Click the **Create New** button in the **New from Existing Page** dialog box. A *copy* of the selected page (not the entire Web) opens in **Page** view.

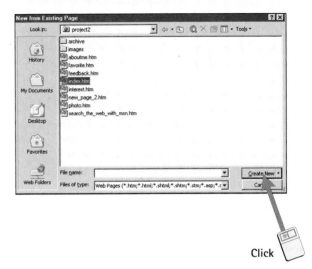

Click

6 Edit and Save the Page

Edit the page to suit your needs. When you are finished, click the **Save** button on the **Standard** toolbar. Because this is the first time you've saved this page, the **Save As** dialog box opens.

Click

7 Title the Page

In the **File name** box, type a name that describes your page. If you like, you can also change the title of the original page to better suit your new, edited page. (You really should. No two documents in your Web should have the same title.) Click the **Change title** button; in the **Set Page Title** dialog box that opens, type a title and click **OK** to save this title. Click **Save** to close the **Save As** dialog box.

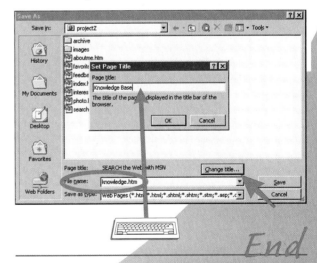

End

How to Move or Copy Pages

Just as you do when adding and deleting pages, you can shuffle pages in a Web. You rearrange Web pages just as you rearrange files in Windows Explorer. FrontPage tracks your changes; if you move a page with hyperlinks, FrontPage updates your links automatically.

Begin

1 Open the Folder List

With the Web you want to modify open in any view, choose **View, Folder List**. The **Folder List** for your Web site opens.

Click

2 Move a Page

To move a page, click and drag the page to the folder where you want it. (For example, you might want to move a picture to the **images** folder.) Creating a set of specific folders for your files makes the files easier to organize and update.

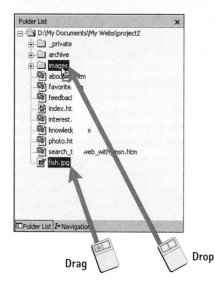

Drag   Drop

3 Copy a Page

You can copy a page to create a duplicate that you can then use as a template for a new page. In the **Folder List**, select the page you want to copy and choose **Edit, Copy** (or press **Ctrl+C**). The file is copied to the Clipboard.

Click

4 Paste a Page

Open the folder in which you want to place the copy of the page you created in Step 3. Choose **Edit**, **Paste** (or press **Ctrl+V**). A new page file appears, bearing the name of the original page with the suffix **_copy(1)**.

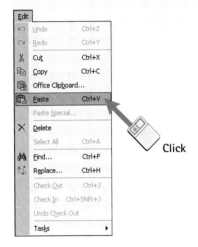

Click

5 Right-Click to Copy or Move

You can use the context menu to move or copy a page: Right-click a file. From the context menu that appears, choose **Cut** (to move the page) or **Copy**. Open the folder in which you want the file to appear. Right-click again and choose **Paste** from the context menu.

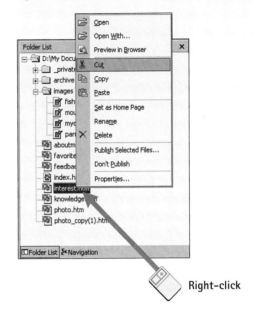

Right-click

How-To Hints

Refresh the View

After making changes and re-sorting files in **Folders** view, you can refresh the view by pressing **F5** on your keyboard or by selecting **View**, **Refresh**. When you work with other people on the same Web, you might have to refresh the view to make sure that you have the most current file list.

The Folder Structure for a Web

When you start a new Web, FrontPage creates at least two folders: **images** and **_private**. You should store your graphics in the **images** folder to keep them organized and easier to find and edit. The **_private** folder can't be opened by visitors. You can use this folder to store data you want to keep hidden, such as the results of forms that visitors fill out. FrontPage also creates folders within your main Web site folder when you set shared borders (**_borders**) or apply a theme (**_themes**).

End

How to Find and Replace Text in a Site

In Part 3, "Working with Text," you learned how to find and replace text on a page. Thankfully, FrontPage can handle bigger jobs; at your request, it can scan an entire site for words to search and replace.

Begin

1 Open a Web

From the menu bar, select **File, Open Web**. Navigate to the Web you want to open, select it, and click **Open**.

Click

2 Choose Replace

From any page in any view, select **Edit, Replace** (or press **Ctrl+H**). The **Find and Replace** dialog box opens.

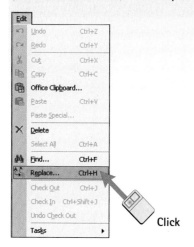

Click

3 Enter Search Terms

Type the word or phrase you are looking for in the **Find what** box. Type the replacement text in the **Replace with** box.

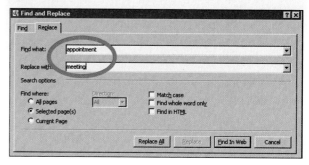

4 Set Options

Set your search options, including whether you want to search all pages or just the selected page. Select **Find in HTML** if you want the Replace tool to find a piece of HTML code (such as hyperlinks or e-mail addresses, which don't necessarily appear as text on any page in your site).

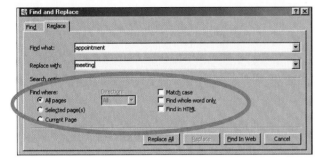

5 Start the Search

If you selected the **Current page** option, click **Find Next** to start the search. Otherwise, click the **Find in Web** button to begin the search.

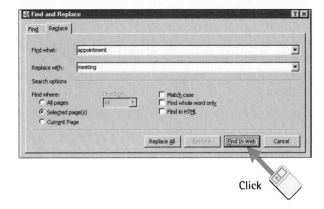

Click

6 Select a File from the List

When the search is complete, the **Find and Replace** dialog box expands to include a list of pages on which the specified text appears. Double-click a page in the list to open it.

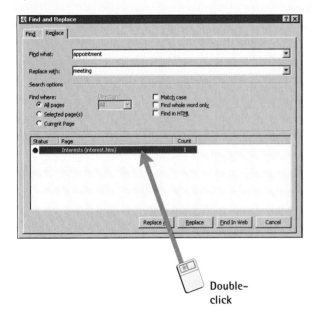

Double-click

7 Replace

The word you were searching for is highlighted on the page. Click **Replace** to substitute this one instance of the word; click **Replace All** to change every occurrence of the word on the page. After you make your selection, the **Finished Checking Pages** dialog box appears. Click **Back to List** to return to the list of pages in which the search text is found.

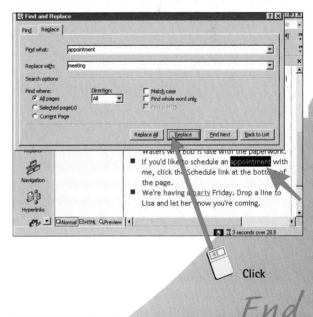

Click

End

How to Use Navigation View

Navigation view is a flowchart-like representation of your site that handles two tasks: First, it gives you a graphical representation of your site, which helps you plan the structure. Second, the view allows you to use automated navigation features, such as the page banner and link bar mentioned in later tasks in this part.

Begin

1 Switch to Navigation View

Open the Web you want to work with. Click the **Navigation** button in the **Views bar** to switch to **Navigation** view. The **Navigation** toolbar also appears on the screen.

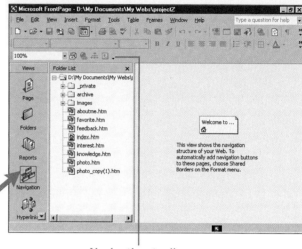

Click

Navigation toolbar

2 Add a Page to Navigation View

Drag a page from the **Folder List** on the left to the pane on the right. (If you don't see the **Folder List** next to the **Views bar**, choose **View, Folder List** to open it.) In this example, FrontPage added the home page to **Navigation** view when it created the Web; here, I drag the page I want to add under the home page.

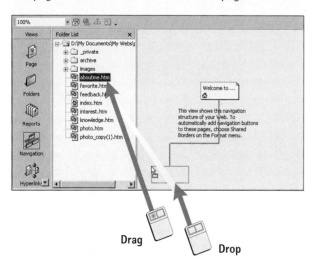

Drag

Drop

3 Set Relationship to Other Pages

Drag a page to adjust its position in the site. If you drag a page *next to* another page, the two pages are considered to be on the same level. Drag a page *under* a page, and the page on top is in the *parent* level; the page below is on the *child* level. Establishing these connections lets you create navigational elements for your site. Learn more in Task 11, "How to Automate Navigation."

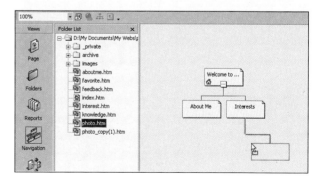

4 Change the View

In the **Navigation** toolbar, you can enter a number in the **Zoom** text box to change the size of the "pages" in the navigation pane. Click the **Portrait/Landscape** button in the **Navigation** toolbar to change the orientation of the pages in the pane. Last, you can right-click a page and choose **View Subtree Only** to hide pages above the one you right-clicked.

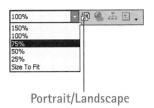

Portrait/Landscape

5 Add a New Page

You can create a new page in **Navigation** view. First, select the page that will be the parent page. Right-click the page and choose **New, Page**. To create a new page at the top level (a "sister" to the home page, as it were), right-click a blank area of the navigation pane and choose **New, Top Page**.

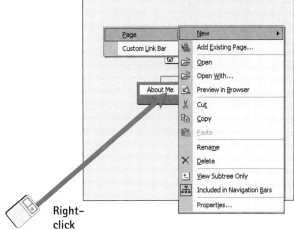

Right-click

6 Open a Page

To open a page in **Navigation** view and begin editing it, double-click the page.

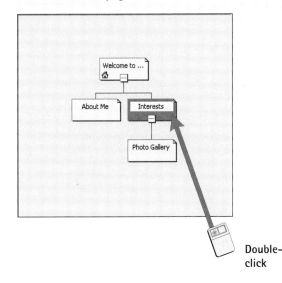

Double-click

7 Delete a Page

To remove a page from **Navigation** view, select it and press the **Delete** key. A confirmation box appears, asking whether you want to remove the page from just **Navigation** view (the default) or to remove the page from the *Web*. If you select to remove the page from the Web, the page is irretrievably lost—so be careful. Click **OK** to delete the page as specified.

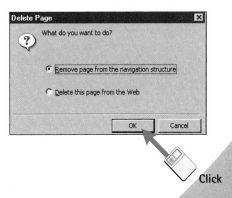

Click

End

10

How to Create Shared Borders

The *shared borders* feature lets you add up to four common areas on each page in your site. You can add text and graphics to the shared border area, and the borders and their contents appear on all the pages of your site. Changing the content in one of those areas on one page affects all the other pages. In the shared borders for your site, you might want to include your address, copyright information, or other content that you update frequently.

Begin

1 Open a Web

Choose **File, Open Web**. Navigate to the Web for which you want to set up shared borders and click **Open**.

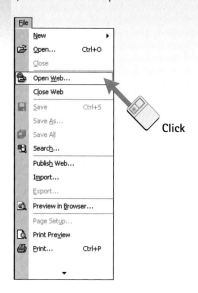

Click

2 Open Shared Borders

Choose **Format, Shared Borders**. The **Shared Borders** dialog box opens. (Note that you don't have to have a page open to change the shared borders.)

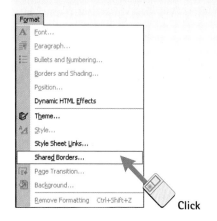

Click

3 Apply to All Pages or the Current Page

Select whether shared borders should be applied to all pages in the site or only to the page or pages you are working on. In general, set shared borders for all pages. Later, you can repeat these steps to remove shared borders on individual pages where you don't want the borders to appear.

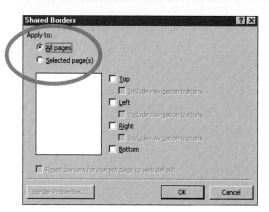

4 Set Borders

Choose the areas where you want the shared borders to be displayed on your page. Watch the preview on the left side of the dialog box. (If you don't want your shared borders to include navigation buttons, deselect the **Include navigation buttons** check boxes.) Save your changes to the shared borders by clicking the **OK** button.

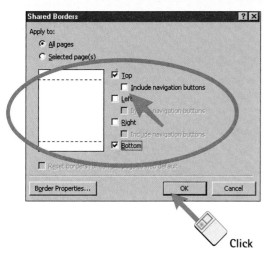

Click

5 Open a Page

Select the **Folders** button in the **Views bar**, and then double-click a page to open it.

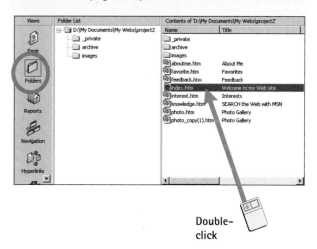

Double-click

6 Make Changes to Page Elements

Note the appearance of the shared borders. Enter text or other page elements in the borders and then examine other pages in the site to make sure that the borders appear on those pages as well.

How-To Hints

Edit Shared Borders

If you decide later to add or remove your shared borders, select **Format, Shared Borders**. Deselect the borders you no longer want and click **OK**. If you want to change the shared borders on just one page, first open that page in **Page** view. Select **Format, Shared Borders**. Choose **Current page**, deselect the borders you want to remove, and click the **OK** button.

End

How to Automate Navigation

Automation is a beautiful thing. Placing a *link bar* (sometimes called a *navigation* bar) on each page in your Web makes the pages in your site much easier to access. A link bar is a set of hyperlinked text or buttons that represents the pages in your site. To create a link bar, you have to use **Navigation** view to tell FrontPage how your site is structured (see Task 9, "How to Use Navigation View"). After you create the site structure, you can insert a link bar on each page in your site.

Begin

1 Open Navigation View

Open the Web you want to work with. Click the **Navigation** button on the **Views bar** to change to **Navigation** view.

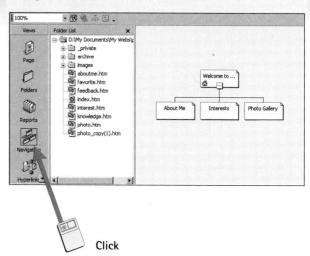

Click

2 Open Shared Borders

To create a link bar on all the pages in the site, you must first create a set of shared borders. These borders appear on every page in your site; the link bar will appear in the border area. (Shared borders are described in detail in the previous task.) Select **Format, Shared Borders**. The **Shared Borders** dialog box opens.

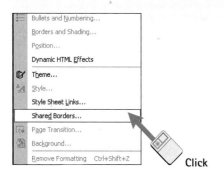

Click

3 Select Pages

Choose whether to apply the shared borders to all pages or to only the selected page or pages. For the purpose of a link bar, select **All pages**.

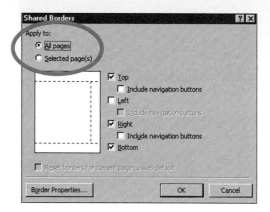

4 Choose the Borders to Display

In this example, I decided to display only a **Top** border. You might want to display your link bar in a shared border in another location. Make sure that the **Include navigation buttons** option is selected for each border location you select. Click **OK** when you finish.

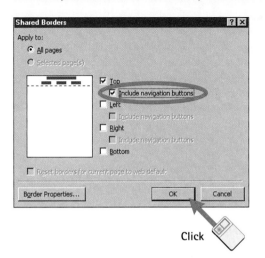

Click

5 Preview Shared Borders

To see your new navigation elements, double-click a page in **Navigation** view to open it in **Page** view.

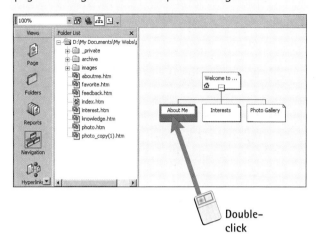

Double-click

6 Open Link Bar Properties

In **Page** view, you can see links for your pages in the border you just added. Double-click a link in the shared border to open the **Link Bar Properties** dialog box.

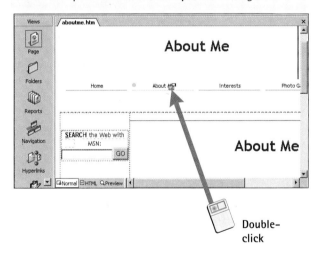

Double-click

7 Set Hyperlinks

Select the hyperlinks you want to appear in the link bar. For example, the **Parent level** option presents links to pages that appear *above* the current page. The **Child level** option displays pages that appear *below* the current page. The **Back and next** option is for pages on the same level that can use **Next** and **Back** buttons (helpful for presentations). To see how each selection affects the links, select a radio button and watch the preview area change.

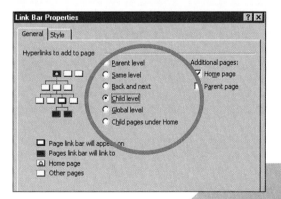

Continues

8 Set Additional Pages

In the **Additional pages** area, select whether you want to display links to the **Parent page** and **Home page** in the link bar.

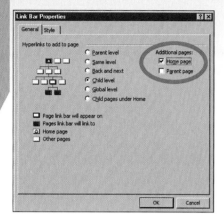

9 Choose Appearance

Click the **Style** tab. In the **Choose a style** area, click to select whether you want the link bar to use the current theme or, instead, another theme that you prefer (see Part 2, Task 4, "How to Choose and Apply a Theme," for more information on choosing themes). This is a new feature of FrontPage 2002, which allows you to apply the look of a theme to the link bar, without forcing you to change the entire page to one theme. Note that, if your page doesn't use a theme, the link bar will appear as a set of text links.

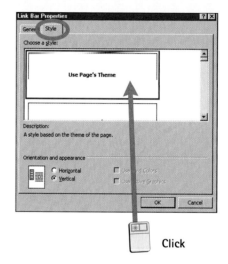

Click

10 Set Orientation

In the **Orientation and appearance** area, choose whether the link bar should be displayed horizontally or vertically in the shared border. Make a selection and preview its effect on the left side of the dialog box. When you finish making changes, click **OK**.

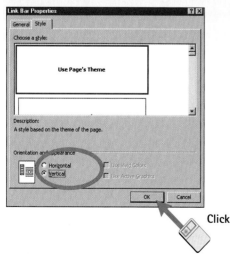

Click

How-To Hints

Link Bars in Shared Borders Share Properties

When you use shared borders, any changes you make to the link bar appear on every page that uses that shared border.

12 Switch to Navigation View

In some cases, you might not want a page to appear in the link bar (a page you use internally, for instance, or a page that is not yet finished). To make this change, first click the **Navigation** button in the **Views bar** to switch to **Navigation** view.

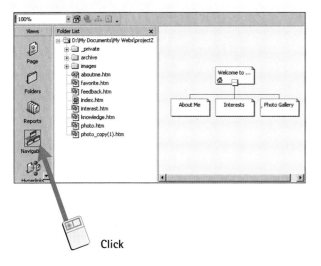

Click

13 Hide a Page from the Link Bar

Right-click the page you want to exclude from the link bar. Deselect the **Included in Navigation Bars** option from the context menu. Hiding this page from the link bars also hides the pages below it. To include pages below this page, right-click those pages in **Navigation** view and select the **Included in Navigation Bars** option for each page.

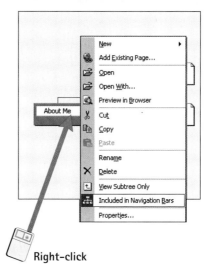

Right-click

How-To Hints

Apply to a Single Page

To apply a link bar to any one page, see Part 9, Task 1, "How to Add a Custom Link Bar."

Remove a Link Bar

To delete the link bar, open the page where the link bar appears, click the link bar to select it, and press **Delete**. If your Web uses shared borders, the link bar will disappear from *all* your pages.

Add a Page from Outside the Web

You can add to your link bar a page that is on the Internet but outside of your Web—for instance, your company's home page. In **Navigation** view, right-click the page under which the link to the external page should appear. Choose **Add Existing Page**. Type the page's URL (or browse to the page if it's on your network) and click the **OK** button.

End

How to Insert a Page Banner

Need to spruce up a page quickly? *Page banners* add a sharp-looking title to your page. If you use a theme, the page banner's font style and graphic look are dictated by the theme. If no theme is applied, you see just text, which you can format. To use a banner, you first should link the page to other pages in your site by changing to **Navigation** view.

Begin

1 Switch to Navigation View

Open the Web you want to work with. Click the **Navigation** button in the **Views bar** to change to **Navigation** view.

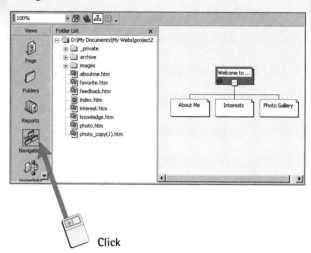

Click

2 Add the Banner Page

Click and drag the page to which you want to add the banner from the **Folder List** to the right pane. For more information, see Task 9, "How to Use Navigation View," earlier in this part.

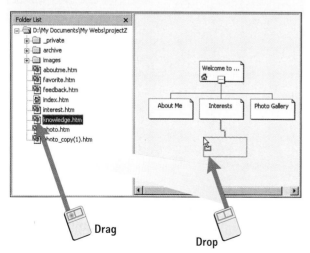

Drag

Drop

3 Open the Page

Double-click the page you just added to **Navigation** view to open it in **Page** view, ready for editing.

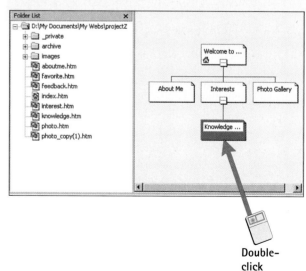

Double-click

4 Choose the Banner Location

Click the page to choose the location for the banner. Choose **Insert, Web Component**. The **Insert Web Component** dialog box opens. Look through the handy list of Web components and pick the right tool for the job: From the **Component type** list, select **Included Content**. Each of the **Included Content** components automates a feature of your Web site. In this case, the **Page Banner** component takes the title of your page and creates a graphic or text label based on the title. Choose **Page Banner** and then click **Finish**.

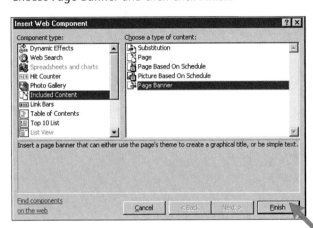

Click

5 Choose a Design

In the **Page Banner Properties** dialog box that opens, choose **Picture** or **Text**. The **Picture** option uses settings from your Web's theme to draw a graphic and place the text on the page. If your Web does not employ a theme, the banner is displayed as simple text, regardless of what you choose here. In the **Page banner** text box, type the title for your banner (by default, FrontPage uses the page title).

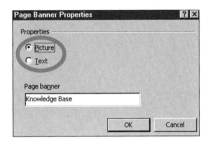

6 Change Banner Text

Click the **OK** button to save your settings. Your new banner appears on the page.

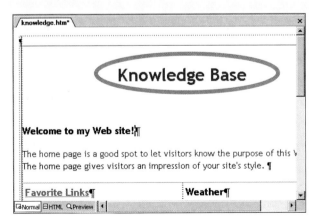

How-To Hints

Edit Page Banner

To edit your page banner later, just double-click the banner. The **Page Banner Properties** dialog box opens, and you can make changes to the text of the banner there. To change the graphic, you have to change the theme.

End

How to Use Tasks View

Tasks view lets you create an intelligent to-do list that comes in handy if you work with groups of people to develop your Web site. You can associate a task with a file and then assign the task to someone in your group. Or you can simply use tasks as reminders of Web chores you have to handle before publishing the site.

Begin

1 Associate the Task with a File

To associate a file with a task, switch to **Folders** view and select a file. From the menu bar, choose **Edit**, **Tasks**, **Add Task**. (You can also associate a task with the currently open file in **Page** view by selecting **Edit**, **Tasks**, **Add Task**.) The **New Task** dialog box opens.

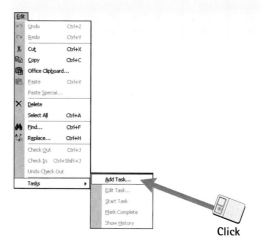

Click

2 Task Settings

Fill in the **Task name** and **Description** text boxes. If you want, type a name in the **Assigned to** text box and assign a **Priority** to the task. When you finish, click the **OK** button.

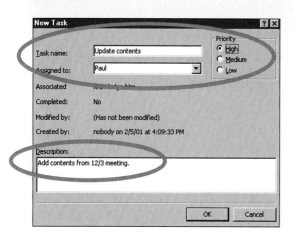

3 Open Tasks View

Click the **Tasks** button in the **Views bar** to open **Tasks** view. **Tasks** view lists all the incomplete tasks for your site.

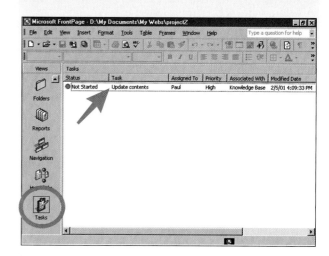

4 Open a Task

Right-click a task and choose **Start Task** to open the page associated with that task in editing mode. Close the page when you finish working on it.

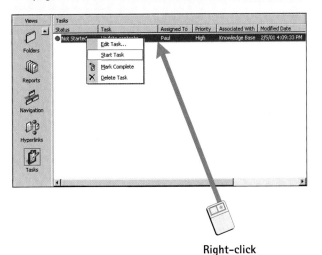

Right-click

5 Mark Task Completed

When you have completed the task, you can mark it complete. Return to **Tasks** view by clicking the **Tasks** button in the **Views bar**. Right-click the task and choose **Mark Complete** from the context menu.

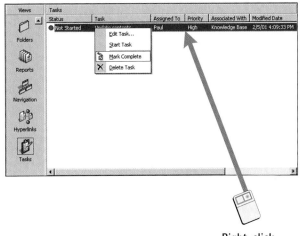

Right-click

6 Delete a Task

To remove a task from the list, right-click the task and choose **Delete Task**.

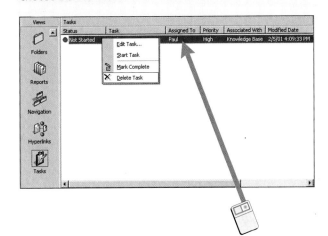

Right-click

How-To Hints

Add a New Task

To begin a new task (without a file association) right-click a blank area of **Tasks** view and choose **Add Task**. The **New Task** dialog box opens.

Show History

By default, **Tasks** view shows only tasks that have yet to be completed. To show a full listing of both completed and uncompleted tasks, right-click a blank area of **Tasks** view and select **Show History**.

End

Project 2

Creating a Company Home Page

In this project, you learn how to create a quick and easy site for your business. To get started, we'll use the **Corporate Web Wizard**. Just answer the questions posed by the wizard, and FrontPage creates the pages for you. Then we'll insert text from a word processing document and add a picture to customize the site. You'll be done in the time it takes to eat two slices of pizza (I tested this myself). For tips on publishing your site, see Part 11, "Preparing to Publish."

Begin

1 Create a New Web

From the **Standard** toolbar, click the **down arrow** to the right of the **New Page** button and select **Web**. The **Web Site Templates** dialog box opens, showing a list of site templates.

Click

2 Select Corporate Presence

From the **Web Sites** list, choose the **Corporate Presence Wizard** template. Type a name in the **Specify the location of the new web** field and click **OK**. The file path fills automatically; all you have to do is add a meaningful name. (In this example, **project2** is appropriate.)

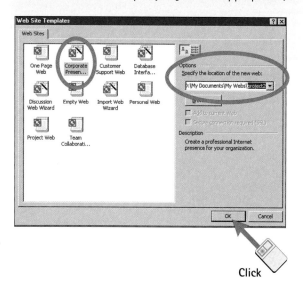

Click

3 Answer the Questions

Answer the questions asked by the wizard to provide contact information and the types of pages you want to include in your Web—and even whether to display an "under construction" sign on the pages. Click **Next** after you complete each section of the wizard. Click **Finish** when you are done answering all the questions. For this project, select the **Show Tasks View after web is uploaded** option at the end of the wizard.

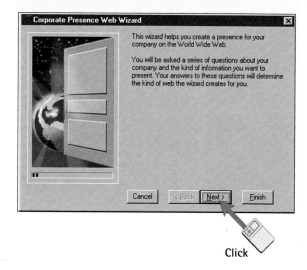

Click

4 Begin a Task

Based on the selections you made in Step 3, your new Web opens in **Tasks** view. Right-click a task and choose **Start Task** to begin working on that page. For this example, right-click **Customize Home Page** and select **Start Task**. The **index.htm** page (the home page) opens in **Page** view.

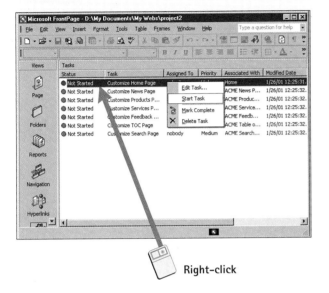

Right-click

5 Insert Text from a File

Now let's add some text from an existing word processing document. For this example, we insert a bit of introductory text. (You can use any existing word processing or text file.) Wherever possible, FrontPage applies the formatting of the Web's theme to your document. Choose **Insert**, **File**. The **Select File** dialog box opens.

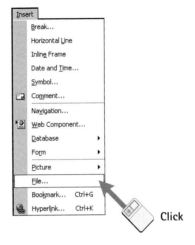

Click

6 Select a File

Navigate to the text file you want to use, select it, and click **Open**. (Note that you might have to select **All Files** from the **Files of type** drop-down list to see your document files.) The text from the selected file appears on the Web page.

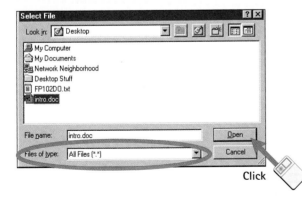

Click

How-To Hints

Creating a Web in a New Location

FrontPage 2002 automatically defaults to the last-used location for a Web. To change this, type the full path (including the drive letter) for the new Web. Click the down arrow next to the **Specify the location of the new web** field in the **Web Site Templates** dialog box (refer to Step 2) to see a list of recently used locations.

Change Between Icon and List Views

By default, FrontPage shows the list of site templates as icons (as shown in Step 2). If you prefer to see the list as text, switch between views by clicking the **Large Icons** button or the **List** button.

Continues

7 Format Text

After the text from the file is inserted on your page, select the text so that you can apply formatting if required. Make selections from the **Font** and **Font Size** menus. If you choose a typeface from the **Font** menu, keep in mind that visitors must have the font you choose installed on their computers; if they don't, they see the default for their own machines (usually Arial or Times New Roman).

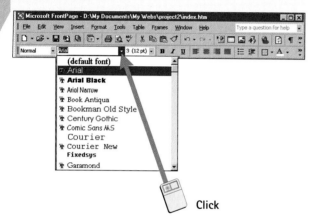

Click

8 Create a Hyperlink

Let's create a link that connects the home page to a page displaying the company's products. Links to other information are essential—and expected—parts of any sophisticated Web site. Select the text you want to link (it can be a single word or a heading) and click the **Hyperlink** button on the **Standard** toolbar. The **Insert Hyperlink** dialog box opens.

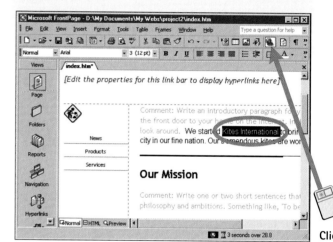

Click

9 Select a Page

In the **Address** field, type the address of the page to which you want to link. Alternatively, you can use the buttons to the right of **Look in** pop-up menu to navigate to the desired file. When the **Address** field has been filled in, click **OK**. Notice that your selected text changes to the default hyperlink color.

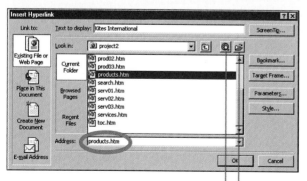

Use your Web browser to select a page or file ———— Make a hyperlink to a file on your computer

10 Insert a Picture

Pictures (graphic images) are expected features of any Web site; they illustrate, add pizzazz, and instruct. To add a graphic image to your home page, first position the insertion point where you want the image to appear. Then click **Insert Picture from File** on the **Standard** toolbar. The **Picture** dialog box opens.

Click

(11) Look for the Picture File

Select the picture file you want and click the **Insert** button to close the **Picture** dialog box and insert the picture on the page. (Note that clicking the **History** button shows you a list of files and folders you have recently opened.)

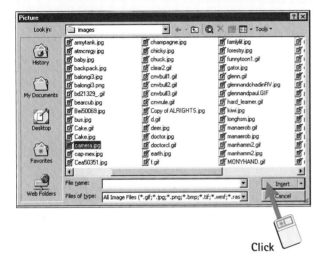

Click

(12) Resize the Picture

Click the picture on the page to select it. A set of handles appears. Drag a corner handle to resize the picture while maintaining its proportions. To resize just one side (and, in the process, distort the picture), drag a middle handle.

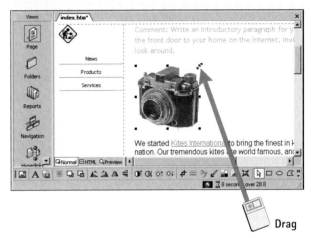

Drag

(13) Resample the Picture

Resizing the picture merely changes the reference to the page, which tells the browser how large to display the image. To eliminate unnecessary data from the picture you just resized, click the **Resample** button on the **Pictures** toolbar.

Click

How-To Hints

Acceptable Image Files

When inserting image files, FrontPage accepts any image files it can read, including clip art files as well as **.gif** and **.jpg** images. FrontPage automatically converts any image file that is not in a Web-acceptable format into either **.gif** or **.jpg** format. Although FrontPage makes the format choice for you, you can change it by right-clicking the picture and choosing **Picture Properties**. Select the **General** tab and select **GIF** or **JPEG**. You can also change the image format when you save your page by clicking the **Picture Options** button in the **Save Embedded Files** dialog box. You can find details about all this and more exciting image action in Part 5, "Working with Graphics."

Continues

14 Set Picture Alignment

For a more professional look, you can align the picture to the left or right so that you can surround it with text. Right-click the picture and choose **Picture Properties**; the **Picture Properties** dialog box opens. Select the **Appearance** tab. In the **Layout** area, make a selection from the **Alignment** drop-down list and click **OK**.

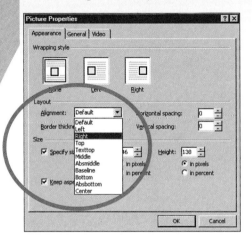

15 Edit Navigation

To further customize the page, let's look at the link bar options (the link bar is also referred to as a *navigation bar*). Right-click the link bar and choose **Link Bar Properties**. The **Link Bar Properties** dialog box opens.

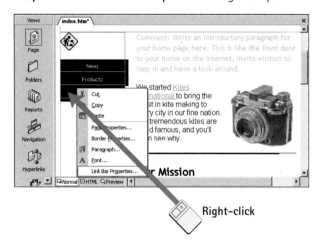

Right-click

16 Set Navigation Options

For details about automating navigation, turn to Part 7, "Working with Webs." For this example, add a home page link to each page. Every page in the site will then have a link back to the home page, but you won't have to edit any page but the home page. This is the first (and most important) part of creating a successful navigation system. When you finish making changes, click **OK**.

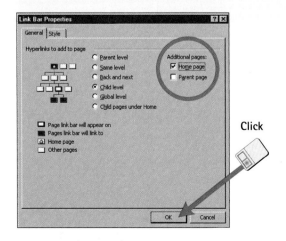

Click

17 Save the File

To save your changes to the home page, click the **Save** button on the **Standard** toolbar. (Alternatively, press **Ctrl+S**.) Because you opened this page from **Tasks** view, you are prompted to mark the task as completed. Click **No** to continue because you will be editing this page further.

Click

18 Save Embedded Files

Whenever you add an image to a page from outside the Web or whenever you have edited an image file, the **Save Embedded Files** dialog box prompts you to save the image into a folder in your Web. Click the **Change Folder** button and select the **images** folder FrontPage created for you. Click **OK** to save the new picture to the Web. Keeping all images in the same folder helps keep the site tidy and well managed.

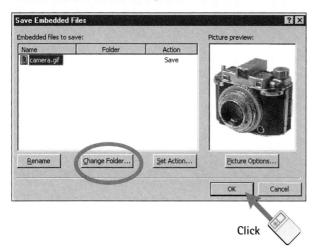

Click

19 Switch to Tasks View

When you've finished customizing the home page that the wizard created for you, you should mark the **Customize Home Page** task as complete. View your list of tasks for this site by clicking the **Tasks** button in the **Views** bar.

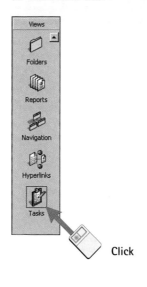

Click

20 Mark Task Completed

Right-click the task you completed (in this case, the **Customize Home Page** task) and choose **Mark Complete** from the shortcut menu.

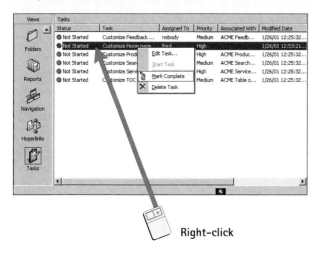

Right-click

21 Close the Web

Choose **File, Close Web**. (If prompted, click **OK** to save changes to any other pages you might have edited.)

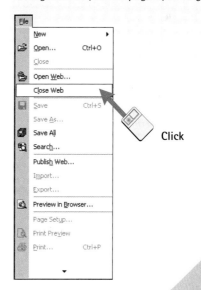

Click

End

Task

1 How to Insert a Video   182

2 How to Set a Background Sound   184

3 How to Use Java Applets   186

4 How to Use a Plug-In   188

5 How to Create a Page Transition   190

PART 8

Adding Multimedia

One of the greatest strengths of the Web is its ability to display multimedia. When your presentation lacks *ooomph* or your personal page seems humdrum, consider adding sound, interactive graphics, or video. With FrontPage, you can easily work with a range of media files:

- **Videos** that you embed in your page.
- Background **sounds** that start playing when a visitor opens a page.
- **Java applets**—small programs that visitors download and view with their browsers. An applet can be a scrolling stock ticker or a calculator. Countless free Java applets are available on the Web.
- Browser add-ons, called **plug-ins**, that play multimedia files (such as audio and video). The browser decides which plug-in to use based on the file type you are trying to access and displays the content of the file within the browser window.
- **Page transitions** that add movie-like effects when a page opens or closes.

Although incorporating these elements is easy in FrontPage, keep in mind that some features might not be useable by all visitors. The tools for inserting videos and sounds, for example, work only with the Microsoft Internet Explorer browser. The best way to ensure compatibility is to create a hyperlink to a multimedia file and then let your visitors choose the program they'll use to open the multimedia file. Refer to Part 4, "Connecting Files with Hyperlinks," for more information.

To ensure compatibility between the Netscape and Internet Explorer browsers, select **Tools, Page Options**. In the dialog box, click the **Compatibility** tab. From the **Browsers** drop-down list box, select **Both Internet Explorer and Navigator**. Then click **OK**. Now, features that aren't supported by *both* browsers will be unavailable (grayed out). It's like signing a peace agreement between the Hatfields and the McCoys.

How to Insert a Video

No doubt about it: Video packs a wallop. A page that *shows* rather than *tells* can have great impact on your visitors. FrontPage provides a way to insert video files directly into the page. (Keep in mind that the motion clips you see in the **Clip Art Gallery** are animated GIFs, not AVI files.)

Begin

1 Select an Insertion Point

Open a Web page and click to position the insertion point where you want the video to appear on the page. When you place the video on the page, you see the first frame of the video if it's a Windows video file (also called an *AVI file*). If the file is in another format, for instance a RealVideo file (which has the extension **.ram**), you'll see a placeholder instead. When visitors view the page, the video appears without controls for playback (unless you add these controls). By default, the video begins playing when the page loads.

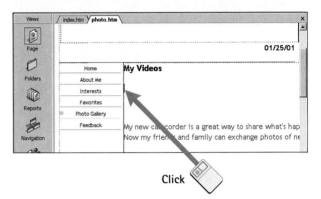

Click

2 Open the Video Dialog Box

From the menu bar, choose **Insert, Picture, Video**.

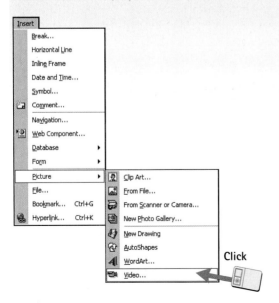

Click

3 Select the Video File

If you have a Web open, the **Video** dialog box opens. Navigate to the video file you want and click the **Open** button. Ideally, the video file you select won't be more than 1MB (still quite hefty, but video files come in only one size—extra large). The first frame of an AVI file, or a video placeholder, appears on your page.

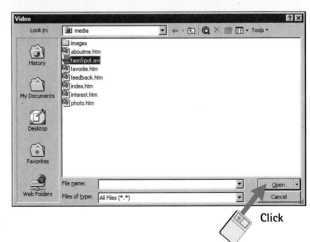

Click

4 Open Picture Properties

You can adjust the position and appearance of the video file just as you can for any graphic image: Right-click the frame of the placeholder and choose **Picture Properties** from the shortcut menu. The **Picture Properties** dialog box opens to the **Video** tab.

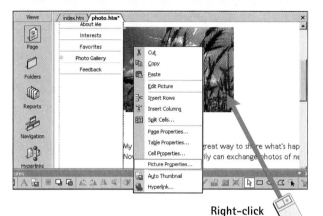

Right-click

5 Set Video Properties

Set the playback options for the video. In the **Repeat** area, set the number of times the video will loop and choose a delay between playbacks (in milliseconds). In the **Start** area, specify whether you want the video to start when the page loads or when the visitor holds the mouse over the image. When you've set the options, click **OK**.

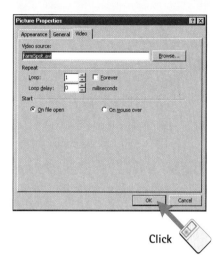

Click

6 Preview the Video

Click the **Preview** tab in **Page** view to view the video. To make the movie play again, you can reload the page by pressing the **F5** key.

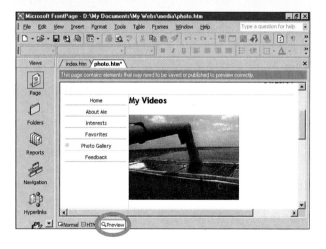

How-To Hints

Download Times

To see how video affects your page size, check the **Estimated Time to Download** area in the status bar at the bottom-right of your screen. By default, the bar shows the number of seconds necessary to download your page over a 28.8Kbps modem. Click the bar to see a menu from which you can select other communications methods (such as a 56.6Kbps modem or a T1 or T3 fast network connection).

End

How to Set a Background Sound

When you add a background sound to a page, the audio file begins playing automatically when the page loads. You can choose from many common audio file formats, including **.wav**, **midi**, **.au**, Real Audio, and **.aif**. However, the FrontPage sound feature works only when you use Internet Explorer 3 or higher as your browser.

Begin

1 Open Page Properties

Right-click a blank area of the page and choose **Page Properties**. (The area you choose to "hold" the background sound file doesn't matter because nothing appears on the page to visually identify the sound file.) The **Page Properties** dialog box opens with the **General** tab selected.

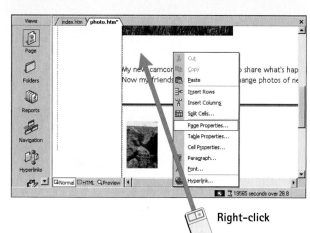

Right-click

2 Browse for a Sound

In the **Background sound** area of the dialog box, click the **Browse** button. The **Background Sound** dialog box opens to help you select a sound file to use as the background for your Web page.

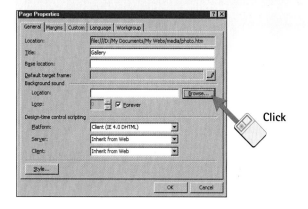

Click

3 Select the Sound

Navigate to the sound file you want to use. If you don't see the type of file you want (for instance, an MP3 audio file), type ***.*** in the **File name** box and press the **Enter** key. This action displays every file in the selected folder. After you have located the desired audio file, click the **Open** button.

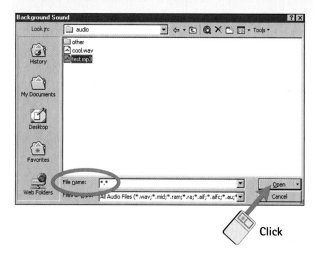

Click

4 Set Loop Options

By default, the sound file is set to repeat indefinitely. To change this setting, deselect the **Forever** box. Type the number of times you want the sound file to repeat in the **Loop** box; leave the setting at **0** if you want the file to play only once. Click **OK** to set your changes.

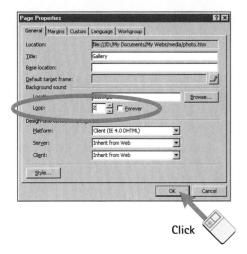

Click

5 Preview the Background Sound

Click the **Preview** tab to test your background sound in Internet Explorer. (You must have IE installed to use the **Preview** tab.)

Click

6 Remove the Background Sound

If you later decide to remove the sound file from your page, open the **Page Properties** dialog box for the page and delete the path and filename from the **Location** box in the **Background sound** area on the **General** tab.

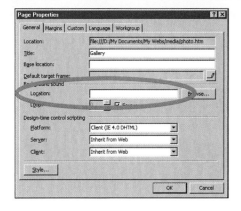

How-To Hints

Sound Alternatives

Visitors using Netscape won't see an error when you set a background sound, but they won't hear your file, either. To make your page's sound available to visitors with browsers other than Internet Explorer 3 or later (such as Netscape Navigator), create a hyperlink to the audio file. You can link your page to a sound file just as you link to a page file (or any other file type). Type some text (or insert an image) that you want to hyperlink to your sound file. Select the text or image and press **Ctrl+K**. Browse to the audio file you want to link to and click the **OK** button. For details, refer to Part 4, "Connecting Files with Hyperlinks."

End

How to Use Java Applets

Java applets offer a simple way to add animation and interactivity to your pages. Unlike other types of multimedia files, Java applets appear the same way to visitors using different types of computers, including PCs, Macintoshes, and UNIX workstations. Java applets don't require a plug-in, just a Java-capable browser (most recent browsers are Java capable). Before you start, you must download a Java applet to your computer. See the "How-To Hints" box on the next page for suggestions on where to find Java applets.

Begin

1 Insert the Applet

Open a Web page and click to position the insertion point where you want the Java applet to appear on the page.

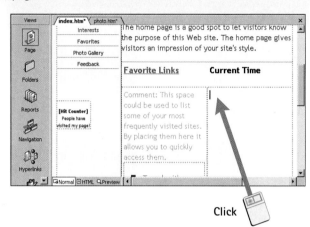

Click

2 Select Java Applet

From the menu bar, select **Insert, Web Component**. The **Insert Web Component** dialog box opens. From the Component type list, select **Advanced Controls**. From the **Choose a control** list, select **Java Applet** and click the **Finish** button. The **Java Applet Properties** dialog box opens.

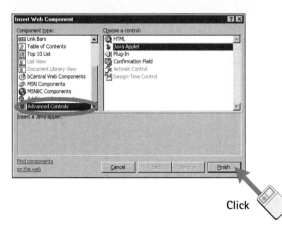

Click

3 Enter Applet Information

In the **Applet source** field, type the name of the Java source file. This file usually ends in the extension **.class**. In this example, the source file is **JavaClock.class**. (Remember that Java filenames are case sensitive.) If your Java applet will not be saved in the same directory as the page on which you are inserting the applet, type the path of the alternative directory in the **Applet base URL** field. In this example, I store my Java applet file in the directory **classes**. If you save the page and applet in the same directory, leave this field blank.

4 Create a Message for Non-Java Browsers

If you want, type a message in the **Message for browsers without Java support** field. This message will appear instead of the applet in the windows of visitors who are using older browsers.

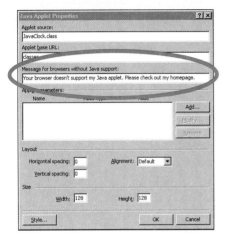

5 Add Parameters

Java applets use *parameters* to define the characteristics of the applet. The programmer sets the parameters, so you'll need to know these before you can add them. (*Hint:* Look for applets that provide a bit of instruction. Sadly, not all applets are well documented.) Click the **Add** button to set a variable and then enter a value as described by the applet's documentation.

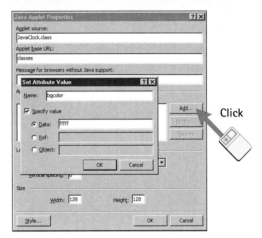

Click

6 Set Size and Layout

Make a selection from the **Alignment** menu to position the applet on your page. Then enter values (in pixels) for the **Height** and **Width** of the applet window on the page. When you finish, click the **OK** button.

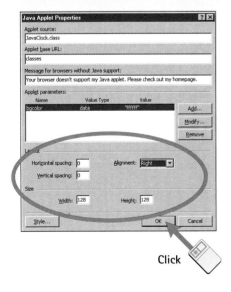

Click

How-To Hints

About Java Applets

Many programmers make their Java applets available on the Web for free. You can find some examples of free applets at **www.jars.com** and **www.java.sun.com/applets**.

Cut and Paste

In many cases, it is easier to cut (**Ctrl+X**) and paste (**Ctrl+V**) a snippet of Java source code provided by the applet designer into **HTML** view in FrontPage. The source code is what allows the applet to run. Most freely distributed Java applets also include basic instructions on how to incorporate the applets into your page.

End

How to Use a Plug-In

Plug-ins help your browser display all sorts of multimedia files. In this example, we'll use the **Plug-In Properties** dialog box to embed a sound file on the page. This reference tells the browser to launch the appropriate plug-in (in this case, a sound file player) and to play the file without launching a separate window.

Begin

1 Select the Insertion Point

Click an area of the page to choose where the plug-in will appear and then choose **Insert, Web Component**. In this example, we point to an audio file that will display sound player controls on the page so that the visitor can start, stop, and adjust the volume of the sound. The controls that appear on the page depend on the player the visitor has configured to open sound files.

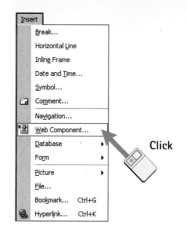

Click

2 Open the Plug-In Properties Dialog Box

From the **Insert Web Component** dialog box that opens, scroll down and select **Advanced Controls** and then choose **Plug-In** from the right pane. Then click **Finish** to open the **Plug-In Properties** dialog box.

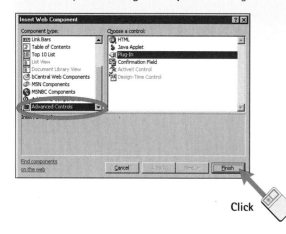

Click

3 Select the File

Click the **Browse** button to open the **Select Plug-In Data Source** dialog box. Navigate to the multimedia file (such as an audio or video file) that you want to insert in your page. Select the file and click the **Open** button.

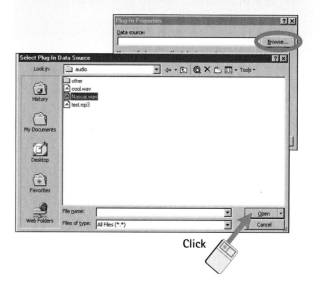

Click

4 Enter an Alternative Message

Back in the **Plug-In Properties** dialog box, type a message that will appear in the browsers of visitors who don't have a plug-in configured for the selected file type.

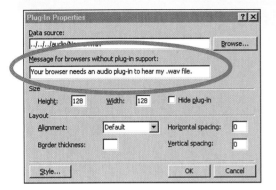

5 Choose Layout Settings

Set the **Alignment** option just as you would with a picture; set the **Horizontal spacing** and **Vertical spacing** options to create whitespace around the plug-in. You can also set a border around your plug-in.

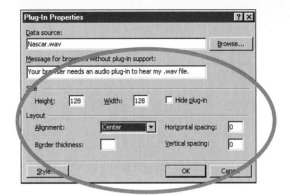

6 Save Your Changes

When you have made all the appropriate changes and selections in the **Plug-In Properties** dialog box, click **OK** to save your changes and insert the reference to the multimedia file into your page. Click the **Preview** tab to see your video or hear your audio file.

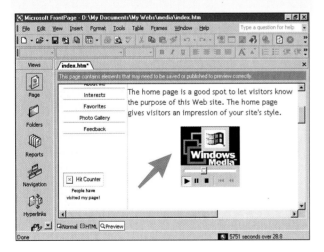

How-To Hints

Considering Compatibility

Keep in mind that your visitors must have their browsers set to open the type of file you embed in your page. Your best bet for compatibility is to create a hyperlink to the multimedia file, as discussed in Part 4, "Connecting Files with Hyperlinks." Don't assume that every visitor's browser will be configured to handle the types of files you insert in your pages.

End

How to Create a Page Transition

FrontPage *page transitions* help visitors move smoothly from one page to another by applying a visual effect each time a page is opened or closed. You can choose an effect that displays your page as if through vertical blinds or in a checkerboard pattern. Transitions are particularly useful for slick presentations—but they may be excessive for simple Web pages. It's important to note that page transitions require Internet Explorer to view them. Visitors with other browsers see no special effects on your pages.

Begin

1 Select Page Transitions

Open the page to which you want to add a page transition and select **Format, Page Transition**. The **Page Transitions** dialog box opens.

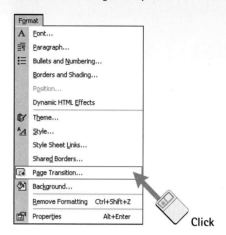

Click

2 Set a Starting Point

From the **Event** drop-down list box, choose the starting point for the transition effect. The transition can start when a visitor enters or exits a page. You can also set the transition to begin when a visitor enters or exits your site.

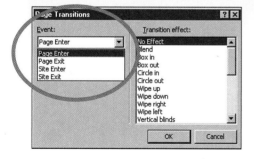

3 Choose a Duration and an Effect

Set the **Duration** (in seconds) for which you want the transition effect to last. Generally, a duration of 3 to 5 seconds is adequate. From the **Transition effect** list, select an effect and then click **OK**. (If you don't like the transition effect you select the first time, it's easy to open this dialog box again and select a different effect.)

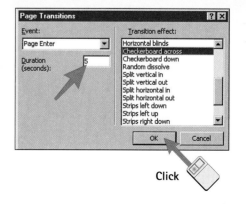

Click

4 Save the File

Before you can preview the transition you have set up, you must first save the file: Click the **Save** icon in the **Standard** toolbar.

Preview in Browser

Click

5 View the Effect

Choose **File, Preview in Browser**. Select **Internet Explorer** and click **Preview**. Note that you might have to open another page first and then open the page you're working on to see the transition. Here you see the end of the **Checkerboard Across** effect.

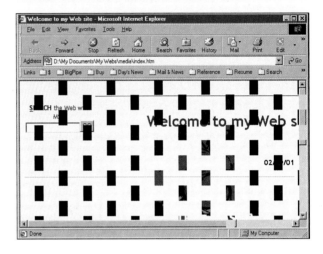

6 Remove the Transition Effect

If you later want to remove the transition effect, open the **Page Transitions** dialog box. From the **Transition effect** list, choose **No Effect** and click **OK**.

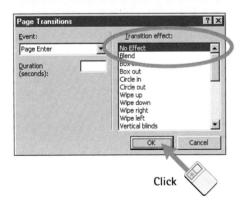

Click

How-To Hints

Browser Watch

Because page transitions require Internet Explorer version 4.0 or higher, the page transition feature is best used for presentations from your hard drive or office network.

End

Project 3

Creating Dynamic Animations

Now we come to the point in the book where we use wildly technical words such as *zoom*, *fly*, and *hop*. These are actual FrontPage terms you use when animating page elements with Dynamic HTML (DHTML).

You create animations by selecting the element you want to animate and then choosing options from the **DHTML Effects** toolbar. The toolbar lets you specify how to start an animation (with a mouse-click, for instance) and what to display (your image sliding onto the page, perhaps).

The only drawback with DHTML is that it won't work in older browsers. You must be certain that visitors will be looking at your pages using version 4 browsers (or later) for your effects to be seen. From the **Tools** menu, select **Page Options** to open the **Page Options** dialog box; then click the **Compatibility** tab. Here you can choose the browsers for which you are designing. If your selection includes older browsers, some effects won't appear on the FrontPage **DHTML Effects** toolbar that you open in Step 4.

Effects range from subtle text-formatting changes to images bouncing like rubber balls onto the page. Point at a picture, and it changes to another picture. Click a paragraph, and it flies off the page. Creating your own DHTML is hard, but using the **DHTML Effects** toolbar is a snap.

Begin

1 Open a New Page

Click the **arrow** next to the **New Page** button in the **Standard** toolbar and choose **Page**. The **Page Templates** dialog box opens. From the **General** tab, select the **Normal Page** template and click **OK** to open the page in **Page** view.

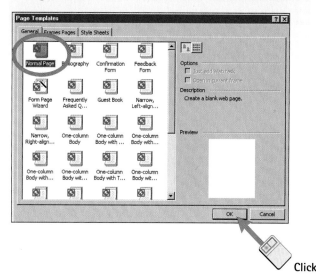

Click

2 Add Text

Type some text on the page and highlight it. For this example, I typed **This text really jumps out at you.**

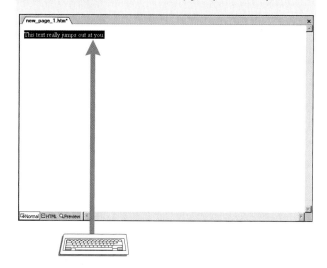

3 Apply Formatting

Add any formatting you want to the text before you animate it. In this example, I chose **Heading 1** from the **Style** menu to increase the font size of the text.

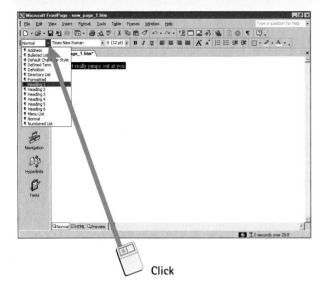

Click

4 Open the DHTML Toolbar

Select **View, Toolbars, DHTML Effects.** The **DHTML Effects** toolbar appears, floating on the screen. You can dock the toolbar at the top of the screen if you want.

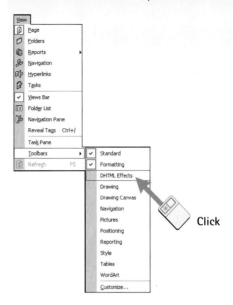

Click

5 Choose the Start Event

Select your text (or any part of it). Now decide on the event that starts the animation of the text. In the **DHTML Effects** toolbar, click the down arrow next to the **On** combo box. Make a selection from the **On** drop-down menu. For this example, I selected the **Page load** option as the event that will start the animation.

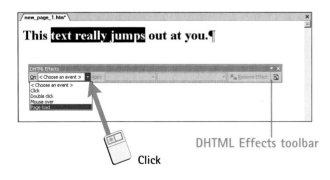

DHTML Effects toolbar

Click

6 Apply an Effect

From the **Apply** menu, choose an animation effect—the action you want the text to "do" when the event you selected in Step 5 happens. *Hmmmmm,* something subtle...how about **Zoom**?

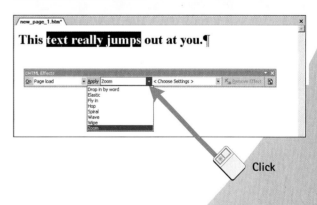

Click

Continues

7 Choose Settings

From the **Effect** menu, select a setting for the effect. Settings vary according to the effect you chose in Step 6 (just as the effects you can choose vary depending on the event selected in Step 5). For this example, I selected In (as in "zoom in"). To see what your animated text can do, click the **Preview** tab. If you don't like your first attempt, make another choice from the menu.

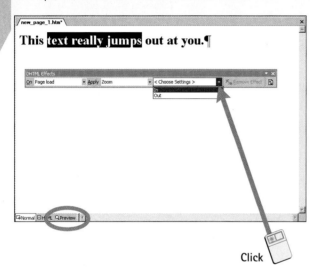

Click

8 Insert an Image

Now let's import a graphic image and animate it. Position the insertion point on the page where you want the image to appear and click the **Insert Picture From File** button on the **Standard** toolbar (or you can select **Insert, Picture** and then choose the type of image you want to use). The **Picture** dialog box opens.

Click

9 Choose the Graphic to Insert

Navigate to the picture file you want to insert. Click the **Insert** button to place the picture on the page.

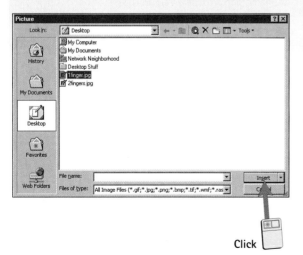

Click

10 Select a Picture for Animation

Of course, you have to select the image before you can animate it. Do so now by clicking the graphic.

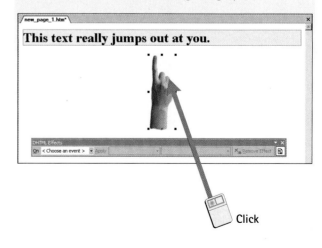

Click

11 Choose the Start Event

In the **DHTML Effects** toolbar, from the **On** menu, choose the action that will start the animation. For this example, I chose **Mouse over**, so that the picture changes when a visitor points at the image with the mouse.

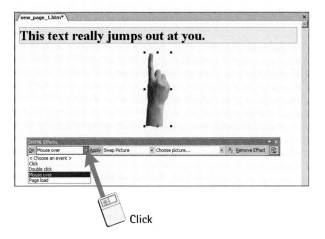

Click

12 Choose an Effect

From the **Apply** menu, select the effect you want to apply to the graphic. For this example, I selected **Swap Picture**. This option creates a cool *rollover* effect; as the name implies, it replaces one picture with another when the visitor moves the mouse over the image.

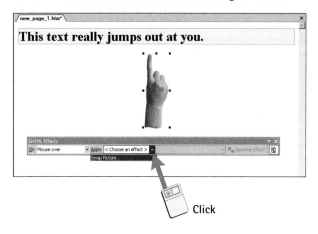

Click

13 Choose the Rollover Picture

Now specify any settings for the effect you selected. For the rollover effect, you must choose the image file that the first picture will change to. Click the **Settings** menu in the **DHTML Effects** toolbar and select **Choose picture**. The **Picture** dialog box appears.

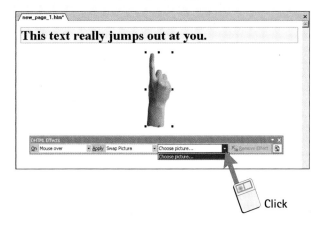

Click

14 Navigate to the Rollover Picture

Browse to the image you want the first picture to swap with. Select it and click **Open**. My initial photo shows one finger; the photo I choose in this step will show two fingers. You often see the rollover effect used to create navigation buttons that supply links to different areas on a Web site.

Click

Continues

15 Add a Caption

Now let's animate a caption under the graphic. Type some text, format it, and select it.

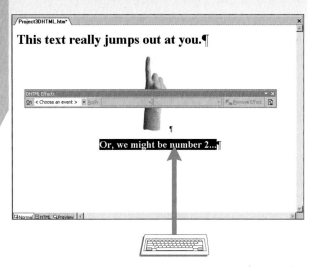

16 Choose the Start Event

From the **On** menu in the **DHTML Effects** toolbar, choose the event that will initiate the animation. For this example, I selected the **Double click** event.

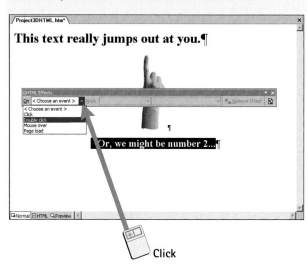

17 Apply the Effect

From the **Apply** menu, select the effect you want to apply to the selected text. For this example, I selected the **Fly out** effect.

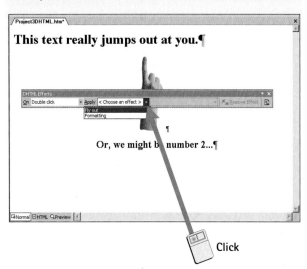

18 Choose Effect Settings

From the **Effect** menu in the **DHTML Effects** toolbar, specify any settings for the selected effect. For the **Fly out** effect, I chose the **To top** option.

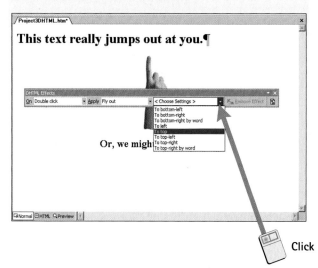

19 Highlight DHTML Effects

In **Page** view, animation effects applied to text are highlighted in blue by default. You can toggle this feature on and off by clicking the **Highlight Dynamic HTML Effects** button in the **DHTML Effects** toolbar.

Click

20 Remove an Animation Effect

If you change your mind and decide to remove an animation effect, select the text or image to which the effect has been applied and click the **Remove Effect** button in the **DHTML Effects** toolbar.

Click

21 Preview the Effects

Click the **Preview in Browser** button on the **Standard** toolbar to view your animation effects. You can also press **Ctrl+Shift+B** to preview these special effects.

How-To Hints

Check for Browser Compatibility

DHTML can behave strangely in different browsers—and won't work at all in older ones. Your best bet is to preview your animated page in several browsers and look for problems. Check well and check often. If you're concerned about browser compatibility, you can turn off Dynamic HTML in the **Page Options** menu and avoid it altogether.

End

Task

1 How to Add a Custom Link Bar   **200**

2 How to Create a Hover Button   **202**

3 How to Rotate Banner Ads   **204**

4 How to Set Pages to Load Automatically   **206**

5 How to Include a Scheduled Picture   **208**

6 How to Add a Top 10 List   **210**

7 How to Add a Photo Gallery Component   **212**

Enhancing Pages with Components

FrontPage includes a handful of objects you can insert in pages that take on specific tasks. These objects, called *Web components*, have duties as varied as collecting your snapshots into a well-designed gallery and updating your site when you go on vacation.

Some of these objects might require that you open a Web to use them (as does the **Top 10 List** component). Others, such as the **Scheduled Picture** component, require that your ISP support the FrontPage Server Extensions. Most components, however, work even if your entire site is just one page.

FrontPage *Server Extensions* are a set of programs installed on a Web server. The extensions make it possible for you to easily insert components (such as a search engine) or to create interactive forms for your pages. You should check with your service provider to see whether the extensions are available on your server.

You add components by choosing **Insert**, **Web Component** or by clicking the **Web Component** button from the **Standard** toolbar and then making a selection.

FrontPage components go a long way toward making your Web site more interactive, more lively, and generally more fun to visit. ●

How to Add a Custom Link Bar

Using FrontPage, you can create a graphic that links to areas of your site or to other Web sites. Such a graphic was previously called a *navigation bar*; Microsoft now calls it a *link bar*. The link bar is a handy and simple way to let visitors browse your site and visit other sites to which you direct them.

Begin

1 Select an Insertion Point

Open the page on which you want to place the link bar and click to select an insertion point. From the menu bar, select **Insert**, **Web Component**. The **Insert Web Component** dialog box opens.

Click

2 Choose Custom Link Bar

From the **Component type** list, choose **Link Bars**. From the dynamic **Choose a type** list on the right, choose a type of link bar (in this example, we're working with the **Bars with custom links** option). Click **Next**.

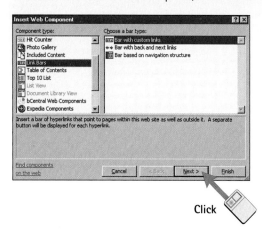
Click

3 Choose a Bar Style

Scroll through the list of graphic examples of link bars. Click one to select it. Notice that some of these link bars are based on themes; if your site uses a theme, consider using the link bar that was designed for that theme. When you're finished, click **Next**.

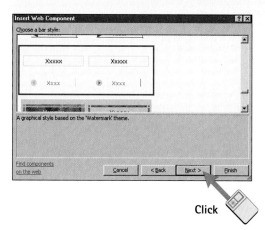
Click

$\mathcal{4}$ Select an Orientation

Choose whether the link bar will appear horizontally or vertically on the page. (If you want the link bar to appear on every page in your site, refer to Part 7, Task 10, "How to Create Shared Borders.") When you have made a selection, click **Finish**. The **Insert Web Component** dialog box closes.

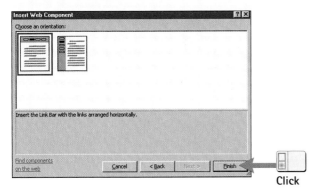

Click

$\mathcal{5}$ Enter a Name

The **Create New Link Bar** dialog box appears, prompting you to name the link bar you have just designed. Do so and click **OK**. Now that you have selected the design options for your link bar, you can start adding links.

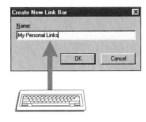

$\mathcal{6}$ Add Links

In the **Link Bar Properties** dialog box that opens, click the **Add link** button. The **Add to Link Bar** dialog box opens. Select a page (or enter a Web address) to which the link will connect when you click it. Repeat this step for each link you want to create in the link bar. If you make a mistake, click the **Remove link** or **Modify link** button and make your changes. You can also set links to your home page or parent page (a page that sits above the current page). When you're done, click **OK**.

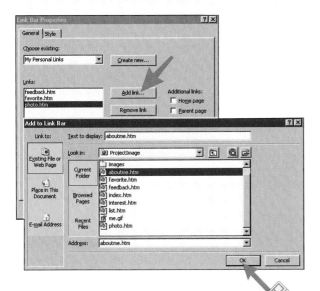

Click

$\mathcal{7}$ Preview the Page

Nice work! Click the **Preview** tab to check out your link bar. Click a link, and the internal browser should display the hyperlinked page.

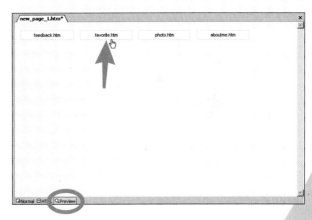

End

How to Create a Hover Button

To add punch to your pages, try inserting an animated hover button. The button changes shape or color when you point at it with a mouse. You can choose special effects for your buttons or add a sound if you want—and then hyperlink the buttons to other pages. Hover buttons help focus visitors' attention on the most important links in your site, and FrontPage handles all the coding for you.

Begin

1 Create the Hover Button

Click the location on your page where you want to place the hover button. From the menu bar, choose **Insert, Web Component**; the **Insert Web Component** dialog box opens. From the **Component type** list on the left, choose **Dynamic Effects**; from the **Choose an effect** list on the right, choose **Hover Button** and click **Finish**. The **Hover Button Properties** dialog box opens.

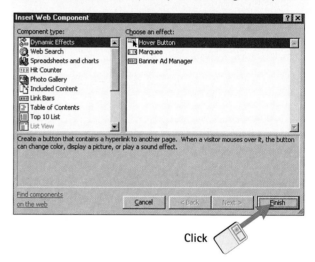

Click

2 Label the Button

In the **Button text** field, type the label that will appear on your button. Short names are best (*Home*, *News*, or *Updates*, for example). If you use a long name, adjust the value in the **Width** field in the **Hover Button Properties** dialog box.

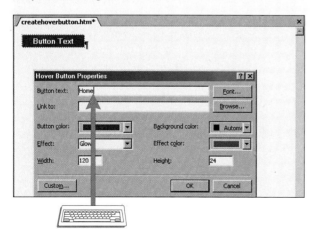

3 Create a Link

To link this button to another page, type a Web address in the **Link to** field. You can link to another page in your site or to an outside Web address (see Part 4, "Connecting Files with Hyperlinks"). Use the **Browse** button to help locate a page address.

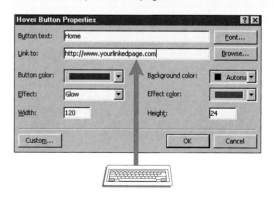

4 Pick an Effect

Make a selection from the **Button color** drop-down list. Then choose from the **Effect** drop-down list. For example, you can make the button glow, or you can add a three-dimensional effect by adding an inward or an outward bevel. For this example, I've selected the **Glow** effect for the hover button. When you're done picking options, click **OK**.

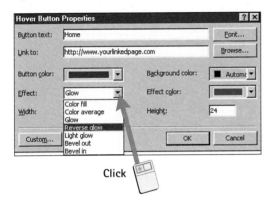

Click

5 Preview the Button

You won't be able to see how your button works until you save the page and preview it. Click the **Save** button in the **Standard** toolbar and select **File, Preview in Browser** from the menu bar. Notice that the button shows a slight "glow" when you move the mouse pointer over the button.

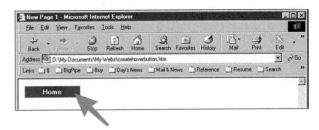

How-To Hints

Choose Your Own Images

If you want to get fancy with hover buttons, pick your own images. You can choose one image to display as the main button and another that appears when a visitor moves the mouse over the button. In the **Hover Button Properties** dialog box, click the **Custom** button. In the **Custom** dialog box, click the **Browse** button next to the **Button** text box and then select the image file you want to display for the main button. Click **Open**. Now choose the image file you want to display when a visitor moves the mouse over the button: Click the **Browse** button next to the **On hover** text box and select the appropriate image file. Click **Open** and then click **OK** to close both dialog boxes.

Try Scrolling

Want a little more action on your page? With the **Scrolling Marquee** component, you can type any text you want into a small box. The box is invisible, but visitors see your text scrolling across the page like a news ticker. Note that the marquee feature does not work with Netscape Navigator. Navigator users see the text, but the text does not scroll. Select **Insert, Web Component** from the menu bar. Choose **Dynamic Effects, Marquee,** and click **Finish**. In the **Marquee Properties** dialog box that opens, type your message in the **Text** box and click **OK**.

End

How to Rotate Banner Ads

If money makes the Web go round, *banner ads* help pay the bills. Usually placed at the top of a page, banner ads feature goods and services. FrontPage enables you to quickly display several banner ads, one at a time, in a rotation you specify. Before you begin this task, you must first create several images that will be the ads; ideally, the images should be all the same size. This task explains how to tell FrontPage to display the ads, after they exist.

Begin

1 Choose the Insertion Point

Click the page at the point where you want the rotating banner ads to appear. Banner ads are usually placed at the top of the page.

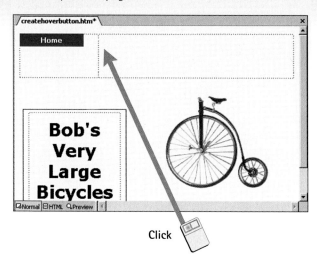

Click

2 Set Banner Properties

From the menu bar, select **Insert, Web Component**. From the **Component type** list, select **Dynamic Effects**; from the **Choose an effect** list, select **Banner Ad Manager**. Click **Finish**. The **Banner Ad Manager Properties** dialog box opens.

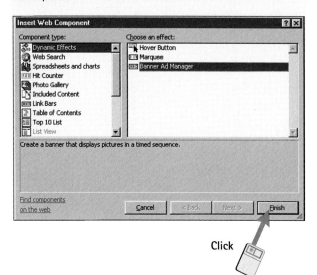

Click

3 Add Height and Width

Set the **Width** and **Height** options to match those of your ad image. A common banner size is 468×60 (pixels). If you want to resize images, see Task 7, "How to Resize and Resample Images," in Part 5, "Working with Graphics."

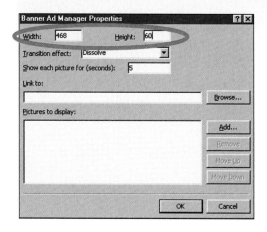

4 Add Images

Click **Add** to open the **Add Picture for Banner Ad** dialog box. You might have to use the **Look in** menu to browse your computer for the image file you want. For more detail on importing images, see Task 1, "How to Import an Image," in Part 5. Choose one of the banner ads you want to rotate through your page and click **Open**. Repeat this step to add as many ad images as necessary.

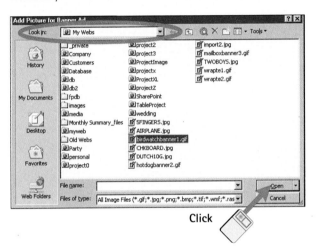

Click

5 Select an Effect

From the **Transition effect** drop-down list box, select the effect you want to use as one ad changes to the next. Choose **None** to display no effect. In the **Show each picture for** field, specify the number of seconds you want each ad to display before transitioning to the next ad.

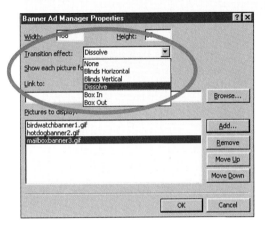

6 Save the Settings and Preview

When you finish setting your banner ad options, click the **OK** button to close the dialog box. Save the file and then preview the page by selecting **File**, **Preview in Browser** from the menu bar (to view this effect, you cannot simply click the **Preview** tab).

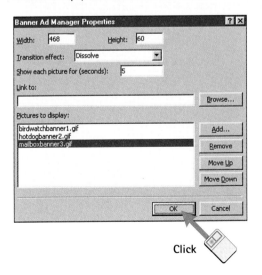

Click

How-To Hints

Clip Art Web Banners

The **Clip Organizer** includes Web banners you can insert on your page. See Part 5, "Working with Graphics," for information on inserting clip art and adding text to images.

Add a Link

You can link an ad image to a Web page by typing an address in the **Link to** box in the **Banner Ad Manager Properties** dialog box. Click the **Browse** button to look for a particular page.

End

How to Set Pages to Load Automatically

Take a break from managing your Web site and let FrontPage handle your page updates. You can insert the contents of one page into another and—better yet—set the time at which a page will be displayed and then disappear. Called a *scheduled include page*, this component saves you time when you want to automatically display a new advertisement, a press release, or any other page that is time sensitive.

Begin

1 Choose the Insertion Point

Click the area of the page where you want the include page to appear.

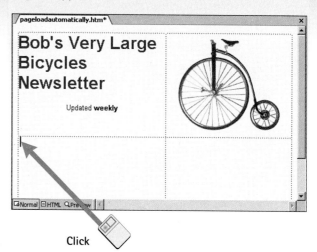

Click

2 Insert the Component

From the menu bar, choose **Insert**, **Web Component**. From the **Component type** list, select **Included Content**. From the **Choose a type of content** list, select **Page Based on Schedule** and click **Finish**. The **Scheduled Include Page Properties** dialog box opens.

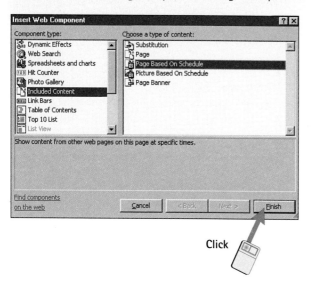

Click

3 Choose the Include Page

In the **During the scheduled time** text box, type the URL of the page you want to display (click the **Browse** button to search for a page on your system or network). If you type a URL, the path must be *relative*. Suppose that your current page is at **www.yoursite.com/homepage.htm,** and you want to include the page at **www.yoursite.com/ads/page1.htm**. The relative path would include just the directory and filename: **ads/page1.htm**.

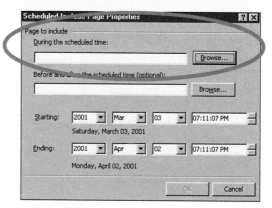

4 Set a Starting Point

In the **Starting** area, choose the date and time at which the specified page should first appear.

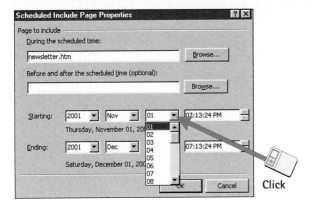

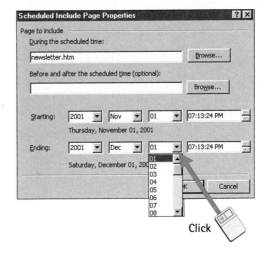

Click

5 Set an Ending Point

In the **Ending** area, select the date and time at which the include page should no longer appear. The Web server to which you publish will stop displaying the page at the time you set here. Your page will either be blank again, or it will show the page you specify in Step 6.

Click

6 Choose an Alternative Page

In the **Before and after the scheduled time** text box, you can provide an optional page that is displayed before and after the include page's specified limit. Type the Web address for this page or click **Browse** to select a page.

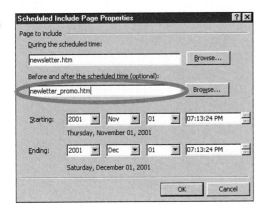

7 Save the Settings

When you finish making changes, click the **OK** button to close the **Properties** dialog box. Save your file and click the **Preview** tab to see your page in the Internet Explorer browser.

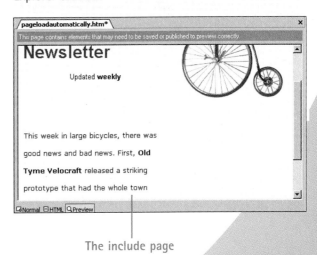

The include page

End

How to Include a Scheduled Picture

Like the scheduled include page, the *scheduled image* shows up on your page when you say so. Pick an image and set starting and ending times. FrontPage handles the rest. Scheduled images are a great way to add fresh content to a page without having to make the update yourself.

Begin

1 Choose an Insertion Point

Click the area on the page where you want the scheduled image to appear.

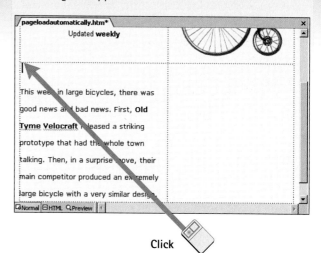

Click

2 Select a Scheduled Picture

From the menu bar, select **Insert, Web Component**. From the **Component type** list, select **Included Content**. From the **Choose a type of content** list, select **Picture Based On Schedule**. Click **Finish**. The **Scheduled Picture Properties** dialog box appears.

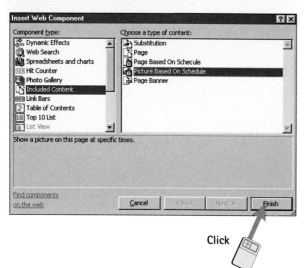

Click

3 Choose an Image

In the **During the scheduled time** text box, type the relative path and filename of the image file you want to display (see Step 3 of the previous task for details). If you want to search your system for the image file, click **Browse**.

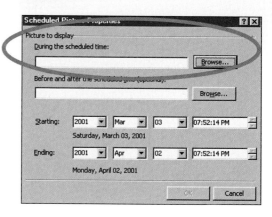

4 Set the Starting Time

In the **Starting** area, choose the date and time at which the specified image should first appear.

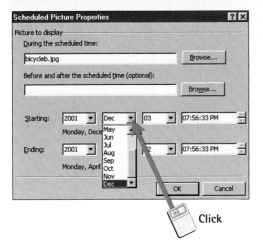

Click

5 Set the Ending Point

In the **Ending** area, select the date and time at which the scheduled picture should disappear.

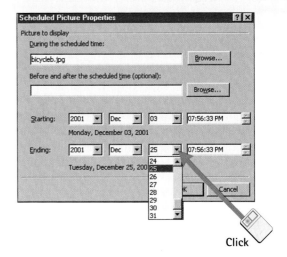

Click

6 Select an Optional Image

In the **Before and after the scheduled time** text box, you can specify an optional image that is displayed before and after the scheduled image's specified limit. Type the URL or click **Browse** to select a picture. You don't have to set start and end times for this image; it appears by default when your scheduled image does not appear.

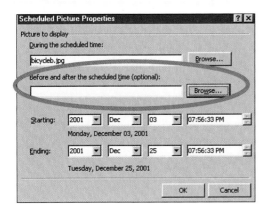

7 Save the Settings

When you finish making changes, click the **OK** button. Save your file and preview the page in your browser.

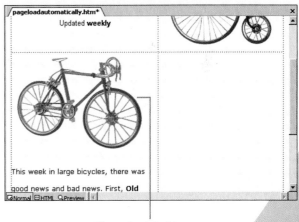

The scheduled image

End

How to Add a Top 10 List

FrontPage can help you find out which of your pages are hits with your visitors. Just add a Top 10 List, a Web component you insert on a page that displays your most frequently visited pages. As you watch the numbers increase over time, you can even let others in on the fun. Just point them to your Top 10 List, which is automatically updated. To use this component, you must publish your page to a Web server that has the FrontPage 2002 Server Extensions. The list won't work on a disk-based Web (that is, a Web that exists on your hard drive).

Begin

1 Insert the Component

From the menu bar, choose Insert, Web Component. The Insert Web Component dialog box opens.

Click

2 Select Top 10

From the Component type list, select the Top 10 List option.

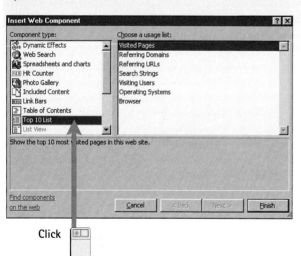

Click

3 Choose a Usage List

From the Choose a usage list pane, select the kind of information you want to collect. Most people want to see the most popular pages on their site and so choose Visited Pages (as we will in this example). You could instead choose Referring Domains to see which Web sites are sending visitors your way. Or choose Browser to see the software your visitors use to browse your site. When you click a selection, a description appears at the bottom of the dialog box. Make a choice and click Finish.

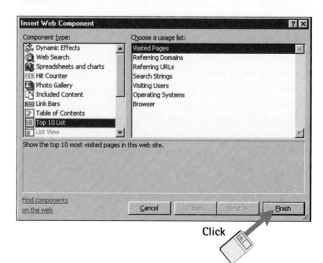

Click

4 Title the Page

The **Top 10 List Properties** dialog box opens. Enter a title if you like, although the default one will do. You can also enable the **Include date usage processing was last run** check box, which tells you how current the list data is.

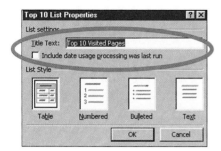

5 Edit Properties

Choose a **List Style** by clicking the sample image that most appeals to you. You can change the properties later by right-clicking the list on your page (in **Normal** view) and choosing **Top 10 List Properties**.

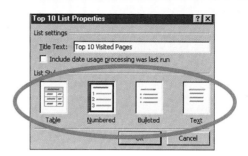

6 Publish the Page

Click **File**, **Publish Web**, enter your publish destination, and click **OK**. When you're ready to check out your list, click **File**, **Preview in Browser**. Note that, in our example, we have fewer than 10 pages that have been accessed, so our list is actually a Top 6.

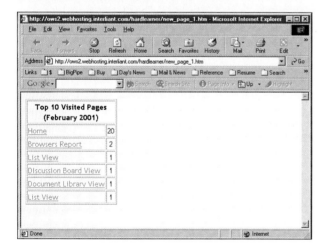

How-To Hints

Add a Hit Counter

Hit counters display the number of people who have opened your page. To add a hit counter to a page, choose **Insert**, **Web Component** from the menu bar. Select **Hit Counter**, and click **Finish**. Choose your hit counter style from the list that appears and click **OK**. Like the Top 10 List, the hit counter does not work until you publish to a Web server that has the FrontPage Server Extensions.

More Web Components

FrontPage 2002 includes a handful of Web components that display current content from Microsoft-owned Web sites, such as the Microsoft Network (MSN), Expedia, MSNBC, and bCentral. You add one of the components to your page by selecting **Insert**, **Web Component**. From the **Component Type** list, make a selection—such as **MSNBC Components** to add news headlines to your page. Make a selection from the **Choose a Component** list on the right, and click **Finish**. The component appears on your page, showing recent news headlines from the category you selected. If you decide to remove the component, just click to select and press **Delete**.

End

TASK 7

How to Add a Photo Gallery Component

Photo galleries are a great way to show snapshots to friends and family members. Typically you create a small *thumbnail* image that your visitor clicks to open a larger version of the same image. Using thumbnails, you can display a series of images on a single page, and your visitors choose which ones they want to view. Until now, it's been quite a hassle setting up all these pages and links. FrontPage 2002 simplifies the job with its handy **Photo Gallery** component.

Begin

1 Insert the Component

Click the **New Page** button to start with a blank page. From the menu bar, choose **Insert, Web Component**. The **Insert Web Component** dialog box opens.

Click

2 Set Up Gallery

From the **Component type** list, select **Photo Gallery**. Pick a photo gallery option from the right pane and notice that the lower pane offers a description of each option you click. When you've made your selection, click **Finish**. The **Photo Gallery Properties** dialog box opens.

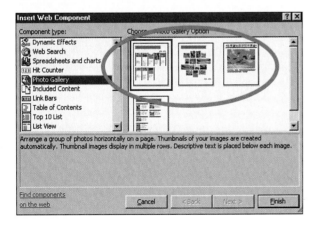

3 Add Photos

Now you can add photos from your hard drive into the gallery. Click the **Add** button and choose **Pictures from Files** to start inserting pictures into the gallery. Keep in mind that you can also acquire photos from a scanner or digital camera attached to your computer by choosing the **Pictures from Scanner or Cameras** option. From the dialog box that appears, click the **Insert** button. FrontPage scans the image and places it on the page. If you choose **Custom Insert**, you can use the software from your scanner or camera to select and insert an image.

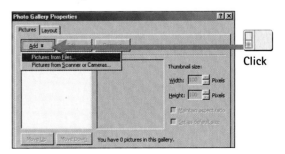

Click

4 Select Images

Navigate to a folder on your hard drive. If you want to select more than one image at a time, press and hold the **Ctrl** key as you select multiple image filenames. When you're done, click **Open**.

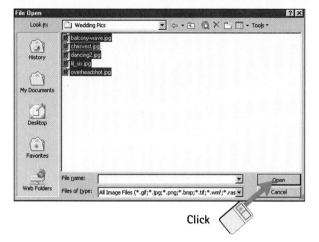

Click

5 Add Captions

The **Photo Gallery Properties** dialog box allows you to rearrange your photos and add captions. Select an image's filename. If you want to add a caption for the selected image, type a few words in the **Caption** field. You can also type a longer description that will appear below the caption. Click **OK** when you're done.

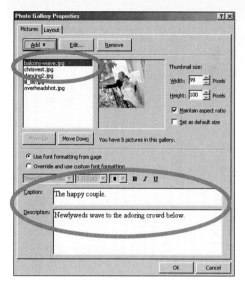

6 Preview the Gallery

FrontPage takes a few seconds to generate the thumbnail images. When the program finishes, click **Preview** to see your images as thumbnails. Click an image to enlarge it. If you later need to add or edit the images that appear in your gallery, just switch to **Normal** view and double-click the photo gallery.

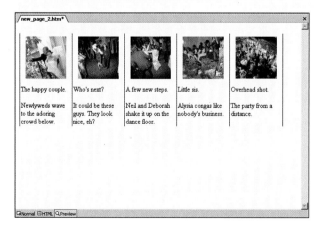

End

Project 4

Creating a Simple Intranet

In this project, we take one of the predesigned Webs that come with FrontPage and use it as a local Web. This is the most basic form of an intranet. An *intranet* is just a Web site used by a select group of folks for the same purpose. As long as you have a Web server installed on your local network, you can share your Web within a closed environment. By following the steps in this project, you end up with a working set of pages that your group's members can publish locally to keep each other informed (see Part 11, "Preparing to Publish," for information on publishing your Web). The pages are searchable, and members can post ideas to the intranet through a discussion board.

Begin

1 Open a New Web

Click the arrow next to the **New Page** icon in the **Standard** toolbar and choose **Web**. The **Web Site Templates** dialog box opens.

Click

2 Select and Name the Web

Select **Project Web** from the list of Web sites that appears. Type a name and location for the Web in the **Specify the location of the new web** text box and click **OK**.

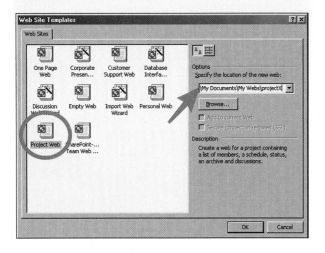

3 Switch to Folders View

The **Project Web Wizard** creates 23 **.htm** files that make up seven complete Web pages. We'll edit just two of the more interesting ones—the Search page and the Discussions page—so that you get a feel for customizing a Web. Click the **Folders** button in the **Views bar** to open the **Folders** view of the Web.

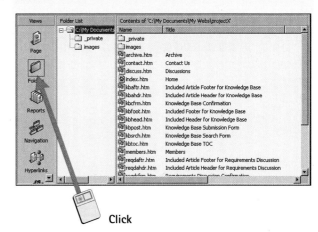

Click

4 Open the Home Page

Double-click the **index.htm** file; the home page opens in **Page** view, ready for editing.

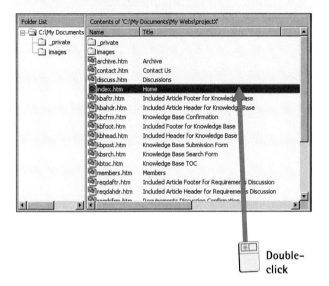

Double-click

5 Edit the Boilerplate Text

Highlight the opening text and personalize the text to suit your project. The **Project** Web home page provides a good structure for introducing your intranet.

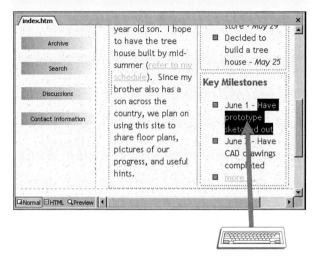

6 Add a Suggestion Box

Let's add a text box in which our intranet users can type suggestions for the site. Click to set the insertion point and type a bit of introductory text. Then choose **Insert**, **Form**, **Text Area**. The text area appears on the page, complete with **Submit** and **Reset** buttons.

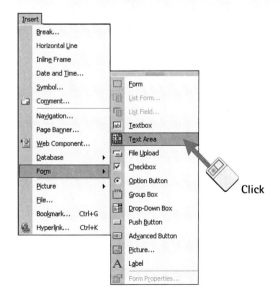

Click

How-To Hints

SharePoint

It's useful to know how to build your own local Web, but there is an easier way. FrontPage now offers a team-intranet service called *SharePoint*. If you have the FrontPage 2002 Server Extensions installed on your network server, you can use a SharePoint site to coordinate events, take surveys, assign tasks, and share documents. The real beauty of SharePoint is that you and your co-workers can create new pages and edit them through a browser. That way, you need fewer copies of FrontPage, and everybody can get involved in an easy-to-use, but very useful, intranet. You'll find more about SharePoint in the final How-To Hint in this project.

Continues

Creating a Simple Intranet Continued

7 Open Form Properties

Let's tell FrontPage how to handle the form. Right-click anywhere inside the text area (the form) and select **Form Properties** from the context menu that appears. The **Form Properties** dialog box opens.

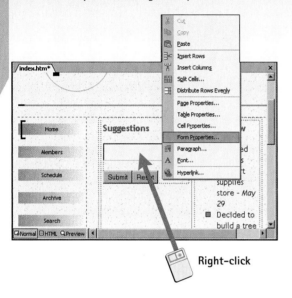

Right-click

8 Set Form Options

By default, FrontPage stores the form results on your Web server in a folder called **_private** in a file called **form_results.csv**. (Any folder starting with an underscore is hidden from users.) For this example, the default pathname is fine. However, I also want the form results e-mailed to the address **yourname@yoursite. com**; type your e-mail address in the **E-mail address** box. When you finish, click the **OK** button.

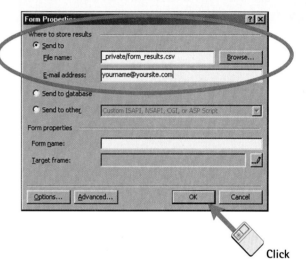

Click

9 Heed the Warning

FrontPage might warn you that your Web is not configured to send e-mail from forms. In this example, I plan to publish the Web locally to my server, which *does* support e-mailed form results. If your Web service provider or local Web server supports forms handling (you might have to ask), click **No** when you get this message.

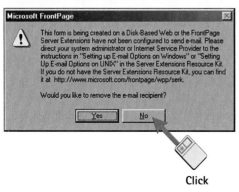

Click

10 Delete the Link Bar

Because there's a link bar in the left shared border on this page, I decided to delete the link bar at the bottom of the page. If you want to keep the link bar at the bottom, double-click it to open the **Link Bar Properties** dialog box, set the properties you want, and click **OK**.

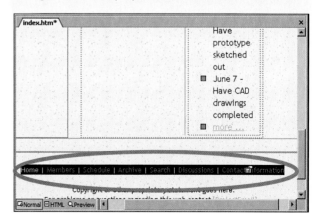

11 Switch to Navigation View

Before you begin editing some of the other pages in the intranet Web, first change to **Navigation** view to get an idea of the layout of the pages in the Web. Click the **Navigation** button in the **Views bar**.

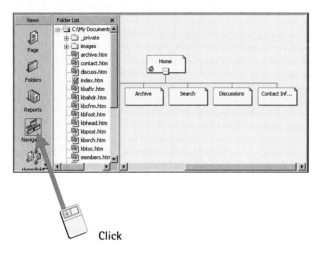

Click

12 Open the Search Page

Look at the arrangement of the pages in the Web you're working on. Double-click the **Search** page to open it in **Page** view, ready for editing.

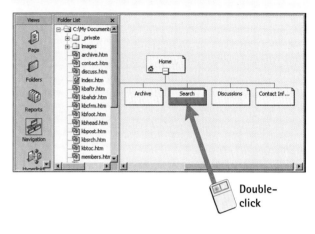

Double-click

13 Modify the Search Page

Highlight some of the text on the **Search** page and replace it with some of your own. The **Search** page's default text contains a useful explanation of the search engine, so you might want to amend rather than replace text on this page.

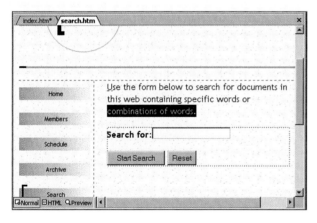

14 Open Link Bar Properties

Notice the link bar in the left column of the page. To customize the navigation tools for the site, double-click the link bar. The **Link Bar Properties** dialog box opens.

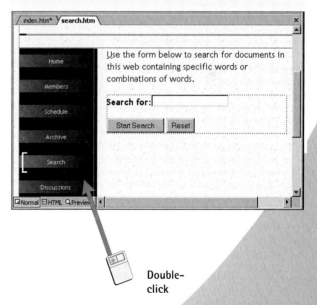

Double-click

Continues

15 Edit the Link Bar

Because no pages exist "below" the **Search** page (refer to the figure in Step 12), I chose to show only parent-level pages as hyperlinks (in this case, just the home page). It's not a bad idea to have a link to each page on your site, from each page on your site. But this example illustrates the level of customization you can choose based on your needs. Set your link bar options and click **OK**.

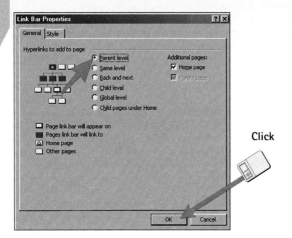

Click

16 Open Folders View

View your changes to the link bar on the **Search** page. Before you can launch another page for editing, you have to switch back to **Folders** view. To do so, click the **Folders** button in the **Views bar**.

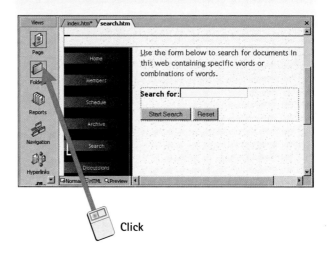

Click

17 Open the Discussions Page

Open the **Discussions** page by double-clicking the file-name **discuss.htm**. The page opens in **Page** view, ready for editing.

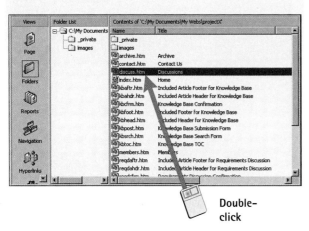

Double-click

18 Modify the Discussions Page

The page you see is the starting point for a well-designed bulletin board. Here, your intranet colleagues can post messages, which are automatically archived (and searchable). Highlight this fairly specific text and replace it with text that meets your needs. FrontPage handles the rest.

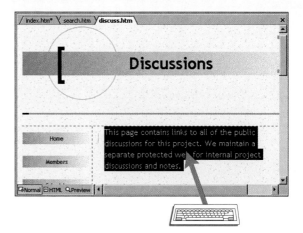

19 Explore the Discussions Page

To check out some of the pages associated with the **Discussions** page (including the posting tools), press the **Ctrl** key and click a link.

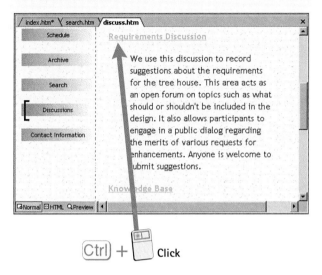

Ctrl + Click

20 Preview the Pages

Click the **Preview** tab to see your **Discussion** pages in action. Note that, although you can click links to see various pages, the Web must be published before you can actually post anything (see Part 11 for information on publishing your Web).

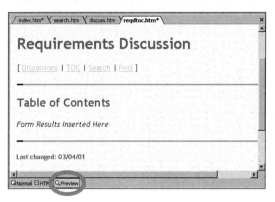

21 Close the Web

To close the Web and all its associated pages, choose **File, Close Web**. If prompted, click **OK** to save changes to any pages you have edited. You now have a Web that can serve as the basis for your own intranet. However, this project has only scratched the surface of how an intranet can really help an organization. Use the following hint to learn more about developing your intranet further.

Click

How-To Hints

More on SharePoint

You can start new SharePoint pages (such as the **List**, **Document Library**, and **Survey Items**) by selecting them from the **File** menu; doing so launches the appropriate wizard for the task. However, if you aren't connected to a SharePoint-based Web, or don't have access to one, you'll get an error message. If your office network isn't running SharePoint, check with your ISP to see whether it provides the SharePoint service. (The ISP might charge you an additional fee for this service.). To access a SharePoint site through FrontPage, select **File, Open Web**. Enter the address of your SharePoint site (ask your network administrator for the address). For example, my ISP-hosted SharePoint site address is **http://ows2.webhosting.interliant.com/heltzel/**. You should be prompted for a username and password. Enter this information and click **Open**. Now you can make changes to the Web and save them directly to the SharePoint-enabled server. Unlike with your other Web projects, you save your work directly to the SharePoint server rather than to your local hard drive and then publish it later.

End

Task

1 How to Use the Form Page Wizard 222

2 How to Use a Predesigned Feedback Form 224

3 How to Insert a Search Form 226

4 How to Create a Guest Book 228

5 How to Design Your Own Form 230

6 How to Create a Drop-Down Menu 232

7 How to Modify Form Fields and Menus 234

8 How to Save or Mail Form Results 236

9 How to Connect a Database to Your Web 238

PART 10

Creating Forms

*I*f you spend any time on the Web, you probably fill out forms almost every day. Checking your mail, shopping, leaving feedback in a guest book—all these activities require you to enter information into Web forms. In this part, we show you how to collect information from visitors by creating your own forms.

You create forms by choosing elements from the **Insert**, **Form** menu. When you do, an outlined box appears with two buttons (one button for submitting information that visitors enter and another button for clearing any entered information). You can start off with a blank form or begin by adding form elements right away.

The elements that make up a form are called *fields*. A field can be a text box in which you type a comment or a check box or menu that offers a handful of choices. Each field has a name that FrontPage automatically assigns (and that you can modify). The information that a user enters into a field is called a *value*.

After you create a form by inserting appropriate fields, you tell FrontPage how to handle the values that visitors provide. You can set up your form to store user data in your Web or to e-mail the results to you.

To handle forms, your Web-hosting service must support the FrontPage Server Extensions. Even if your Web provider has FrontPage support, you should check to make sure that your account is set up for forms handling. And in some cases, such as when you use the **Database Interface Wizard**, your server will need support for *Active Server Pages (ASP)*. ASP is a technology that allows a Web page to interact with a program—in this case, a database. You won't have to worry about creating code to make your database available online, though. FrontPage handles the tough part behind the scenes. ●

How to Use the Form Page Wizard

The **Form Page Wizard** helps you create a custom form using prewritten questions. This timesaver might not serve every need, but it's a handy way to get started quickly.

Begin

1 Select a New Page

To create a new form page, click the down-pointing arrow next to the **New Page** button and choose **Page**. The **Page Templates** dialog box opens. (Note that if you click the **New Page** button itself in the **Standard** toolbar, you don't get the opportunity to select a template.)

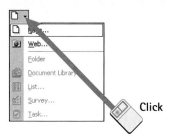

Click

2 Select the Form Page Wizard

From the list of templates, select **Form Page Wizard** and click the **OK** button. The introductory screen of the wizard opens.

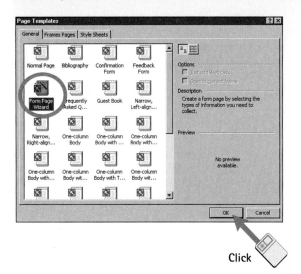

Click

3 Start the Wizard

Click **Next** to start the wizard. On the second page of the wizard, click **Add** to begin entering new questions to your form.

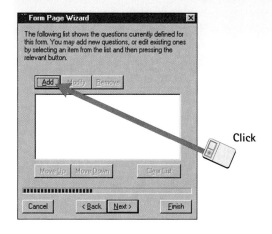

Click

4 Select the Form Type

The wizard provides a list of common form types, such as **product information** and **contact information**. Select the type of information you want this form to gather. Every form needs a bit of introduction. FrontPage provides some default text in the **Edit the prompt for this question** box. Change or delete this text as necessary and click **Next**.

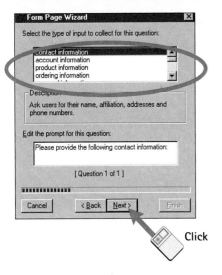

Click

5 Choose Questions

Choose from the list of items that the user will be prompted to provide. Don't worry about the text in the **Enter the base name for this group of variables** text box. FrontPage uses the text in this text box to create the first part of the field names in your form. Click **Next** when you are done.

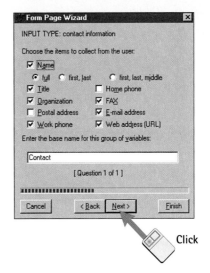

Click

6 Finish the Form

If you have additional information you want to collect, click **Add** and repeat Steps 3 through 5. When you have finished setting options for the form, click **Finish**. The new form opens in **Page** view.

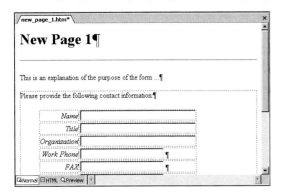

How-To Hints

Form Handling

You can choose later how you want to collect the form results. You can save the input visitors provide to a file on your server or have the responses e-mailed to you. To see how the form is processed, check out Task 8, "How to Save or Mail Form Results."

End

How to Use a Predesigned Feedback Form

After you publish your site, you might want to collect visitor feedback to fine-tune your pages. The **Feedback Form** template creates a basic way for visitors to contact you; you can customize the form after you create it.

Begin

1 Open a New Page

From the **Standard** toolbar, click the down-pointing arrow next to the **New Page** button and choose **Page**. The **Page Templates** dialog box opens. (Note that if you click the **New Page** button itself in the **Standard** toolbar, you don't get the opportunity to select a template.)

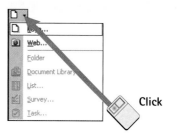

Click

2 Choose Feedback Form

Select **Feedback Form** from the list of page templates and click **OK**. A new feedback form opens in **Page** view.

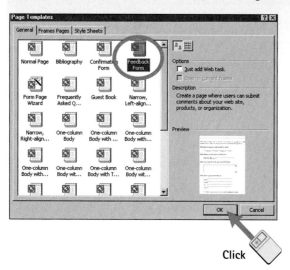

Click

3 Edit Text

Highlight and edit the message that precedes the form.

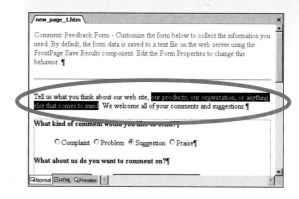

4 Edit the Form Text

You can customize the elements of the form itself. Select the text from the form and change the wording to suit your needs.

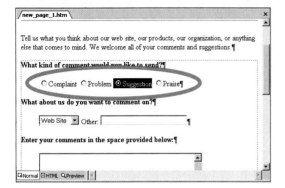

5 Remove Form Elements

You can also delete unnecessary parts of the form. Highlight form elements and text you want to remove and press **Delete** or **Backspace** to eliminate these elements.

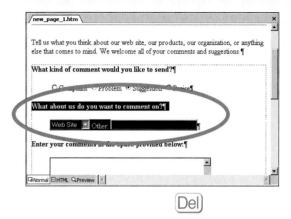

How-To Hints

Comments

The *comment* at the top of the **Feedback Form** page is a bit of text that appears only when you edit the page. Because comments are hidden in the HTML code that generates the page, you can see them only when you are editing (or when viewing the source code in a browser). Click the **Preview** tab to see that the internal browser hides the comment. To remove the comment, select the comment area and press **Delete**. To change the comment, double-click the text and type a new message in the dialog box that appears. Click **OK** when you are done.

End

How to Insert a Search Form

To help visitors navigate your site, consider adding a *search form*. This component creates a list of the words on every page in your site. The visitor enters a word in the search form and clicks a button; the result appears at the bottom of the same page. After inserting the search form on a page, you must publish the page to see the search in action.

Begin

1 Select the Insertion Point

Open the page on which you want to place the search form. Click to position the cursor where you want the search form to appear. (If you want a separate search page, click the arrow next to the **New Page** button, and select **Page**; choose **Search Page** from the list of templates, and click **OK**.)

Click

2 Insert the Search Form

From the menu bar, choose **Insert, Web Component**. From the **Component type** list, select **Web Search** and then click **Finish**. The **Search Form Properties** dialog box opens. (If you created a separate search page in Step 1, double-click the search form to open the **Search Form Properties** dialog box.)

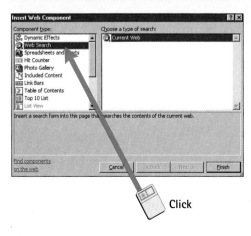

Click

3 Change the Input and Width

You can customize several elements of the search form. By default, the words **Search for:** appear in front of the search text box. Type a new label if you want something more descriptive. You can also set the form width in characters.

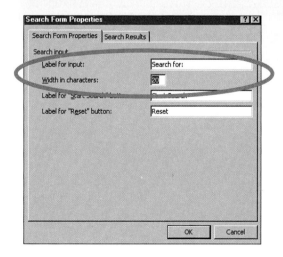

4 Name the Start and Clear Buttons

Two buttons appear on the search form: one to start a search and another to clear the form. You can rename the **Start Search** and **Reset** buttons; just type new labels into the appropriate text boxes. Consider *Submit* or *Go!* as alternative labels for the **Start Search** button. *Clear* also works for buttons that reset a form.

5 Click the Search Results Tab

You can customize the result that displays when a visitor runs a search. By default, when the word the visitor types is found, the title of that page appears in the search result. To change the display of the result, click the **Search Results** tab.

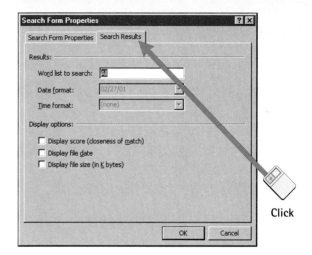

Click

6 Set Display Options

In the **Display options** area, select boxes to show the relevancy of a match (its *score*), the size of the file, and the date it was last modified. If you select **Display file date**, you can also set a **Date format** and a **Time format**.

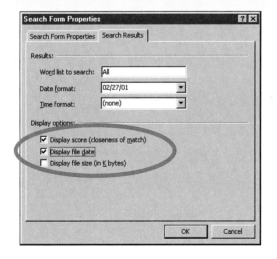

7 Save the Settings

Click **OK** to save your settings and see your search form in **Page** view.

End

How to Create a Guest Book

To record visitors' comments about your site, you can easily set up a *guest book*. Your visitor types comments into a text box and clicks a button; the results appear on the same page. Creating a guest book is as simple as creating a new page.

Begin

1 Open a New Page

Start by creating a new page for your site: Click the down-pointing arrow next to the **New Page** button and choose **Page**. The **Page Templates** dialog box opens. (Note that if you click the **New Page** button itself, you don't get the opportunity to select a template.)

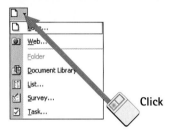

Click

2 Select the Guest Book Template

On the **General** tab, select the **Guest Book** template and click the **OK** button. Your new guest book page opens in **Page** view, ready for editing.

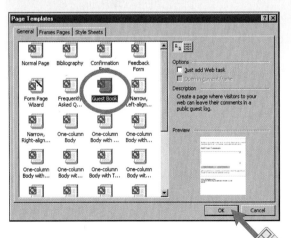

Click

3 Edit the Comment

The comment at the top of the page appears only when you are editing. (Visitors will not see it; click the **Preview** tab to see the page without the comment.) You can highlight and delete the comment or edit it to add more detailed information for your personal reference.

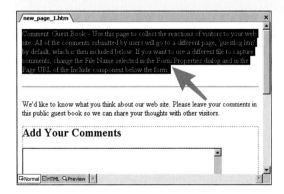

4 Edit the Introductory Text

If you want to personalize the boilerplate text that appears above the guest book itself, highlight and modify it.

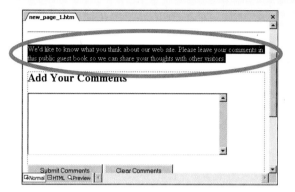

5 Edit the Form Text

You also can edit the text within the form or adjust the size of the guest book text box. See Task 7, "How to Modify Form Fields and Menus," for details about modifying forms.

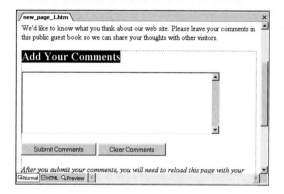

6 Preview the Guest Book

Click the **Preview** tab to view your guest book. Note that you must publish the page to a Web server before viewers can actually add comments to the page.

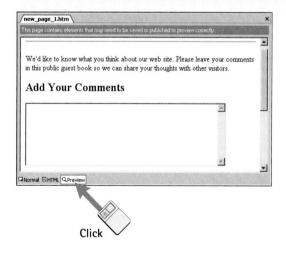

Click

How-To Hints

Guest Books a Go-Go

Beyond the obvious uses for a guest book, this component provides an easy way for others to publish to your site. Let co-workers or friends publish memos, press releases, or events. You won't have to teach anyone else FrontPage or worry about files being accidentally deleted. Everybody gets in on the action, stress-free, when you use a guest book in this way.

End

How to Design Your Own Form

For every form you create, FrontPage provides two buttons: **Submit** and **Reset**. Aside from these two obligatory form fields on the page, the rest of a page's content is up to you. You can collect feedback from visitors using text boxes, clickable check boxes and buttons, or menus that offer choices from which the user can select.

1 Choose the Insertion Point

Open the page on which you want the new form to appear. Click to position the insertion point where the new form is to go. **Important:** If you click a blank area of a page, choose **Insert, Form** and make a selection, a new form is created. If you click inside an existing form, you simply add another field to the existing form.

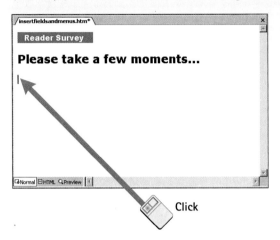

Click

2 Insert a Text Box

If you want visitors to enter a small bit of text, such as an address, add a one-line text box. Choose **Insert, Form, Textbox**. (Before inserting any form field, you might want to add a bit of descriptive text that identifies the field. But you can always add that later.)

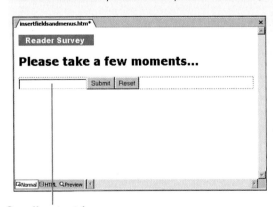

One-line text box

3 Insert a Scrolling Text Box

To collect lengthy information, such as a comment about your site, try a scrolling text box. First, press **Enter** to start a new line on the form. Then choose **Insert, Form, Text Area**.

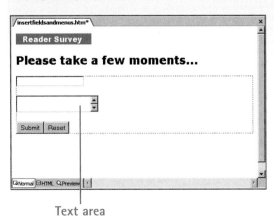

Text area

4 Insert Check Boxes

You can make things easier on your visitors by providing a set of selections to choose from. If your page offers a service with several options, check boxes are often handy because they allow visitors to sign up for more than one option. To insert a check box, select **Insert, Form, Check Box**. To add another check box on a separate line, press **Enter** (press **Shift+Enter** to create a line break) and repeat this step.

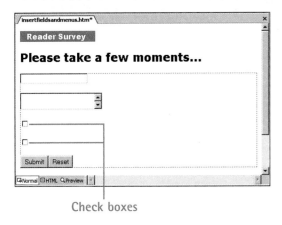

Check boxes

5 Insert Radio Buttons

Radio buttons (frequently called option buttons) are helpful when several choices are offered from which only one can be selected. Add radio buttons by selecting **Insert, Form, Option Button**. Repeat this step for each radio button you want to insert.

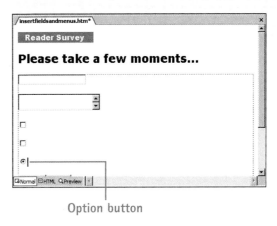

Option button

6 Insert a File Upload Area

You can place a field in your form that will allow visitors to upload a file to your Web server. Insert a file upload field by choosing **Insert, Form, File Upload**. A **Browse** button appears on the form. Visitors will click this button if they want to navigate to their hard drives for a file they want to copy to your site. Unlike other form controls, the **File Upload** feature requires that you have access to a remote Web (not a disk-based Web on your hard drive). See the following How-To Hint for details. Don't forget to click the **Preview** tab to see your form as it will appear in a browser.

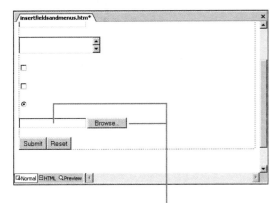

File Upload button
and text field

How-To Hints

Form Validation for Menus

To make the **File Upload** feature work, you have to open your server remotely (choose **File, Open Web**; enter the address of your site—such as **http://www.yoursite.com**—and click **Open**). Then type your username and password.

You must then create a new folder in your Web, in which the uploaded files will be stored. Right-click the new folder, choose **Properties**, and deselect the **Allow programs to be run** option. Select the **Allow scripts to be run** and **Allow files to be browsed** options.

Right-click the **File Upload** control you added in Step 6 and select **Form Properties**. Click **Options** and select the **File Upload** tab. Click **Browse** and navigate to the new upload folder you created. Click **OK** twice to finish. You should now be able to upload files to your site. Remember that you must open the Web remotely to make these changes; you cannot make them to a disk-based Web.

End

TASK 6

How to Create a Drop-Down Menu

In this task, we show you how to offer visitors multiple choices from a drop-down menu. This example illustrates the basic concepts you'll use (with some variation) each time you make a form.

Begin

1 Set the Insertion Point

Open the page on which you want to add the customized form. Click to position the insertion point where you want the drop-down list to appear.

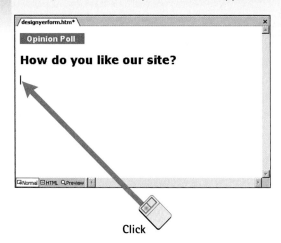

Click

2 Insert a Drop-Down Menu

From the menu bar, select **Insert**, **Form**, **Drop-Down Box**. A blank drop-down menu appears on the page, complete with **Submit** and **Reset** buttons. We will customize the menu by adding choices in the next few steps.

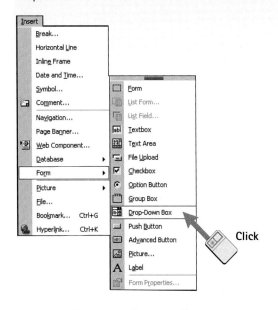

Click

3 Open Form Properties

Double-click the down arrow next to the menu you just inserted to open the **Drop-Down Box Properties** dialog box. (Alternatively, right-click the menu and choose **Form Field Properties** from the shortcut menu to open the dialog box.)

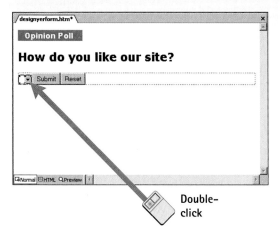

Double-click

232   PART 10: CREATING FORMS

4 Add a Selection

Now you have to build a list of options that will appear when the user clicks the down arrow next to the menu box. To add a selection to the menu, click the **Add** button. The **Add Choice** dialog box opens.

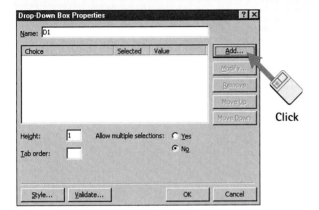

Click

5 Enter Selection Text

In the **Choice** text box, type the text for the first item you want to appear in the menu list. Click **OK** to add this option to the list.

Click

6 Save and Preview

Repeat Steps 4 and 5 to add additional options to the menu list. Click **OK** to close the **Drop-Down Box Properties** dialog box. To preview your new menu, click the **Preview** tab in **Page** view. Click the menu's arrow and make selections to see your new form at work.

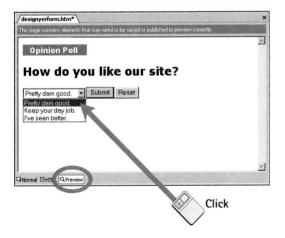

Click

How-To Hints

Menu Options

The **Drop-Down Box Properties** dialog box has a number of options you can set. If you set **Height** to a number greater than 1, the menu appears as a scrolling list rather than as a drop-down menu. If you change the height, you can allow the visitor to select more than one option by clicking the **Yes** radio button. In the **Add Choice** dialog box (click **Add** to launch it from the **Drop-Down Box Properties** dialog box), you can specify more options for each choice. By default, FrontPage uses the name you entered for a choice as its value (the information stored when a user makes a selection on the form). To create a value other than the name of the choice, select **Specify Value** and enter a word. If you want a choice to be selected by default, click the **Selected** radio button. Entering a number in the **Tab Order** text box tells FrontPage the order in which this field should come up when users press the **Tab** key on their keyboards. You can enter **-1** if you want the **Tab** key to skip over this field.

End

How to Modify Form Fields and Menus

After you insert form fields on the page, you might want to modify them (including resizing them). Often, the default settings work just fine, but you can set individual field properties or change the properties for the entire form by following a few simple steps.

Begin

1 Resize the Form Field

You can resize a form field just as you would a picture. Click the form field; a set of handles appears around the edges. Select a handle and drag until the field reaches the size you want. If you resize a drop-down menu, you can show more than one option at a time.

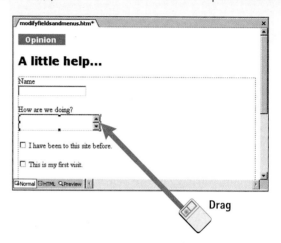

Drag

2 Select Form Field Properties

To perform more detailed customization on a form field, right-click the field and choose **Form Field Properties**. The **<Field Type> Properties** dialog box opens.

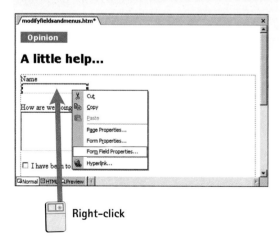

Right-click

3 Change Form Field Properties

Depending on the type of field you are working with, you can set an initial value (or *state*). For a text box or drop-down menu, you can type a value (in characters) that appears by default in the field (for example, **Type here** or **Make a selection**). For a group of check boxes or radio buttons, you can set the initial state of each button or box as checked or unchecked. You can also set the width of the field. When you finish, click the **OK** button.

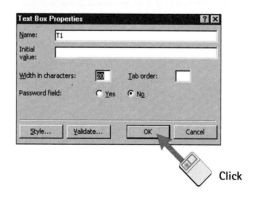

Click

4 Select Form Properties

In addition to modifying the individual fields on a form, you can modify the properties of the entire form itself. Right-click any open area on the form and choose **Form Properties**. The **Form Properties** dialog box opens.

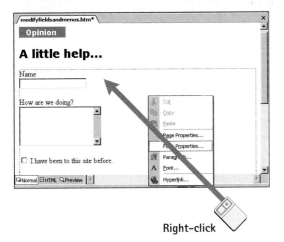

Right-click

5 Set Form Options

Use the form options to set how the data that visitors enter is handled. When a visitor types information into a form field, the data can be e-mailed to someone or can be stored in your Web. You also can store results in a database or with a custom script, but creating your own script is beyond the scope of this book. We do, however, show you how to use a FrontPage wizard to add a database to your Web site in Task 9, "How to Connect a Database to Your Web." See the next task to learn how to work with form results.

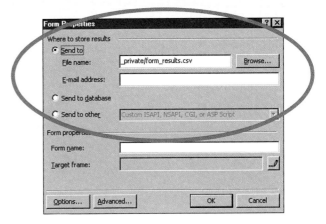

6 Save the Properties

Click **OK** to save any changes you have made and close the **Form Properties** dialog box.

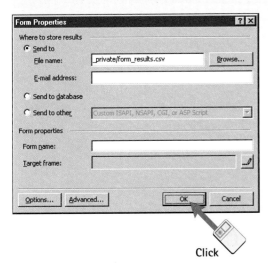

Click

How-To Hints

Form Validation

As an option, you might want to *require* that your visitors fill in a particular field. For instance, you can require a visitor to fill in a name or address field. If a visitor clicks the **Submit** button on a form without making a choice or entering information in the required field, an error message appears. To make a field required, right-click the field and choose **Form Field Properties** from the context menu. From the dialog box that appears, select the appropriate options to require data.

End

How to Save or Mail Form Results

After you create a form, you can tell FrontPage how to collect the data that visitors will enter into the form. After it's entered into a form, information can be automatically input to a text file in your Web. Alternatively, you can have the results e-mailed to you. Consider this last option carefully because the messages do tend to pile up. If you want to collect your form data in a database, see the next task, "How to Connect a Database to Your Web."

Begin

1 Change Form Properties

Open the page on which the form appears. Right-click any open area on the form and select **Form Properties** from the shortcut menu that appears. The **Form Properties** dialog box opens.

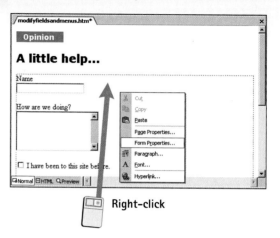

Right-click

2 Store Results in a File

By default, FrontPage creates a file in your Web to store the results. The file is called **form_results.csv** and is stored in a directory called **_private** (which visitors cannot see) in your Web. You can modify the filename here or delete the entry if you don't want the form results stored in that file.

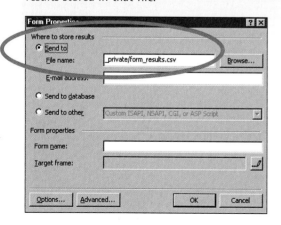

3 E-mail the Results

To have the form results e-mailed to you, fill in the **E-mail address** text box. If you enter an e-mail address, the data results will be mailed to the address you specify.

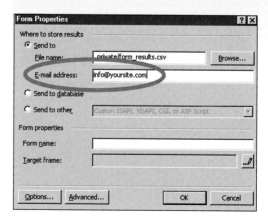

4 Click Options

Click the **Options** button. The **Saving Results** dialog box opens, showing more form settings.

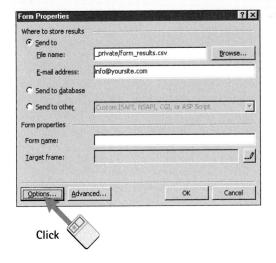

Click

5 Set File Results

On the **File Results** tab, from the **File format** list, select the format in which you want to store the form results. For example, you might want to store the results in HTML format if you plan to view them on the Web. You can choose a text format if you plan to import the results into a database.

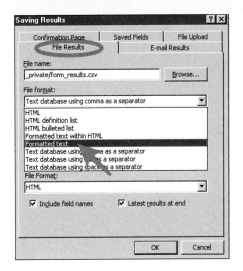

6 Select E-mail Results

Click the **E-mail Results** tab. You can change the e-mail address to which the results are sent. From the **E-mail format** drop-down list, you can choose to send the results as plain text or as HTML-formatted text (if your e-mail client supports HTML). You can also set the **Subject** and **Reply-to** lines you'll see for the message in your Inbox. Click **OK** to save any changes.

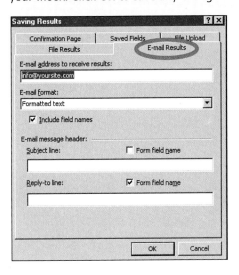

How-To Hints

Specify a Subject Line

If you decide to have form results e-mailed to you, consider setting the **Subject** line so that you can filter your form results with your e-mail program. On the **E-mail Results** tab of the **Saving Results** dialog box, enter a **Subject** line (type **Opinion Poll** or **Suggestions**, for example). Now, when you get e-mail, you'll be able to quickly identify the mail sent from your form.

End

How to Connect a Database to Your Web

FrontPage 2002 offers a new feature that lets you quickly create a Web-based database. The **Database Interface Wizard** simplifies what is typically a complicated job for any Web designer. With just a few clicks, you'll be able to enter and edit information into your database through the Web. A Web-based database is handy because you can update records from anywhere that you have access to the Internet. Co-workers can work on the database from work or from home, as long as they have a Web browser and an Internet connection. Keep in mind, though, that you need a server that supports Active Server Pages (ASP). Not all Web service providers offer this feature, so you should first check with your provider.

Begin

1 Start a New Web

If you want to add the database to a Web you have created, open it now. If you are starting a new Web, click the arrow next to **New Page** icon and select **Web** to open the **Web Site Templates** dialog box. Choose the **Database Interface Wizard**. If you are creating a completely new Web, type the path and name for your new Web in the **Options** area. If you want to add the database to a Web you have open, select the **Add to current Web** option. Click **OK**.

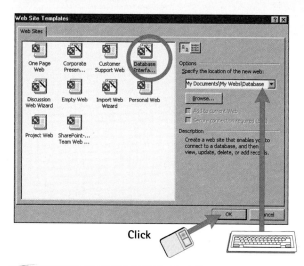

Click

2 Create a New Access Database

Select **Create a new Access database within your web**. You choose the information collected by your new database in the next few steps. You can also choose **Use a sample database connection**, which creates a database for a fictitious company (Northwind) that you can edit to suit your needs. This second option can be a handy way to get started, but, for this example, we'll start from scratch. Click **Next**.

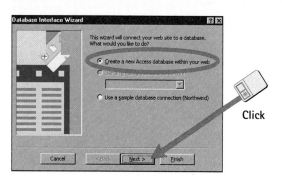

Click

3 Name Your Database

Type a descriptive name for your database. The name should be one word (you can't use spaces, but you can use capital letters to set off words, if you want). Click **Next**.

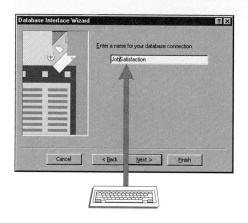

4 Select Information Collected

In the next wizard screen, you edit the type of information collected by your database. Right now, the database will prompt users to enter a Name, Address, and a Choice (users are given the options 1, 2, or 3). Click **Add** to enter a new column that will collect a phone number.

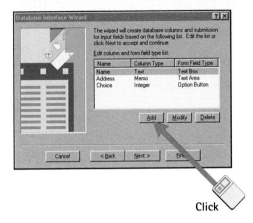

Click

5 Collect a Phone Number

Now we'll identify the column in the database that will store phone numbers. Under **Column name**, type **PhoneNumber** (with no spaces). We need to tell FrontPage what kind of information will be collected. From **Column type**, select **Text**. In the **Form field input type** drop-down list, leave **Text Box** selected. Click **OK** and then click **Next**. You will see a confirmation message that your database has been established. Click **Next** again.

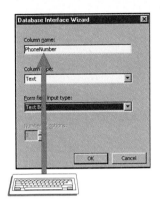

6 Choose Pages

Choose the types of pages that will display your database information. The **Results Page** shows the entries (or records) in your database. The **Submission Form** lets you enter a new record. The **Database Editor** lets you add and delete records. If you select this last option, you'll be prompted to create a name and password for the database administrator, or select an option that lets anyone edit the database. (Leave the **Database Editor** option deselected if you don't need to edit records through your Web site). When you are done making your selections, click **Finish**.

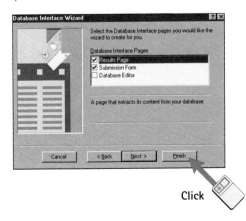

Click

7 Test Database Connection

You can't see your database in action if your Web is on your hard drive (unless you're running a server). Publish your Web site by choosing **File, Publish Web**. Then click **File, Preview in Browser** to view your database. If your server supports Active Server Pages, you should be able to view records from your database and add new ones over the Web.

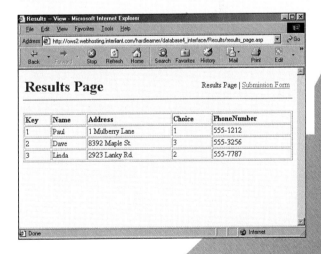

End

Task

1 How to Find a Web Service Provider That Supports FrontPage   **242**

2 How to Use a Web Service Provider That Doesn't Support FrontPage   **244**

3 How to Check Your Site's Health with Reports View   **246**

4 How to Repair and Update Links   **250**

5 How to Spell Check the Entire Site   **252**

6 How to Back Up a Web Site   **254**

7 How to Publish Your Site   **256**

8 How to Track Visitors to Your Site   **260**

PART 11

Preparing to Publish

Here's the first task in this part: Pat yourself on the back. In the previous 10 parts, you've designed, linked, previewed, found, replaced, and applied themes until you can apply no more. Now, the payoff—publishing your site for the world to see.

First, you have to ready pages for uploading to a dedicated server. To get a snapshot of the site's vital signs, the **Reports** view can be invaluable. After consulting the **Reports** view, you can fix any problems you might have overlooked during the page-building process.

Confident that the site is free from typos, broken links, and slow-loading pages, you move on to uploading. Even if your Web server does not support the FrontPage Server Extensions (and many do not), we can get you up and running. And, once your site is up, we'll show you how to find out who's visiting your site—and how often.

How to Find a Web Service Provider That Supports FrontPage

The first thing you have to do before you publish your newly developed Web site is find a company that has Internet access and that will host your site on its server. If you have the option, the company you pick should also support FrontPage Server Extensions (some of the features that make your FrontPage pages so much fun require these server extensions). Microsoft maintains a list of FrontPage-savvy host companies you can search. You can also search independent Web sites that offer listings and rankings of FrontPage-enabled, Web-hosting services.

Begin

1 Open Office on the Web

If your computer isn't set up to automatically establish an Internet connection, you must first establish your Internet connection and then select **Help, Office on the Web** from the FrontPage menu bar. The **Office Update** site opens in your default browser. Here you'll find listings of FrontPage-enabled Web hosts that Microsoft recommends.

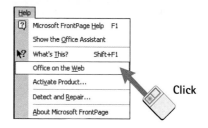

Click

2 Open the Microsoft WPP Site

You can also open Microsoft's **Web Presence Provider** site directly. Launch your browser and enter **www.microsoftwpp.com** in the **Address** bar.

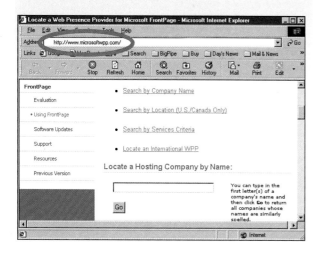

3 Search ISPs

Try searching for a FrontPage-enabled Web host by name, location, and type of services the hosts offer. For instance, some hosts offer free, advertiser-supported Web hosting. Others focus on small businesses or corporate Web sites; these kinds of sites might cost more and provide more services than a personal site. Note that Microsoft's sites change relatively frequently, so the page might look somewhat different than it does here.

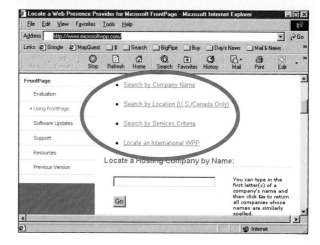

4 Find an Independent Source

To see user ratings of available ISPs, check out CNET's **Web Services** site. Open your browser and enter the following address: **http://webhostlist.internetlist.com**.

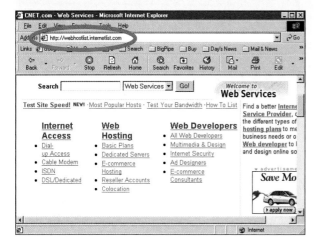

5 Investigate Hosts

The **Host Investigator** site lets you find hosting services based on cost and services offered. The site also provides customer reviews. Open your browser to **www.hostinvestigator.com** and then check out Web site host rankings based on customer service, reliability, and price.

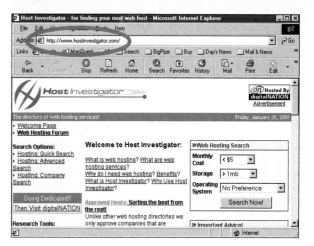

6 Check the Top 25

Another independent service is **TopHosts.com**, which reviews and ranks hosting services. Open your browser to **www.tophosts.com** to see the site's Top 25 recommended hosting services.

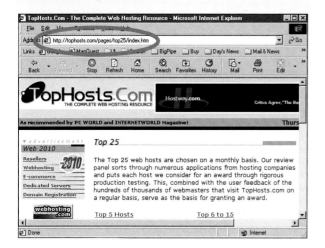

How-To Hints

Free Stuff

If you are looking for free hosts that support FrontPage, check out Tripod (**www.tripod.com**) and Yahoo! GeoCities (**geocities.yahoo.com**). For listings and reviews of free Web hosts, check out the Free Webpage Provider Review (**www.fwpreview.com**).

End

How to Use a Web Service Provider That Doesn't Support FrontPage

If your Web service provider does not support the FrontPage Server Extensions, you can still create a sharp-looking Web site. You will miss out on a few components, however, such as the hit counter and search form. This task explains how to set FrontPage to display only the features available on the server you use. Unavailable features will be grayed out in FrontPage menus.

Begin

1 Open Page Options

With the Web you want to affect open, select **Tools**, **Page Options**. The **Page Options** dialog box opens.

Click

2 Choose Compatibility

Click the **Compatibility** tab to bring it forward.

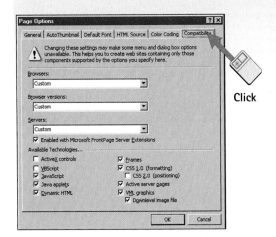

Click

3 Deselect Server Extensions

Deselect the **Enabled with Microsoft FrontPage Server Extensions** option.

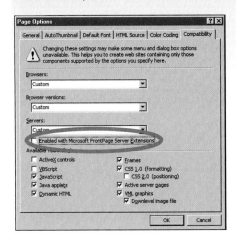

4 Deselect Technologies

You can also turn off certain features you don't want FrontPage to use. Deselect the **JavaScript** and **Java applets** options, for instance, if you don't want to use those technologies. Components—such as hover buttons and the banner ad manager (which uses Java)—will then be disabled in the **Insert, Web Component** menu.

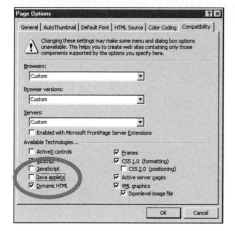

5 Save the Settings

Click **OK** when you finish changing settings. FrontPage is now configured to offer only those options that don't rely on Server Extensions.

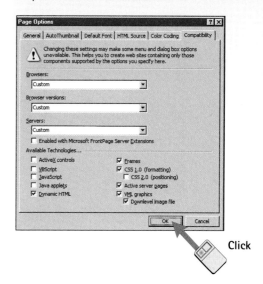

Click

How-To Hints

Publishing Without Extensions

You can use the default settings in FrontPage, even if you don't use a Web host that supports Server Extensions. When you publish your site to that Web host's server, however, you will get a warning that some features might not work on the server.

End

How to Check Your Site's Health with Reports View

The **Reports** view presents a quick rundown of your site's vital information. In addition, **Reports** view points out potential hang-ups in your pages and acts as a central point for fixing these problems.

Begin

1 Open a Web

Choose **File**, **Open Web**, and then navigate to the Web you want to check and click the **Open** button.

Click

2 Switch to Reports View

Click the **Reports** button in the **Views bar** to open the **Site Summary** in **Reports** view. The **Site Summary** offers a lot of site information in a small space. You can quickly see how many files you have in your Web and how much space they take up. The **Site Summary** points out slow-loading pages, broken hyperlinks, and unlinked (or orphan) files in your Web that cannot be reached by a link.

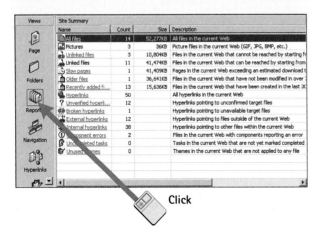

Click

3 Sort Files

To view more information about any one of these reports, double-click the report name (or choose **View**, **Reports** and select the desired report name from the submenus).

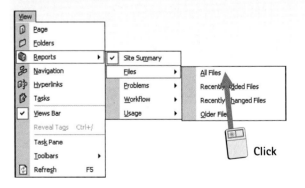

Click

4 Display the Reporting Toolbar

You can display the **Reporting** toolbar to make it easier for you to quickly jump to different reports. Choose **View, Toolbars, Reporting**.

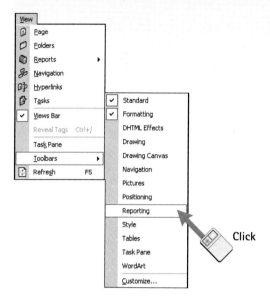

Click

5 Open a Report

From the **Reporting** toolbar, click the arrow next to the **Reports** drop-down list box and choose the report you want to view. In this example, the **Slow Pages** report is selected.

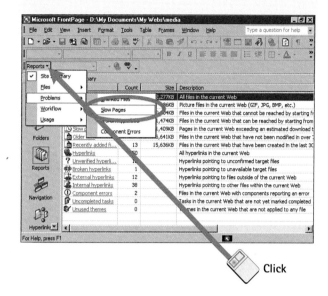

Click

6 Change Report Setting

Many of the reports offer a setting you can adjust to refine the report. In the **Slow Pages** report, for example, you can adjust the number of seconds used to determine a "slow" page. Open the **Report Setting** drop-down list in the **Reporting** toolbar and select a number of seconds. The report adjusts to incorporate this new setting.

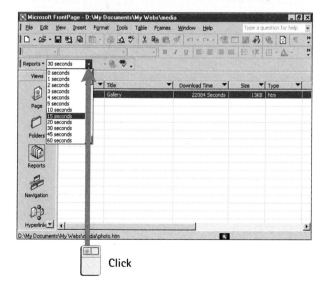

Click

How-To Hints

How to Read a Report

Each report lists pages from the site that are relevant to the specific report. (For example, the **Unlinked Files** report shows files in the Web's folders that have no links to other pages.) Open the **Slow Pages** report (select **View, Reports, Problems, Slow Pages**) to see pages that are slow to download. From this view, click an item in the list and press **F2** to rename a file or page title. The **Broken Hyperlinks** report shows a list of pages that have broken links or that have not yet been verified (see Task 4, "How to Repair and Update Links").

Continues

7 Change Publish Status

From **Reports** view, you can also view and change the publishing status of pages. The publishing status of a page can be either **Publish** or **Don't Publish**. If you want to work on a page for some time before uploading it to your site, you should mark it as **Don't Publish**. To do so, first select **Workflow, Publish Status** from the **Reports** drop-down list in the **Reporting** toolbar.

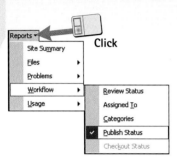

Click

8 Choose Page Properties

Select the pages you don't yet want to publish (press **Shift** while selecting multiple pages). Right-click the selected pages and select **Properties** from the context menu. The **Properties** dialog box opens for the selected files.

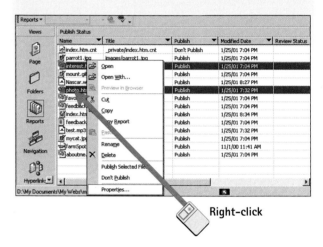

Right-click

9 Select the Workgroup Tab

Click the **Workgroup** tab to bring it forward.

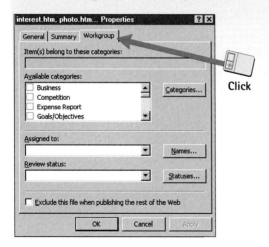

Click

10 Set the Publishing Status

Select the **Exclude this file when publishing the rest of the Web** option to mark the file. Then click the **OK** button. Now when you publish your Web, these pages will not upload to the server.

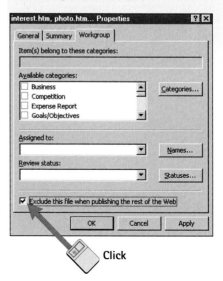

Click

11 Change Report Options

You can customize some of the report options to fit your needs. Choose **Tools**, **Options** to open the **Options** dialog box; click the **Reports View** tab to bring it forward. On this tab, adjust the settings to define recent files, older files, and slow pages. You can also set the modem speed used to determine a slow page, and you can choose the number of months shown in your usage reports.

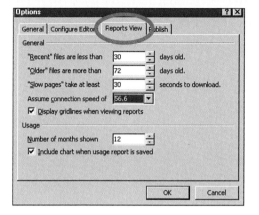

12 Save the Settings

Click **OK** when you finish making adjustments to the settings in the **Options** dialog box. The report options you specified are immediately applied to any new reports you view.

Click

13 Edit a File

From **Reports** view, you can open any file so that you can edit it. Double-click the filename you want to work on. The file opens in **Page** view.

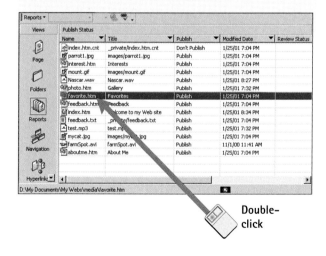

Double-click

How-To Hints

Publish Status Shortcut

There's a faster way to mark a page that you don't want published: In **Reports** view, choose **View**, **Reports**, **Publishing Status** from the menu bar. Click the file to highlight the entire line; click the word (it will be either **Publish** or **Don't Publish**) in the **Publish** column to activate the drop-down menu. Choose **Don't Publish** from the drop-down list to make the page unavailable for publishing; choose **Publish** if you want to publish the page.

End

How to Repair and Update Links

Like your personal cleaning crew, FrontPage scans for broken links and helps you fix them. To make sure that your links are up to date, you'll want to use the **Verify Hyperlinks** tool, which checks internal links as well as links from your site to outside Web pages. If the tool can't find a link, it reports the link as broken.

Begin

1 Open a Web

Choose **File, Open Web**. In the **Open** dialog box, navigate to the Web whose links you want to check and click the **Open** button. The **Recalculate Hyperlinks** tool is available only from the **Reporting** toolbar. To open the toolbar, select **View, Toolbars, Reporting**.

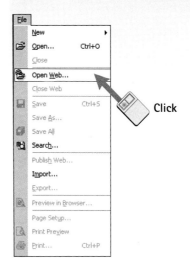

Click

2 Verify Hyperlinks

If your Web includes hyperlinks to other sites on the Internet, you should establish your Internet connection now. FrontPage will check these external links for you (but it will report the links as broken if it cannot find an Internet connection). To start the housecleaning, click the **Verify Hyperlinks** button on the **Reporting** toolbar. The **Verify Hyperlinks** dialog box opens.

Click

3 Click Start

You can choose **Verify only unknown hyperlinks**—links FrontPage hasn't yet checked, such as links to outside Web sites (this option can save time). Or you can check **Verify all hyperlinks**. Click **Start** to begin checking the hyperlinks in the current Web. When the check is complete, the **Broken Hyperlinks** report is displayed, listing all the pages that contain broken links.

Click

4 Select a Page

From the list of Broken Hyperlinks, select a page to fix and click the **Edit Hyperlink** button on the **Reporting** toolbar. Alternatively, select the page, right-click it, and choose **Edit Hyperlink** from the context menu. The **Edit Hyperlink** dialog box opens.

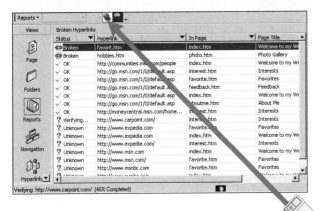

Click

5 Fix a Link

In the **Replace hyperlink with** field, type the address of the page to which you want to link. Alternatively, click **Browse** and navigate to the page that should be linked.

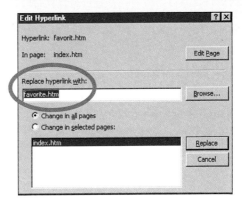

6 Replace All Broken Links

If this link appears in multiple locations, select the **Change in all pages** option and click **Replace**. Every place the broken link appears is replaced with the link you specified in Step 5.

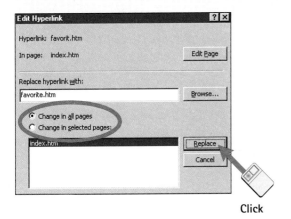

Click

How-To Hints

Recalculate Hyperlinks

FrontPage keeps an internal index of all the links in your Web. To make sure that the list is up to date (especially after importing new pages or making changes with an external editor), use the **Recalculate Hyperlinks** tool. The tool checks your Web for broken links, repairs links, and deletes unnecessary files (such as unused themes). Choose **Tools, Recalculate Hyperlinks**. When the Recalculate Hyperlinks dialog box opens, click **Yes**.

End

How to Spell Check the Entire Site

In Part 3, "Working with Text," you used the spell checker to find spelling errors on a page. In this task, you learn how to scan the entire site for spelling errors. When a potential misspelling is found, you can jump right to the page to fix it.

Begin

1 Open the Spell Checker

Open the Web you want to spell check. Then select **Tools, Spelling**. The **Spelling** dialog box opens.

Click

2 Select the Entire Web

Choose whether you want to spell check the **Entire web** or a **Selected page**. (By default, the checker is set to scan the entire site.)

3 Add to the Tasks List

If you want to add a task to your task list to remind yourself to correct the errors in each page that contains a typo or a misspelling, select the **Add a task for each page with misspellings** option. Task lists are described in Part 7, "Working with Webs." The task list provides a way to see all the corrections that were made to the site after the fact. You also might find the task list useful if you need to finish the corrections later.

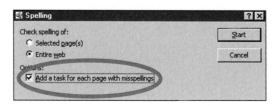

4 Start the Check

Click the **Start** button to start the spell checker, using the options you selected.

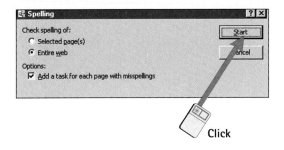

Click

5 Open a Page

When it has scanned the entire site, the spell checker presents a list of pages that contain potential spelling errors. Double-click a page to open it.

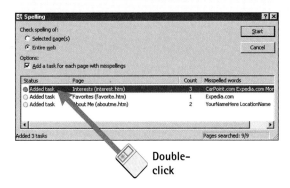

Double-click

6 Choose a Correction Option

The selected page opens in **Page** view. The first misspelled word is highlighted, and the spelling checker is open. Click the appropriate button to **Ignore**, **Change**, or **Add** the highlighted word to the spelling dictionary.

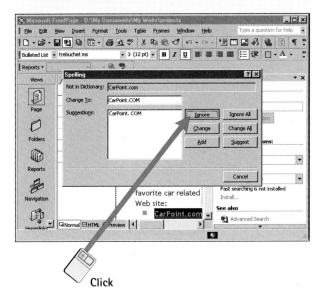

Click

7 Check the Next Document

When the spelling checker finishes with the current page, you are prompted to continue checking more documents. Click **Next Page** to start the correction process on the next page in your site that contains misspellings. You can also choose **Back to List** to select a page to open and review for potential misspellings.

Click

End

How to Back Up a Web Site

Data loss is painful and often unnecessary. To protect your Web, back it up to a separate drive, removable media, or your office network, depending on your hardware setup. In FrontPage, you back up your site by "publishing it" to the backup media.

Begin

1 Choose Publish Web

Open the Web site you want to back up. Next, select **File**, **Publish Web** to open the **Publish Web** and **Publish Destination** dialog boxes.

Click

2 Enter the Backup Path

In the **Enter publish destination** field, type the location where you want to back up your Web. Alternatively, click the **Browse** button and navigate to the location; FrontPage fills in the path for you. Click the **Open** button to choose your folder. Then click the **OK** button to get things started. You might be prompted to create a Web in the location you chose; if so, click **OK**.

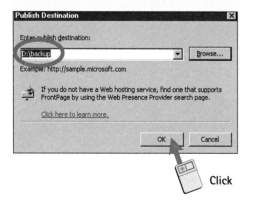

Click

3 Click Options

There are other options you can specify when "publishing" a Web to backup media. Click the **Options** button in the **Publish Web** dialog box; the **Options** dialog box opens and expands to show a list of publishing settings.

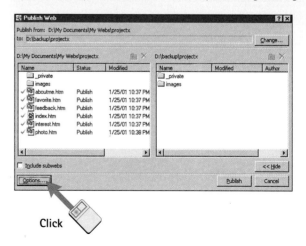

Click

4 Select Backup Options

Decide whether you want to publish all pages or only those that have changed recently. If you are backing up for the first time, select **All pages**. The publish options are set by default to check for differences between the pages you are publishing and the pages that might exist at the destination folder. They also log the publishing details to a text file by default, so that you can view them later in case there is an error. When you finish setting options, click **OK**.

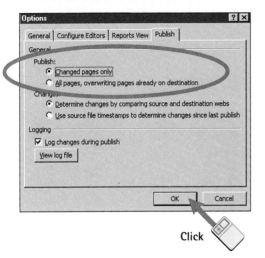

Click

5 Back Up

Start the backup by clicking the **Publish** button in the **Publish Web** dialog box. A backup of a small site should take under a minute. Larger sites—and slower processors—lengthen the backup time, but the process is generally quick and painless. A dialog box with a thermometer-style progress bar appears to show the progress of your backup.

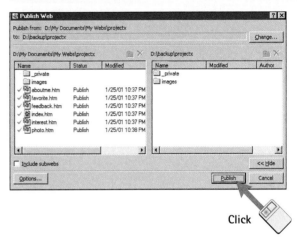

Click

6 Choose Done

When your Web is backed up (FrontPage says that the site has "published successfully"), a dialog box appears. Click **Done** to finish.

Click

How-To Hints

Backup Options

In general, you're better off backing up to a removable-media drive (such as an Iomega Zip drive) rather than publishing to your hard drive. Of course, if you publish often to a server on the Web, you already have a backup: One copy is on your computer, and the other is on your Web server. If you lose your Web because of hard drive failure or some other calamity, import the site from the Internet using the **Import Web Wizard**. See Task 3, "How to Import an Existing Web Site," in Part 7.

End

7

How to Publish Your Site

FrontPage provides everything you need to publish your files to a Web server. You can copy the entire Web to your server, or, to save time, you can upload only the files that have changed since you last published the site. Then sit back, open the frosty beverage of your choice, and let FrontPage handle the rest.

Begin

1 Open the Publish Web Dialog Box

Open the Web you want to publish. Then choose **File**, **Publish Web**. The **Publish Web** and **Publish Destination** dialog boxes open.

Click

2 Search for a Provider

If you don't have a Web service provider, click the **Click here to learn more** link and refer to Task 1, "How to Find a Web Service Provider That Supports FrontPage."

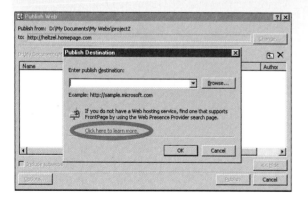

3 Enter the Location

In the **Enter publish destination** field, type the location of the server to which you're publishing. The address should be in the form **http://www.*sitename*.com/ *yourwebname***. Note that you might not have to include the directory *yourwebname* if you own your own domain name. A *domain name* is an Internet address of your choosing, such as *yoursite.com* (or **.edu**, **.org**, or **.net**, among other options). Note that not all servers require you to type **www** before the domain name (as in our example). When you have entered your site name, click **OK**.

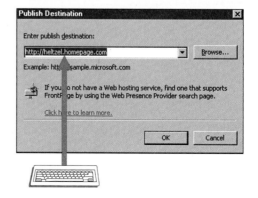

4 Enter a Password

If your server host requires authentication, you might be prompted to enter a username and password. The person or service hosting your site will provide this information. Enter your information and, to save time, select **Save this password in your password list**. Click **OK**.

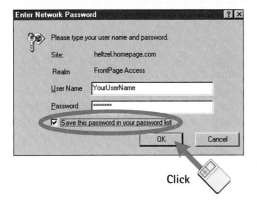

Click

5 Include Subwebs

The **Publish Web** dialog box appears and shows you both the files on your hard drive and those on the site to which you are publishing (in this example, we're publishing the site for the first time). Select the **Include subwebs** option if you have created separate Webs within the Web you are publishing.

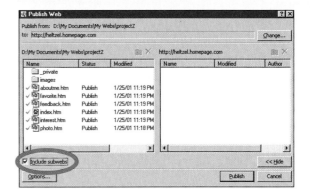

6 Set Publishing Options

Click the **Options** button at the bottom of the **Publish Web** dialog box to display all your publishing options. Choose whether to publish all the pages in the site or to publish only the pages that have changed since the last time you uploaded the site to the server. (It's usually much faster to publish only the changed pages.) In addition to publishing the entire site for the first time, you might also want to publish the entire site (over-writing any previous versions of the entire site) after moving to a new server or after making a complete redesign of your site.

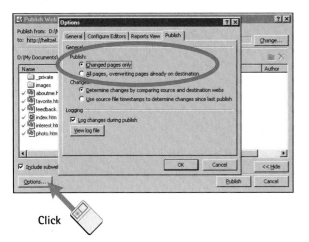

Click

How-To Hints

What's a Subweb?

When publishing, you might have to tell FrontPage to include subwebs (Webs within another Web, as discussed in Step 5). You should select the **Include subwebs** option, for instance, if you've added a Discussion Web. (This is a pre-designed discussion group you can insert into your current Web by choosing **File, New, Web** and selecting it from the **Web Sites** list. Then you select **Add to current Web** and click **OK**.) Subwebs are sometimes used in intranet environments, where each subweb in the intranet has different properties and access rights set by the server administrator.

Continues

How to Publish Your Site Continued

7 Set Change Options

In the **Changes** area of the **Options** dialog box, you will typically want to use the default selection, which lets FrontPage compare differences between the files you are uploading and the files that exist on the server to which you're publishing.

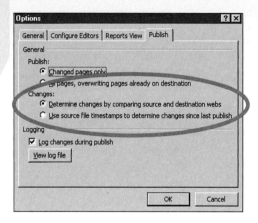

8 Publish to a Server Without Extensions

If your server doesn't support FrontPage Server Extensions, you have to make some changes. In the **Enter publish destination** field of the **Publish Destination** dialog box, replace **http** with **ftp** and replace the **www** with **ftp**. In other words, enter **ftp://ftp.yourftpsite.com**. (Check with your provider to find the correct address for your FTP site.)

9 Publish Locally

If you are publishing your site to a location on your computer or network (for instance, to back up the site), click **Browse**. See the previous task, "How to Back Up a Web Site," for information about publishing the site locally.

Click

10 Click Publish

All set for liftoff? Click the **Publish** button. A dialog box appears, showing the upload progress of your site. If you are publishing for the first time, take five. This will likely be the longest upload you'll have to sit through. The speed of transfer depends on the size of your files and your bandwidth.

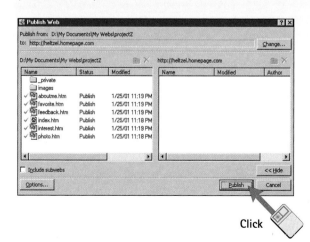

Click

11 Click Done

FrontPage connects to the specified server and copies your pages to the Web. When the upload is complete (that is, when it has "published successfully"), you'll see a message to that effect. Click **Done**. Congrats!

Click

12 A Publishing Shortcut

To publish the site to the same location later, click the **Publish Web** button on the **Standard** toolbar. Only pages that have changed since the last time you uploaded the site will be published.

Click

How-To Hints

FTP Servers

If your Web service provider doesn't support the FrontPage Server Extensions, you'll publish to a File Transfer Protocol (FTP) server. FTP is a protocol that has long been used to transfer files from one computer to another over the Internet. If you publish your files to an FTP server, some FrontPage components such as the hit counter and some form elements such as the search form will not work.

Publish History

If you publish Webs to more than one site, FrontPage keeps a list of all the sites. From the **Publish Destination** dialog box, click the down arrow to the left of the **Browse** button and select a site name as the one to publish to.

End

How to Track Visitors to Your Site

For my Web-publishing dollar, the best new feature in FrontPage is one you use after all your designing and publishing is done. *Usage analysis reports* tell you who visits your site and how often. To use this feature, you need to publish to a server with the FrontPage 2002 Server Extensions installed. To view the reports, you must also open the Web from that server. Usage analysis reports are a great way to see how well your Web site is attracting visitors over time.

Begin

1 Open a Web

To check out a usage report, you must first open a Web. Choose **File**, **Open Web**, select the Web you want to work with, and click **Open**. The Web server to which you publish must support the FrontPage 2002 Server Extensions because this feature was not offered in earlier versions of FrontPage. Let's take a look at a summary of how the site is doing. Select **View, Reports, Usage, Usage Summary**.

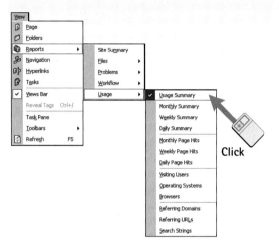

Click

2 Take an Overall Look

Among other information, the **Usage Summary** report shows the number of visits by individual users and the number of pages in your site that were viewed (hits). This information is calculated from the time that you first published the site with FrontPage 2002.

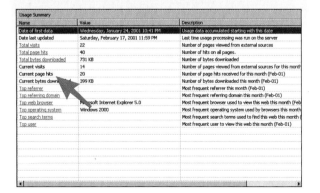

3 Switch the Time Period

For a more specific look at your stats, you can see reports for how many times a page was viewed in one day, one week, or one month. Choose **View, Reports, Usage, Monthly Page Hits, Weekly Page Hits**, or **Daily Page Hits**.

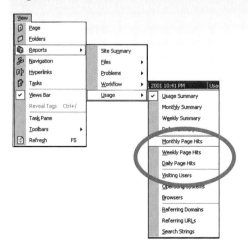

4 Get Browser Information

You can also take a look at the browsers your visitors use. Select **View, Reports, Usage, Browsers** to see a list of the types and versions of browsers with which visitors have viewed your site, and what percentage of your visitors are using each type of browser.

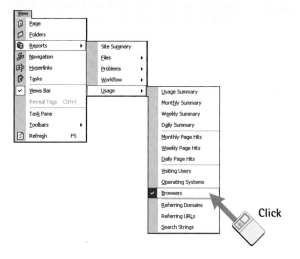

Click

5 View the Report as a Chart

From the **Usage Chart** toolbar button menu in the **Reports**, select a chart type. For this example, I selected the **3D Pie Chart** to see the breakdown of operating systems that have been used to visit my site.

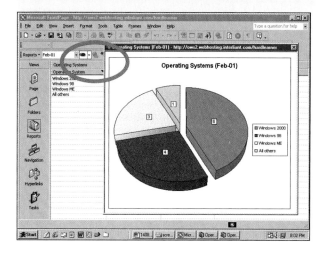

6 Change Report Settings

Click the **Report Setting** button and make a selection. For example, if you have tracked user information since January 2001, you can select **Jan-01** from the drop-down list to view the browser information report (or a chart) from that month.

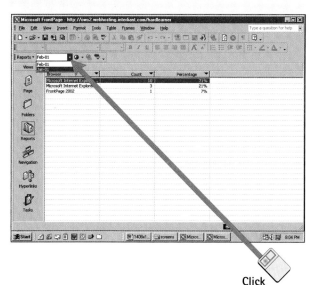

Click

How-To Hints

Tracking Page Hits

To view information about page visits on your Web site, you can also insert a component on a Web page that will display your site's 10 most popular pages. For more information, see Task 6, "How to Add a Top-Ten List," in Part 9, "Enhancing Pages with Components."

End

Glossary

absolute positioning   A way to place page elements precisely—and even layer them on top of each other.

active hyperlink color   The color a link takes on when it is clicked.

Active Server Pages (ASP)   A Microsoft technology that lets HTML pages interact with programs such as databases. ASP can be used to create dynamic pages, which are created when the browser requests a page. Active Server Pages have an `.asp` extension when you see them on the World Wide Web.

anchor   The common name for the navigation aid FrontPage calls a *bookmark*.

applet   A small program written in the Java programming language that can provide interactive functionality to a Web page. Because applets have received bad press as carriers of Internet viruses, you might want to carefully consider whether you include an applet on your Web page.

AVI (Audio Video Interleaved) file   The standard format for a Windows video file.

banner ad   An advertisement for which merchants might be willing to pay, usually placed at the top of a page. With FrontPage, you can display several banner ads, one at a time, in a specific order.

bookmark   A link to a specific location, usually in the same page. Bookmarks are helpful when you want to create a link that jumps to a specific location in a lengthy document. A bookmark is more commonly referred to as an *anchor* or a *target*.

border   The outline of an area, such as around a table or a frame. You can specify the thickness of the line used to border a selected area; generally, a 1-pixel or 2-pixel rule is adequate.

brightness   A characteristic of a graphic image, indicating its overall level of light.

browser   An application used to surf the Web. The browser interprets the HTML code that defines a Web page and displays the page in the format you're used to seeing—complete with graphics, styled text, and colored links. FrontPage uses Microsoft Internet Explorer (version 3.0 or later) as the internal browser when you click the Preview tab in Page view.

bullet   A typographic element used to emphasize points in a list. The standard bullet character is a solid dot to the left of an indented list item. With FrontPage, you can use any character—or a piece of clip art or any other small graphic—for a bullet.

cell padding   A buffer of whitespace around text or an image in a table cell.

cell spacing   The number of pixels between cells in a table.

child level   A page that is below another page in the vertical hierarchy of pages in a Web site.

clip art   Royalty-free images that can be "clipped" from the source location and insert into Web pages. FrontPage comes with clip art files that include images for a variety of business and personal projects. This collection includes Web-specific images, such as banners, buttons, and backgrounds.

close box   The × button that appears on the title bar of an application or the top bar of a window within the application. When you click the close box, the window or the application closes. (If you haven't saved changes, you are given the opportunity to save before the window closes.)

collapsible list   An "animated" nested list. Clicking a primary entry in the list makes all the subentries appear; clicking the primary entry again makes the subentries collapse (disappear) beneath the main entry.

component   Objects that can be inserted into pages to perform specific tasks. Some components need to be used in a FrontPage Web, and others require the use of a Web server running the FrontPage Server Extensions. Components come in all shapes and sizes; they include the hit counter, the search form, and the marquee.

contrast   An adjustable characteristic of a graphic image that affects the difference between the lightest and darkest areas of a picture.

default hyperlink color   The color a link takes on when the link hasn't yet been clicked. This is the color seen most of the time.

dock   To position a floating toolbar in a fixed position. Drag the floating toolbar until it snaps into place. You can dock toolbars at the top of the screen (just under the menu bar) or at the left, right, or bottom edge of the screen.

domain name   An Internet address for a site, such as `yoursite.com`. The first part of the address usually identifies a particular computer. The second part indicates what kind of organization is in charge. Commercial sites use `.com` or `.net` (for networks), organizations use `.org`, and schools use `.edu`.

Dynamic HTML (DHTML)   An enhancement to HTML that allows animation of page elements. DHTML animations require Microsoft Internet Explorer or Netscape Navigator version 4.0 (or later). Some DHTML animations, such as page transitions, work only with Internet Explorer.

field   An element of a form that standardizes the way information is provided (for example, a `LastName` field and a `FirstName` field). A field can be completed by means of a text box in which you type a comment or a check box or menu that offers a handful of choices.

Folders view   A Windows Explorer–like tree of the files and folders in a site. In Folders view, you can move, copy, and delete pages.

form   An online device, much like the ubiquitous paper variety, used to gather information. The fields in a form standardize the way information is submitted, making it easier to store that information into a database. A common element of a Web site, a form is almost required if your Web site offers products or information for sale.

frame   A way to view multiple pages in a single browser window.

frames page   A browser window that can display the contents of several Web pages. Each page is held in a frame, which functions like a miniature window. To view a frames page, your visitor needs a frames-capable browser.

FrontPage Web   The collection of pages, pictures, and other elements that make up a FrontPage site.

FTP (File Transfer Protocol)   Used to transfer files from one computer to another over the Internet. If you publish your files to an FTP server, some FrontPage components that rely on the Server Extensions (such as the hit counter and some form elements such as the search form) will not work.

GIF (Graphics Interchange Format) image   A compressed graphics format that displays images in a maximum 256 colors. Most images that require fewer than 256 colors—such as stylized text created in a graphics editor—use the GIF format. The GIF format is also used for animation. A series of individual images that display in sequence is called an *animated GIF*.

guest book   A standard feature of Web sites that allows a visitor to enter comments about the site and read other visitors' comments. A visitor types comments in a text box and clicks a button; the text appears on a page with other comments.

hit counter   A component that tracks and displays the number of visitors to a page.

home page   The first page visitors see when they view a Web site. The home page FrontPage designates when you create a new Web site is named `index.htm`.

hotlink   *See* hyperlink.

hover   To hold the mouse pointer over an image on a page without clicking. Typically, the name of the graphic (not necessarily its filename) appears in a ScreenTip-like box next to or on top of the graphic when the mouse pointer passes over the graphic area. You can add this alternative text in the Picture Properties dialog box (right-click an image and select Picture Properties to open the dialog box).

hyperlink   Text or a graphic that a user clicks to open another object. Clicking a hyperlink might open a Web page, download a file, or launch a program to handle files of many different types, such as an e-mail client or a multimedia player. Also called a *hot spot* or *hotlink*.

hyperlink rollover   A special effect by which the text of a hyperlink will change appearance when a mouse hovers over it (for example, a hyperlink might change color or turn bold).

Hyperlinks view   A visual overview of the hyperlinks in a Web site's pages. The view also identifies any links the pages have to other sites on the World Wide Web.

imagemap   A standard graphic with hyperlink images that might (or might not) be symbolic of the sites they represent. For example, in an image of a pirate ship, the Jolly Roger flag might have a link to a page of other flags and banners; the treasure chest on the deck might link to a sterling silver charm home page. In effect, the entire graphic becomes a navigation tool.

import   To bring an existing text or graphics file into a Web site or place it on an individual page. For example, you might want to import text from a word processing file into a Web page, or import a page you created with another program into your FrontPage Web.

inline frame   A feature that allows a user to place a frame within a new or existing page. An inline frame can display dynamic information changes without affecting the rest of the page. Inline frames can also be used to link to somebody else's page from within your own page. Note that this practice is frowned on unless you have permission from the other site.

intranet   A local Web site on a network, as in a company. If you are publishing information for use on an intranet, you will have more information about the browsers and connection speeds of the users than if you are publishing to the Internet.

Java applets   *See* applet.

JPEG (Joint Photographic Experts Group) format   A common graphics format that enables an image to display thousands or millions of colors. Typically best for photographs.

link   *See* hyperlink.

link bar   A set of hyperlinked text or buttons that represent the pages in a Web site; formerly called a *navigation bar*. Visitors to a site can click the buttons or text in the link bar to jump to the individual pages in the site.

marquee   An invisible text box in which text scrolls across the face of the box, much like lights appear to scroll around a theatre marquee.

navigation bar   *See* link bar.

Navigation view   The pages in a Web site in a flowchart-like display. In the Navigation view, you can rearrange pages and automatically link them together.

nested list   A list in which some items are subordinate to others. For example, in a daily to-do list, the primary entries might be the days of the week, and the subordinate items might include the activities of each day. *See also* collapsible list.

page   The most basic unit you work with in FrontPage. A page contains text, graphics, and animations that inform, entertain, or direct the visitor to additional information. Although a Web site can consist of a single page, most successful Web sites contain multiple pages linked together using hyperlinks or other navigation tools.

page title   Identity of a Web site page that appears at the top left of a visitor's browser window, in the same bar as the close box.

page transition   A visual effect that appears each time a Web site page is opened or closed, helping move a visitor smoothly from one page to another. You can choose an effect that displays your page in a checkerboard pattern or as if viewed through vertical blinds. Transitions are particularly useful for slick presentations—but they might be excessive for simple Web pages. Page transitions require Internet Explorer to view them; visitors with other browsers see no special effects on your pages.

Page view   The most commonly used FrontPage view. In Page view, you can enter text and insert images to create pages and preview your work.

parameters   Settings that define certain characteristics of an applet. You might set a parameter to change the way an applet is displayed, for example, or choose a sound for an applet that plays audio files. The Java programmer defines which parameters you can configure;

check the documentation for information about the parameters for a particular applet.

parent level   A page that is above another in the vertical hierarchy of pages in a site.

picture properties   The characteristics of any graphic image located on a Web page. These properties include the filename of the image; the type of image it is (GIF, JPEG, or PNG); the resolution at which it appears; the text that appears when a visitor hovers over the image; the size of the image; its position on the page; whether it has a border, and so on.

pixel   The smallest unit of measurement on a display screen.

plug-ins   Browser add-ons that allow a user to view multimedia or other content (audio files and streaming videos, for example). A browser decides which plug-in to use, based on the file type you are trying to access, and displays the content of the file within the browser window.

publish   The process of copying a Web site and pages from a local computer system to a Web server with a direct connection to the Internet (or a local intranet).

relative path   Text that specifies the location of a file in relation to the current working directory. If you are pointing to a file called `index.htm` in the same directory as the page with which you are working, the relative path would simply be `index.htm`. In contrast, a full path for the same file might be `http://www.yoursite.com/index.htm`.

Reports view   A summary of a Web site, including the size of its files. Reports view indicates pages in a site that have problems (such as poor download speeds or broken links).

resample   To change the appearance of an image and the amount of data it takes to display the image. For example, if you resize a graphic image so that it takes up only half the original space, it makes sense to shrink the graphic file's size as well by resampling the image.

resize   To change the size of an image. Resizing does not reduce the amount of data it takes to display the image. For example, if you resize a graphic image so that it takes up only half the original space, the graphic file does not change size. *See also* resample.

rollover   *See* hyperlink rollover.

scheduled image   A FrontPage feature that lets a user set the time at which an image will be displayed and then disappear from a page. Scheduled images are a great way to add fresh content to a page without having to make the update yourself.

scheduled include page   A FrontPage feature that lets a user set the time at which a page will be displayed and then disappear. This feature lets you automatically display a new advertisement, a press release, or any other page that is time sensitive.

ScreenTip   A feature that displays the name of a toolbar button when the mouse pointer is positioned over a button. A ScreenTip looks like a hovering yellow sticky note.

search form   A FrontPage feature that lets visitors search for words that appear on a Web site. FrontPage automatically creates a list of every word found in a Web. Visitors can enter a word in the search form and click a button; the locations of the word appear at the bottom of the page.

server   A computer connected to a network (such as the Internet or an office intranet) to which Web pages can be published and to which visitors can connect to view the pages.

Server Extensions   A group of programs installed on a Web server that makes it possible to insert components such as a search engine or create interactive forms for pages. The FrontPage Server Extensions also simplify managing and publishing a site.

shared borders   Areas that appear on multiple pages of a Web site. Text or graphics you place within the border on one page automatically appear in the same place on all other pages that share that border. A shared border is commonly used as the location of a site's link bar.

site   Several Web pages linked together with hyperlinks or other navigation tools. A (Web) site is your ultimate goal when working with FrontPage.

source code   The programming text a Web browser reads to display Web pages. Hypertext Markup Language (HTML) is the programming language used to create and display Web pages. When you create Web pages in

FrontPage, FrontPage generates the HTML source code for you.

table   A way to organize data by placing it in rows and columns.

target frame   On a frames page, the frame in which a linked page opens.

Tasks view   A FrontPage view in which a user can create a to-do list for a project and assign different tasks to different members of the project team. Everyone working on a project can view the tasks and check them off as they are completed.

template   Any one of several pattern pages provided by FrontPage. You can select a template as the basis of a new Web page. The template sets up the basic formatting for the page, which you can then alter until the new page is exactly what you want it to be.

text file   An unformatted text document. A text file might be one that was created in a word processor but saved in text-only format (`.txt`). It also might have been created in Notepad or another text editor that does not save text formatting such as font style, italics, bold text, or other attributes.

theme   A predesigned scheme of color and graphic elements that sets the look for a Web page or for an entire Web site. A theme might set the background for pages to off-yellow and format all the text in dark blue Arial font. As you add pages to your site, the new pages take on the same properties. You can even apply a theme to a template (a customizable sample page provided by FrontPage).

tile   To repeat an image over the surface of an area, much like identical ceramic tiles are laid in rows and columns over a surface. Tiling an image is one way to create a background graphic for a Web page.

time stamp   A component that automatically inserts text that specifies the date and time at which a page was last edited and saved.

transparent color   A selected color that will disappear from a picture so that the background of a Web page shows through parts of the graphic. An image with transparent color appears to float on the page.

URL (uniform resource locator)   The Web address at which a file exists. The URL is what you enter to go to a site when you surf the Web (for example, `http://www.myfavorites.com`). A hyperlink requires a URL so that it knows what file (or page) to open when the link is activated.

usage analysis report   A new feature in FrontPage 2002 that logs who visits a site and how often. To use this feature, you must publish to a server that has the FrontPage 2002 Server Extensions installed. Usage analysis reports are a great way to see how well your Web site is attracting visitors over time.

value   The data a user enters into a form's field. If a user enters **Jones** in a **LastName** field, for example, the value for that field is **Jones**.

view   Any of six different on-screen displays of a FrontPage Web site's pages, accessed from the Views bar. Although each view is necessary in developing your Web site, you will spend most of your time in Page view.

Views bar   The link bar at the left edge of the FrontPage screen. Click the buttons in this bar to display your Web pages in different views.

visited hyperlink color   The color a link takes on when a user has clicked the link previously.

Web   *See* FrontPage Web.

word processing file   A file created by a word processor, and usually containing formatting (such as font size, italic or bold text, and other attributes), that you can import into FrontPage.

Index

A

absolute positioning, 142-143, 263

accessing
  Clip Art Gallery, 86
  Office Assistant, 15
  views
    Folders, 8, 147, 218
    Hyperlinks, 9
    Navigation, 9, 217
    Page, 6, 8
    Reports, 9
    Tasks, 9, 179
  Views bar, 8
  WordArt Gallery, 58

Active Graphics theme, 27, 61

Active Server Pages (ASP), 263

adding
  background sound, 184-185
  borders, 65
  browsers, 33
  buttons to toolbars, 11
  captions to tables, 125
  columns (tables), 124-125
  comments to files, 153
  page titles, 36-37
  pages in Navigation view, 162
  photo galleries, 212-213
  rows (tables), 124-125
  scheduled images, 208-209
  search forms, 226-227
  text to images, 102-103
  text boxes, 111
  Top 10 lists, 210-211
  Web pages, 154-155

ads banner ads, 204-205

Align Left button (Formatting toolbar), 50

Align Right button (Formatting toolbar), 50

aligning
  horizontal lines, 131
  pictures, 178
  tables, 118-121
  text, 50-51, 63

anchors. See bookmarks

animated images, 87

animations, 192-197

Answer Wizard, 14-15

applets (Java), 186-187, 263-265

applications (browsers), 263

applying themes, 26-27

Ask A Question (Standard toolbar), 13

ASP (Active Server Pages), 263

associating files with tasks, 172-173

audio (background sound), 184-185

audio files, 76-77

automatically loading pages, 206-207

Auto Thumbnail button (Pictures toolbar), 97

AutoFit to Contents button (Tables toolbar), 121

automating navigation, 166-169

AVI (Audio Video Interleaved) file, 263

B

Background command (Format menu), 47, 114

Background picture theme, 27, 61

background sound, 184-185

Background Sound dialog box, 184

backgrounds, 114-115, 128-129

backing up Webs, 254-255

Banner Ad Manager Properties dialog box, 204-205

banner ads, 204-205

banners, 170-171

bars
  link bars, 168-169, 216-217
  navigation. *See* link bars
  Views, 267

Bevel button (Pictures toolbar), 105

beveled edges (images), 105

black and white, converting images to, 101

blank pages, linking to, 73

Bold button (Formatting toolbar), 46, 62

Bookmark command (Insert menu), 74

Bookmark dialog box, 74

bookmarks, 74-75, 263

borders
  adding, 65
  frames, 136-137
  images, 99
  removing, 65
  shared, 164-167, 266
  tables, 119, 126-127

boxes. 21. *See also* text boxes

brightness (images), 100-101

Bring Forward button (Positioning toolbar), 143

Broken Hyperlinks report, 250
broken hyperlinks, viewing, 155
browsers, 263
 adding, 33
 choosing, 32-33
 internal, 34
 naming, 33
 plug-ins, 188-189
 previewing pages in, 32-33
 tracking, 261
bullets, 52-53
Bullets and Numbering command (Format menu), 53
Bullets button (Formatting toolbar), 52, 63

C

captions, 125, 213
Cascading Style Sheets (CSS), 27
cell padding (tables), 119, 263
Cell Properties dialog box, 127
cell spacing (tables), 119, 263
cells (tables), 121-123, 127-129
Center button (Formatting toolbar), 50
checking spelling, 56, 63-64
 suggestions, 57
 Webs, 252-253
child level pages, 162, 263
Choose Download Amount dialog box, 151
clip art, 263, 86-87
Clip Art Gallery, 86
Clipboard, managing, 16
close boxes, 21
Close Web command (File menu), 149, 179
closing
 FrontPage, 5
 pages, 21, 38-39
code, source code, 266
collapsible lists, 263
collapsible outlines, 54-55

collecting information, 239
color (text), modifying, 47
Color button (Pictures toolbar), 101
color palette, 114
color schemes, previewing, 29
coloring shapes, 110
colors, 62-63
 custom, 62, 116-117
 tables, 121
 themes, 28
 transparent, 267
columns (tables), 124-125
comments, 153 225
company home pages, 174-179
compatibility
 inline frames, 141
 plug-ins, 189
connecting databases to Webs, 238-239
connections
 establishing Internet, 242
 pages, 162
contrast (images), 100-101, 264
Convert Text dialog box, 45
converting images to black and white, 101
copies of pages, saving, 37
Copy command (Edit menu), 16, 158
copying
 images, 85
 paragraph formats, 49
 text, 43
 Web pages, 158-159
Corporate Presence Wizard, 174-179
counters, hit counters, 211
Crop tool (Pictures toolbar), 92
cropping images, 92-93
CSS (Cascading Style Sheets), 27
custom colors, 62, 116-117
custom link bars, 200-201

D

Database Interface Wizard, 238
databases, testing, 239
Decrease Indent button (Formatting toolbar), 50-51
Delete Cells (Tables toolbar), 125
Delete Cells command (Table menu), 125
Delete Frames command (Frames menu), 135
deleting
 background sound, 185
 borders, 99, 136-137
 cells (tables), 121
 frames, 135
 hyperlinks, 71
 link bars, 169, 216
 page transitions, 191
 pages, 154-155, 163
 tasks, 173
 Webs, 147
DHTML (Dynamic HTML), 192, 197, 264
DHTML Effects toolbar, 197
disabling ScreenTips, 11
Discussion page, 218
Distribute Columns Evenly command (Table menu), 123
Distribute Rows Evenly command (Table menu), 123
docking toolbars, 11, 264
drawing, 110, 121
Drawing toolbar, 110-111
Drop-Down Box Properties dialog box, 232-233
drop-down menus, 232-233
duration of page transitions, 190
dynamic animations, 192-197
dynamic resizing (tables), 119

E

e-mail, linking to, 72, 99
e-mailing form results, 236-237
Edit Hyperlink button (Reporting toolbar), 251

Edit Hyperlink dialog box, 71

editing. See modifying

effects, 195-197, 203-205

elements, positioning, 142-143

embedded files, 37, 65, 179

Enable Collapsible Outlines check box, 55

Enabled with Microsoft FrontPage Server Extensions check box, 244

enabling ScreenTips, 11

entering text, 42-43, 120

establishing Internet connections, 242

events, start (dynamic animations), 193-197

existing backgrounds, 115

Exit command (File menu), 5

exiting. See closing

extensions
    Server Extensions, 266
    Webs, publishing without, 245, 258

external hyperlinks, 72-73

eyedropper tool, 63

F

feedback forms, 224-225

<Field Type> dialog box, 234

fields, form fields, 234-235

File command (Insert menu), 44

File Transfer Protocol (FTP)

File Upload option, 231

files
    adding comments, 153
    associating with tasks, 172-173
    audio, linking to, 76-77
    AVI, 263
    linking to, 72
    modifying, 249
    multiple
    opening, 39
    saving, 37, 65, 178-179
    searching, 17
    sorting, 153
    summaries, 153

Find and Replace dialog box, 160-161

Find command (Edit menu), 43

finding. See searching

Flip Horizontal button (Pictures toolbar), 95

Flip Vertical button (Pictures toolbar), 95

flipping images, 95

floating toolbars, 10

Folder List command (View menu), 153

folder structures (Web sites), 159

folders, 152-153

Folders button (Views bar), 8, 152, 218

Folders view, 8, 147, 152-153, 218, 264

Font Color button (Formatting toolbar), 62, 116

Font command (Format menu), 47

Font dialog box, 47

Font list (Formatting toolbar), 46

Font menu (Formatting toolbar), 62

Font Size menu (Formatting toolbar), 62

font styles, setting, 62

fonts, themes, 30

Form, Check Box command (Insert menu), 231

Form, Drop-Down Box command (Insert menu), 232

Form, Option Button command (Insert menu), 231

Form Page Wizard, 222-223

Form Properties dialog box, 216

Form, Text Area commands (Insert menu), 230

Form, Textbox commands (Insert menu), 230

Format Painter, 48-49

Format Painter button (Standard toolbar), 49

formatting
    applets, 187
    drop-down menus, 233
    links, 78-79
    paragraphs, 48-49
    plug-ins, 189
    search forms, 226
    tables, 121
    text, 46-47, 176

forms, 222-231, 234-237, 264

Frame Properties dialog box, 134-136

frames, 133-141, 264

Frames menu commands, 135

frames pages, 132-136

From, Text Area command (Insert menu), 215

FrontPage
    Answer Wizard, 14-15
    closing, 5
    Help, 12-13
    navigating, 6-7
    opening, 4

FrontPage Web, 264

FrontPage-enabled Web hosts, 242-243

FTP (File Transfer Protocol), 264

G-H

galleries, photo, 212-213

GIFs (Graphics Interchange Format images), 264

Guest Book template, 228

guest books, 228-229

handling form results, 235-237

headings (paragraphs), 48

Help, 12-15

hiding
    pages, 169
    toolbars, 10

Highlight button (Formatting toolbar), 47

Highlight Dynamic HTML Effects button (DHTML Effects toolbar), 197

highlighting, 47, 197

history (tasks), viewing, 173

hit counters, 211

home pages
creating, 60-65, 174-179
opening, 23
saving, 64-65
templates, 60
titling, 64

Horizontal Line command (Insert menu), 130

Horizontal Line Properties dialog box, 130

horizontal lines, 130-131

horizontal spacing (images), 107

hosts (Webs), 242-245

hotlinks. See hyperlinks

hotspots (imagemaps), 108-109

hover buttons, 202-203

HTML source code, 266

HTML tab (Page view), 25

HTML tags, 25

hyperlink rollover, 79

hyperlinks, 265
broken, 155
creating, 70-73, 176
deleting, 71
in frames, 138-139
modifying, 70-71
navigating, 80-81
repairing, 250-251
testing, 71, 80-81
updating, 250-251
viewing, 69

Hyperlinks button (Standard toolbar), 70

Hyperlinks button (Views bar), 9

Hyperlinks view, 9, 68-69, 265

I

imagemaps, 108-109, 265

images
animated, 87
aligning, 178
backgrounds, 115, 129
beveled edges, 105
borders, 99
brightness, 100-101
clip art, 86-87, 263
contrast, 100-101, 264
converting to black and white, 101
copying, 85
cropping, 92-93
flipping, 95
formats, 91
GIFs, 264
importing, 84-85
inserting, 176-178, 194
JPEGs, 265
linking, 98-99
pasting, 85
properties, 90-91
resampling, 96-97, 177, 266
resizing, 96-97
restoring, 101
rotating, 94-95
scanned, 88-89
scheduled, 208-209, 266
spacing, 107
in tables, 120
text, 102-103, 106-107
themes, 30
thumbnails, 97, 212
transparent, 104-105
washing out, 101

Import command (File menu), 150

Import Web Wizard, 150-151

importing
images, 84-85, 88-89
pages, 155
text, 44-45
Webs, 150-151

Increase Indent button (Formatting toolbar), 50-51

indenting text, 50-51

information, collecting, 239

Initially Collapsed dialog box, 55

Inline Frame Properties dialog box, 141

inline frames, 140-141, 265

Inline Frames command (Insert menu), 140

Insert, Caption command (Table menu), 125

Insert Columns (Tables toolbar), 124

Insert Hyperlink button (Standard toolbar), 138

Insert Hyperlink dialog box, 70-71, 98-99, 138

Insert Picture From File button (Standard toolbar), 84, 194

Insert Picture From Scanner or Camera dialog box, 88-89

Insert Rows (Tables toolbar), 124

Insert, Rows or Columns command (Table menu), 125

Insert Table button (Standard toolbar), 121

Insert, Table command (Table menu), 118

Insert Table dialog box, 118

Insert Web Component dialog box, 171, 200

inserting
applets, 186
clip art, 86-87
horizontal lines, 130-131
images, 120, 176-178, 194
inline frames, 140-141
page banners, 170-171
tables, 118-121
videos, 182-183

Install Additional Themes option (Themes dialog box), 61

internal browsers, 34

internal hyperlinks, 72-73

Internet connections, 242

intranets, 214-219, 265

Italic button (Formatting toolbar), 46, 62

J-L

Java Applet Properties dialog box, 186

Java applets, 263-265

JPEGs (Joint Photographic Experts Group format), 265

launching. See opening

Less Brightness button (Pictures toolbar), 100

Less Contrast button (Pictures toolbar), 100

line breaks (text), 43

line spacing, 51

lines, horizontal. See horizontal lines

Link bar, modifying, 218

Link Bar Properties dialog box, 167, 178, 216

link bars, 169, 200-201, 216, 265

linking
    to blank pages, 73
    to e-mail, 72, 99
    to files, 72, 76-77
    graphics, 98-99
    hover buttons, 202
    to movies, 76-77
    to Web sites, 73

links. See hyperlinks

lists
    bullets, 52-53
    collapsible, 263
    creating, 52-53, 63
    nested, 53
    numbering, 53
    sublists, 53
    Top 10, 210-211
    usage, 210

loading pages automatically, 206-207

location of Webs, specifying, 175

looping background sound, 185

M

managing Clipboard, 16

marquees, scrolling, 203

menus, 232-235

Merge Cells button (Tables toolbar), 123

merging cells (tables), 122-123

messages, No-Frames, 135

Microsoft FrontPage 2002. See FrontPage

Microsoft FrontPage Help command (Help menu), 12

Modify Theme dialog box, 28-30

modifying
    backgrounds, 114-115, 128-129
    borders, 136-137, 165
    color, 47, 121
    Discussion pages, 218
    files, 249
    form fields, 234-235
    forms, 224-225, 228-229
    horizontal lines, 130-131
    hyperlinks, 70-71
    link bars, 168, 218
    menus, 234-235
    page banners, 171
    publishing status (pages), 248
    reports, 247
    Search page, 217
    shapes, 111
    tables, 126-127
    text, 43
    themes, 28-31
    troubleshooting, 29
    toolbars, 11
    WordArt, 58-59

More Brightness button (Pictures toolbar), 100

More Colors dialog box, 63, 116-117

More Contrast button (Pictures toolbar), 100

movies, linking to, 76-77

moving
    text, 43
    Web pages, 158-159

multiple files, opening, 39

N

naming
    browsers, 33
    folders, 152
    frames, 134
    link bars, 201
    pages, 36-37, 64
    Webs, 23, 146

navigating
    FrontPage, 6-7
    hyperlinks, 80-81
    Hyperlinks view, 68-69
    Web, 263

navigation, automating, 166-169

navigation bars. See link bars

Navigation button (Views bar), 9, 162, 217

Navigation view, 9, 162-163, 217, 265

nested lists, 53

New from Existing Page dialog box, 156-157

New, Folder command (File menu), 152

New Page button (Standard toolbar), 6, 20, 60

New, Page or Web command (File menu), 22, 156

new windows, targeting, 139

No-Frames message, 135

Normal tab (Page view), 25

numbering lists, 53

O-P

objects, 111

Office Assistant, 15

Open command (File menu), 24, 38

Open File dialog box, 24, 38-39

Open Web command (File menu), 148, 164

Open Web dialog box, 148

opening
    Front Page, 4
    Help, 12, 14
    home pages, 23
    multiple files, 39
    pages, 38-39, 218-219
    reports, 247
    Search page, 217
    Web sites, 148-149
    Task Pane, 16

orientation (pages), 163

outlines, 54-55

padding, 119, 263

Page Banner Properties dialog box, 171

page banners, 170-171

Page button (Views bar), 8

Page icon (View bar), 4

Page Options command (Tools menu), 192

Page Options dialog box, 192

Page Properties dialog box, 114

Page Templates dialog box, 20-21, 60

page titles, 36-37

Page Transition command (Format menu), 190

Page Transition dialog box, 190

page transitions, 190-191, 265

Page view, 6-8, 20, 24-25, 265

pages
   adding, 154-155, 162
   automatically loading, 206-207
   blank, 73
   child level, 162, 263
   closing, 21, 38-39
   connections, 162
   copies, 37
   copying, 158-159
   creating, 20-21, 154-157
   deleting, 154-155, 163
   Discussions, 218
   frames pages, 132-135
   hiding, 169
   home pages. See home pages
   importing, 155
   modifying, 214-219
   moving, 158-159
   naming, 36-37
   opening, 38-39
   orientation, 163
   parent level, 162
   pasting, 159
   previewing, 24-25, 32-35
   publishing, 248
   saving, 5, 36-37
   Search pages, 217

SharePoint, 219
themes, 26-31
zooming, 163

palettes, color palette, 114

panes, Task Pane, 16-17

Paragraph command (Format menu), 48, 51

Paragraph dialog box, 48

paragraphs, 48-49

parameters (applets), 187, 265

parent level pages, 162

Paste command (Edit menu), 159

pasting
   images, 85
   Web pages, 159

paths, relative, 266

photo galleries, 212-213

Photo Gallery Properties dialog box, 212-213

Picture, Clip Art command (Insert menu), 86

Picture command (Insert menu), 194

Picture dialog box, 84, 194

Picture, From Scanner or Camera command (Insert menu), 88

Picture Properties dialog box, 90-91, 97, 178, 183

Picture, Video command (Insert menu), 182

Picture, WordArt command (Insert menu), 58

pictures. See images

pixels, 266

Plug-In Properties dialog box, 188-189

plug-ins, 188-189, 266

populating
   forms, 223
   link bars, 201

Position Absolutely button (Positioning toolbar), 142

positioning, 142-143, 263

Positioning toolbar buttons, 142-143

predesigned sites, 146-147

Preview in Browser command (File menu), 33-34

Preview in Browser dialog box, 33-35

Preview tab (Page view), 25

previewing
   background sound, 185
   bookmarks, 75
   clip art, 87
   color schemes, 29
   effects, 197
   forms, 229
   hover buttons, 203
   outlines, 55
   page transitions, 191
   pages, 24-25, 32-35
   photo galleries, 213
   shared borders, 167
   themes, 61
   transparent images, 105
   video, 183
   Webs, 23

Print Topics dialog box, 15

programs (applets), 263

Programs, Microsoft FrontPage 2002 (Start menu), 4

Project Web Wizard, 214-219

Publish Destination dialog box, 256

Publish Web button (Standard toolbar), 259

Publish Web command (File menu), 7, 254-256

Publish Web dialog box, 254-256

publishing status (pages), 248

publishing Webs, 245, 256-259

R

radio buttons, 231

reading reports, 247

Recalculate Hyperlinks tool (Reporting toolbar), 250-251

Recent Files command (File menu), 38

Recent Webs command (File menu), 148

Redo button (Standard toolbar), 43

Refresh command (View menu), 159

refreshing views, 159

relative paths, 266

Remove Formatting command (Format menu), 45

removing
  borders, 65
  bullets, 53
  columns (tables), 124-125
  effects, 197
  rows (tables), 124-125

repairing hyperlinks, 250-251

Replace command (Edit menu), 160

replacing text, 43, 160-161

Reporting toolbars, 247

reports, 247, 250, 260-261, 267

Reports button (Views bar), 9, 246

Reports command (View menu), 246

Reports, Problems, Broken Hyperlinks command (View menu), 155

Reports, Publishing Status command (View menu), 249

Reports, Usage, Usage Summary command (View menu), 260

Reports view, 9, 246-249, 266

Resample button (Pictures toolbar), 97, 177

resampling, 96-97, 177, 266

Reset button, 227

Resizable in browser option (Frame Properties dialog box), 136

resizing
  form fields, 234
  frames, 133, 141
  images, 96-97
  tables, 119-121
  WordArt, 59

resolution (pages), 35

restoring images, 101

results of forms, 235-237

Reveal Tags command (View menu), 25

rollover effects, 195-196

rollovers, hyperlink rollover, 79

Rotate Left button (Pictures toolbar), 94

Rotate Right button (Pictures toolbar), 94

rotating
  banner ads, 204-205
  images, 94-95

rows (tables), 124-125

S

sampling colors, 63, 116-117

Save As dialog box, 5, 36, 64

Save button (Standard toolbar), 64

Save command (File menu), 5, 36

Save Embedded Files dialog box, 95, 177, 179

Save Themes dialog box, 31

saving
  files, 37, 65, 178-179
  home pages, 64-65
  pages, 36-37
  themes, 31
  pages, 5
  Webs, 148-149

Saving Results dialog box, 237

scanned images, importing, 88-89

scheduled images, 208-209, 266

Scheduled Include Page Properties dialog box, 206

Scheduled Picture Properties dialog box, 208-209

schemes, color schemes, 29

ScreenTips, 10-11, 266

scrolling frames pages, 136

scrolling marquees, 203

scrolling text boxes, 230

Search Form Properties dialog box, 226

search forms, 226-227

Search page, 217

searching
  clip art, 86-87
  files, 17
  Help, 12-13
  hosts, 242-245
  text, 43, 160-161

Select File dialog box, 44-45

selecting
  backgrounds, 114-115
  bookmarks, 75
  browsers, 32-33
  colors, 62
  templates, 60
  themes, 7

Send Backward button (Positioning toolbar), 143

Server Extensions, 266

servers, 266

Set Page title dialog box, 64

setting
  alignment, 178
  colors, 62
  font styles, 62
  line spacing, 51
  properties, 90-91, 183
  width (tables), 119

shadows (objects), 111

shapes, 110-111

Share Point, 215

shared borders, 164-167, 266

Shared Borders command (Format menu), 164

Shared Borders dialog box, 164-169

SharePoint, 219

shortcuts, 5

Show All button (Standard toolbar), 42

Show the Office Assistant command (Help menu), 15

Site Summary, 246

sorting files, 153

sound. See audio

source code, 266

spacing
cell spacing (tables), 119, 263
frames, 137
horizontal, 107
lines, 51
paragraphs, 48
vertical, 107

specifying location of Webs, 175

spell checking, 56-57, 63-64, 252-253

Spelling button (Standard toolbar), 63

Spelling command (Tools menu), 57, 252

Spelling dialog box, 64, 252-253

Split Cells button (Tables toolbar), 122

Split Cells dialog box, 122

Split Frames command (Frames menu), 135

splitting
cells (tables), 122-123
frames, 135

start events (dynamic animations), 193-197

Start menu (Programs, Microsoft FrontPage 2002 command), 4

Start Search button, 227

starting. See opening

storing form results, 236-237

structures, folder structure (Webs), 159

styles
font, 62
paragraphs, 48-49
text, 31

subfolders, 152

sublists, 53

subwebs (Webs), 257

summaries (files), 153

switching between views, 175

T

tables
aligning, 118-121
backgrounds, 128-129
borders, 119, 126-127
captions, 125
cells, 119-123, 127-129
columns, 124-125
drawing, 121
formatting, 121
horizontal lines, 130-131
modifying, 130-131
images, 120
inserting, 118-121
recoloring, 121
resizing, 119-121
rows, 124-125
text, 120
width, 119

tags (HTML), viewing, 25

Target Frame dialog box, 139

target frames, 138-139, 267

targeting new windows, 139

Task Pane, 16-17

Task Pane command (View menu), 16

Task view, 179

tasks
associating files with, 172-173
deleting, 173
history, 173
starting, 175

Tasks button (Views bar), 9, 179

Tasks view, 9, 172-173, 267

Tasks, Add Tasks command (Edit menu), 172

templates, 23, 146
choosing, 20-22
Guest Book, 228
selecting, 60

testing
databases, 239
hyperlinks, 71, 80-81

text
aligning, 50-51, 63
color, 47
copying, 43

entering, 42-43, 120
finding/replacing, 43, 160-161
formatting, 46-47, 176
highlighting, 47
images, 102-103, 106-107
importing, 44-45
indenting, 50-51
line breaks, 43
modifying, 43
moving, 43
underlined, 62

text boxes, 111, 230

Text button (Pictures toolbar), 102

text styles, 31

Theme command (Format menu), 60-61, 115

themes, 23
applying, 26-27
fonts, 30
graphics, 30
horizontal lines, 131
link bars, 200
modifying, 28-31
previewing, 61
saving, 31
selecting, 7
text styles, 31
viewing, 26

Themes command (Format menu), 7, 26

Themes dialog box, 26-29, 60

three-dimensional objects, 111

thumbnails (images), 97, 212

time stamp, 267

titles, adding, 36-37

titling pages, 64

Toolbars, DHTML Effects command (View menu), 193

Toolbars, Drawing command (View menu), 110

Toolbars, Formatting command (View menu), 46

Toolbars, Positioning command (View menu), 142

Toolbars, Reporting command (View menu), 247

Toolbars, Tables command (View menu), 120

Toolbars, WordArt command (View menu), 59

Top 10 List Properties dialog box, 211

Top 10 lists, adding, 210-211

tracking visitors, 260-261

transitions, page transitions, 190-191, 265

Transparent Color button (Pictures toolbar), 104

transparent colors, 267

transparent images, 104-105

troubleshooting
    applets, 187
    background sound, 185
    close boxes, 21
    collapsible outlines, 54
    DHTML, 192, 197
    Format Painter, 49
    frames, 133
    themes, 29
    underlined text, 62

two-color borders (tables), 127

U-V

Underline button (Formatting toolbar), 46, 62

underlined text 62

underscore symbol (_), 216

Undo button (Standard toolbar), 43

updating hyperlinks, 250-251

URLs (uniform resource locators), 267

usage analysis reports, 267

usage lists, 210

Usage Summary report, 260-261

validating forms, 235

Verify Hyperlinks dialog box, 250

Verify Hyperlinks tool (Reporting toolbar), 250

vertical spacing (images), 107

vertically aligning tables, 120

video, 182-183

Video dialog box, 182-183

View bar (Reports button), 246

viewing
    folders, 153
    history, 173
    HTML tags, 25
    hyperlinks, 69, 155
    themes, 26
    toolbars, 10

views
    Folders, 8, 147, 152-15, 218, 264
    Hyperlinks. See Hyperlinks view
    Navigation. See Navigation view
    Page, 6-8, 265
    Page view, 20, 24-25
    refreshing, 159
    Reports. See Reports view
    switching between, 175
    Task, 179
    Task Pane, 16
    Tasks. See Tasks view

Views Bar command (View menu), 8

visitors, tracking, 260-261

Vivid colors option (themes), 61

Vivid Colors theme, 26

W-Z

washing out images, 101

Watermark (backgrounds), 115

Web Component command (Insert menu), 171, 186

Web pages. See pages

Web Site Templates dialog box, 6, 146, 174-176, 178-179

Web sites. See Webs

Webs
    backing up, 254-255
    creating, 6-7, 22-23, 147
    databases, connecting, 238-239
    deleting, 147
    finding/replacing text, 160-161
    folder structures, 159
    FrontPage Web, 264
    hosts, 242-245
    importing, 150-151

    linking to, 73
    locations, 175
    naming, 23, 146
    navigating, 263
    opening, 148-149
    predesigned, 146-147
    previewing, 23
    publishing, 245, 256-259
    saving, 148-149
    spell checking, 252-253
    themes, 23
    visitors, 260-261

windows, targeting new, 139

wizards
    Corporate Presence, 174-179
    Database Interface, 238
    Form Page, 222-223
    Import Web, 150-151
    Project Web, 214-219

WordArt, 58-59

WordArt Gallery, 58

wrapping text around images, 106-107

zooming pages, 163

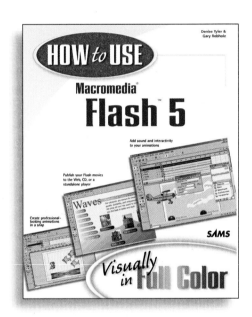